Management and Regional Science
for Economic Development

Studies in Applied Regional Science

Editor-in-Chief:

P. Nijkamp, Free University, Amsterdam

Editorial Board:

Management and Regional Science for Economic Development

Manas Chatterji
Professor of Management
State University of New York at Binghamton

Kluwer Nijhoff Publishing
Boston/The Hague/London

To my wife Pradipta

Distributors for North America:
Kluwer.Nijhoff Publishing
Kluwer Boston, Inc.
190 Old Derby Street
Hingham, Massachusetts 02043, U.S.A.

Distributors outside North America:
Kluwer Academic Publishers Group
Distribution Centre
P.O. Box 322
3300AH Dordrecht, The Netherlands

Library of Congress Cataloging in Publication Data

Chatterji, Manas, 1937–
   Management and regional science for economic development.
   (Studies in applied regional science)
   Includes bibliographical references and indexes.
   1. Economic development. 2. Regional economics. 3. Regional planning—India—Calcutta Region.
4. Calcutta Region (India)—Industries. I. Title. II. Series
HD82.C465   338.9   82-15182
ISBN 0-89838-108-8   AACR2

Printed in the United States of America

Contents

List of Figures

List of Tables

PREFACE

The greatest challenge facing mankind today is the immense disparity in the levels of income among people in different parts of the globe. The growth rate of income of the poor countries is consistantly far below the rate of the advanced, industrialized nations. Due to low income and a high propensity to consume, there is very little left in these countries for investment. A major portion of the resources available is devoted to military expenditures. This continual decline in the standard of living, coupled with poverty and unemployment, will lead to social and political upheaval in these countries, which affects developed countries. Because of high capacity and low population growth, the market of the developed countries is already saturated. To maintain the high standard of living in the developed countries it is necessary to have a strong and stable developing world. It is gratifying to see that both groups of countries see the need for peaceful economic growth; however, the amount of cooperation between countries and the material help from the developed countries are far from satisfactory.

The economic and social scientists have investigated the best way to achieve the transformation from a poverty-ridden condition to a decent existence. Their studies have proceeded in two different directions. One is a more descriptive, historical analysis and the other is theoretical model-building. Although these studies have achieved a relatively high level of perfection, one significant factor is sometimes missing. This factor is "space" and the conflicts that go with it—agricultural vs. urban, the capital city vs. the rest of the nation, areas inhabited by tribal groups and minorities vs. the other areas, and so on. These oppositions have great implications for political and social stability in the developing countries.

This book addresses the problem of development from spatial and regional aspects. The emphasis is on practical applications. Although standard techniques of management have been presented in their sophistication, how these techniques can be used to solve practical problems is also shown. The starting point is population and migration. It is not an understatement to say that a large present population and excessive population growth are the basic reasons for low economic development. Definitions of measurement of key indices of demography are given and how different techniques can be used to project population and migration are shown. Spatial regularities of population distribution are fully explored; then the determinants of location and measurement of economic activities are presented.

Economic activities have intricate forms of interdependence. To capture the nature of this interdependence, input/output analysis is presented and how this technique can be used to project scenarios in the future is shown. This model has also been extended to include other factors, such as environmental pollution. The developing countries face different kinds of economic resource constraints. To devise optimum strategy it is thus necessary for us to use optimization techniques. So we have presented the programming models and indicated how they can be transformed to create a control theory framework.

Besides most input-output and programming models, another technique that is used often is econometric modeling. How regional econometric models can be developed to project economic activities is shown. Shortages of resources, such as energy and minerals, are going to pose serious problems for development. Integrated energy econometric modeling examples are given.

Planning and decisions are made in the context of political realities, such as ideology and popular participation. After population, these factors are most important. It is often said that planning in underdeveloped countries is based on sound principles but is managed very badly. Here the management of the planning process is emphasized.

Although the first concern of this book is developing countries, the material can also be used for developed countries, particularly for their underdeveloped areas, depressed central cities, declining areas (such as the Northeastern United States), and agricultural regions.

I would like to thank Peter Christensen for his editorial assistance. My thanks also goes to Peggy Nitto for excellent typing services and to Dan Loetterle for his help in drawing the figures.

1 THE PROBLEM AND THE SETTING

Introduction

One of the most important problems facing humanity today is the immense disparity in the level of income and, consequently, in the standard of living among the people in different parts of the world. What is more disheartening is that the growth rate of income of the poor countries is consistently far below the rate of economically advanced countries. Based on the resulting difference of income, countries are generally divided into two groups: developed and underdeveloped.

The term *underdeveloped* has been used with different connotations in the literature of economic development. Sometimes it means a low ratio of population to area, sometimes a scarcity of capital as indicated by the prevalence of high interest rates, and sometimes a low ratio of industrial output to total output. A reasonably satisfactory definition of an underdeveloped country seems to be a country that has good potential prospects for using more capital and labor and/or more available natural resources to support its present population at a higher level of living; or, if its per capita income level is already fairly high, to support a larger population at a level of living no lower than at present. The reasons for underdevelopment include poor natural environments, severe climatic conditions, niggardly endowment of resources, past social and cultural development, and restrictive religious practices. All these factors confine production far within the maximum possible frontier, leading to low output. Frequently, the result is a vicious circle of low output, high propensity to consume and low levels of savings and capital accumulation (Meier 1963).

Another dimension of the problem of economic development is regional or spatial. Unfortunately, insufficient attention was paid to this area until recently. Considerable theoretical and empirical work has been done on the problem of allocation of resources over time, but not over space. Clearly, the spatial aspect is also important. This is particularly true for a country like India, which is striving for economic growth despite extreme regional variations within a framework of a federal democratic system of government. The situation is basically the same in all the so-called poor countries, especially those that were under foreign rule for a long time. Examples are Indonesia (Java versus the other islands), Burma and Thailand (capital cities and rice growing areas versus up-country), Brazil (Northeast versus Central-South area), and so forth.

The formation of Bangladesh from former East Pakistan is a classic example of regional divisiveness. The general pattern is one of economic disparity between the capital or port city and the rest of the country. Look at the economic history of any of these countries. Typically, industrialization has started at a few focal points, mostly port cities. These were points deemed convenient to the rulers, not necessarily optimum locations. In addition to economic development, these points got an earlier start with respect to education, health care facilities, and all the other benefits and drawbacks of Western civilization. The cases of Calcutta, Bombay, and Madras in India are good illustrations.

This regional variation can also be observed in regions of developed countries, such as the United States, the United Kingdom, Western Europe, the USSR, and the like. In the United States, for example, the central cities, Appalachia, the northern Michigan and Minnesota regions, and other areas provide clear examples of poverty and underdevelopment in the midst of affluence and prosperity. Although on the absolute level there is no comparison between this underdevelopment and that of the developing countries, in relative terms it is nevertheless very striking.

There are many reasons for the growth and decay of a region: economic, social, and political. One factor that has become prominent in recent years is the availability of resources, particularly energy. Scarcity of energy, its high price, and the development of new sources are going to have a profound impact on regional growth and decline. For example, the northeastern United

States is in decline and is in need of reindustrialization, whereas the South and Southwest are growing and need management of this growth.

The spatial dimension is also highlighted by the continuous confrontation between developing and developed countries (North versus South); between ethnic, racial, linguistic, and religious groups; and, more recently, between ecological and development goals. Historically, this phenomenon of conflict and its resolution has not been integrated into social science theory. Consequently, the solutions obtained from such an analysis, though optimal, in an economic, social, or political perspective, have not been found to be practical in terms of policy.

Regional Science as a Discipline

It is thus abundantly clear that to understand this process of regional transformation and predict the scenarios both in time and space, we need a different orientation in the social sciences, one that incorporates space as a crucial dimension. This is provided by *regional science.*[a]

Regional science, like all social sciences, is concerned with the study of people and their continuous interaction with and adaptation to their physical environment. However, regional science limits itself to the study of problems for which a spatial or regional focus is central. It concerns research and studies on the structure, function, and operation of regions from an economic, social, and political point of view. In several important ways regional science is related to other social sciences such as economics, geography, sociology, political science, and anthropology. Each of these disciplines involves the study of humans in relationship with their physical environment.

In economics, the emphasis is on scarce resources, the pricing mechanism by which these scarce resources are allocated to diverse uses, and the associated income-determining and distributing processes. Economics is among those social sciences that have achieved a significant depth of analysis. However, the core area, at which it achieves maximum penetration, is primarily centered around the behavior of business concerns, consumers, and financial and government institutions. Until recently, economics has only infrequently broached the broad influence of space and physical environment on human behavior and land utilization patterns.

Geography is concerned "with the arrangement of things on the face of earth and with the associations of things that give character to particular places" (James and Jones 1954). Nonetheless and almost by definition, pure

---

[a]Part of this chapter is heavily drawn from Isard and Chatterji (1968) and Isard (1957).

statistical and regional theorizing, whether static or dynamic, has been generally excluded from the field of geography. The central focus of sociology is humanity and its interaction with and adaptation to the physical environment as embodied in social group activities and problems. Spatial aspects of social organizations are rarely central. The same is true for political science, where we are interested in political activities of human beings and their relation to different governmental institutions; and for anthropology, where we are more interested in the mutual relations between humans and environment.

In contrast with geography, anthropology, and political science, regional science—much like economics and to a lesser extent sociology—finds a basic thread in a methodology that embraces (1) the construction of theoretical models of various degrees of abstraction, based either on intuitive hypotheses or hypotheses suggested by the previous accumulation and processing of empirical materials; and (2) the testing of these models against statistically valid materials; the refinement and reformulation of these models in the light of the results; and, in nonending succession, the retesting and restructuring of the models.

Basic to regional science is the concept of *region*. At the present stage of scientific development, this concept is elusive. Though inescapable as a tool, the region acquires a concrete form and character only with respect to a given problem, whether the problem concerns the testing of pure spatial models at one end of the continuum or a pressing situation of reality at the other end. In this sense the set of regions (or hierarchy of sets of regions) associated with each problem at a given time is unique. Yet we may anticipate that as regional science develops and becomes better able to cope with problems of a more general nature, the diverse sets (or hierarchies of sets) of regions will tend to blend into one another to yield, ultimately, the best set (or hierarchy of sets), constantly changing over time.

The concept of *regional structure* is as relativistic as that of region. Again, at this stage in the development of regional science, the nature of the problem dictates the analytic framework, the manner of degree of disaggregation, and hence the particular notion of regional structure to be employed. Of the several valid types of sector breakdowns, analytical frameworks, and theoretical models, no one can be said to be superior in general to all the others. Each is best with respect to specific problems only. Yet, ultimately, as regional science matures, we may be able to approach general purpose regional structures that would be associated with a more satisfactory general type of theory. Such a theory would capture the essence of a region as a dynamic organism, identify its basic interaction matrix, and take us far beyond the crude conceptions we obtain by the piecemeal summation of regional studies in the several social sciences.

Techniques of Regional Science

Over the last two decades, the literature on regional science has increased considerably. The methods and techniques employed in this field have been published in books and professional journals and discussed in scholarly meetings. Much of the existing material is yet to be published.

It is not possible to catalog rigidly the different techniques of regional science, since by nature it has an interdisciplinary focus. However, we can group them conveniently under the following headings.

1. Location theory and comparative cost analysis.
2. Regional demography.
3. Regional and urban history approach.
4. Economic base and related urban growth theories.
5. Regional and interregional social accounting, intergovernmental transfer.
6. Regional and interregional input-output models.
7. Interregional programming and other optimization techniques.
8. Industrial and urban complex analysis.
9. Interregional multiplier and business cycle analysis.
10. Central place theories and application of classification techniques such as factor analysis and discriminant analysis to analyze regional problems.
11. Spatial regularity models.
12. Regional systems and simulation.
13. Regional econometric model building.
14. Interregional general equilibrium theory with political, social, economic, and ecological variables.
15. Spatial organization theory, graph theory application to regional problems.
16. Nearest-neighbor approach. Point distribution, pattern recognition, and application of mathematics of topology to point distribution, remote sensing, and other abstract models.
17. Regional allocation of resources within a fixed time horizon.
18. Survey methods in regional planning, problems of implementation.
19. Transportation studies and diffusion models.

20. Housing and rent studies.
21. General areas of management of public systems, such as hospitals, educational administration, and the like.
22. Regional and interregional energy modeling.
23. Entropy and its application.
24. Fuzzy systems and their application.
25. Catastrophe theory and its relevance in regional decline.
26. Statistical ecology.
27. Application of mathematical biology to regional growth.
28. Application of conflict management to regional systems.
29. Regional groupings of nations.
30. Multinational corporations and regional growth.

Objective of the Book

The objective of this book is to discuss briefly the different techniques listed in the previous section and to show how they can be used to attack real problems of both developed and developing countries. For a developed country, the example used will most often be the United States. For a developing country it will most often be India, particularly the Calcutta Industrial Region.

This region, termed the CIR (see Figure 1–1), consists of Calcutta City and thirty-four towns. It is probably the largest urban agglomeration in the world, and it is facing stupendous problems—economic, social, and political. The importance of this region for the economy of West Bengal, and India as well, need not be emphasized. The region's problems are also examined elsewhere (Park 1962) and will not be repeated here. There is one point on which there can be no disagreement, however: the need for comprehensive regional planning in this area.

In the planning problems of Calcutta, demographic, social, political, economic, and other factors are interrelated in a complex fashion. I do not intend to imply that the solution of these problems can be made only with the development of mathematical models, but I do believe that these models, embodying the diverse factors at work, can help us do the job better when accompanied by practical policies, such as zoning regulations, transportation planning, housing policy, and so on.

The situation in Calcutta can be viewed from three dimensions of analysis, which are nevertheless not independent. The first dimension concerns Calcutta City itself. The problems are those of housing, transportation, health, employment, and so on. The second is the relationship between the

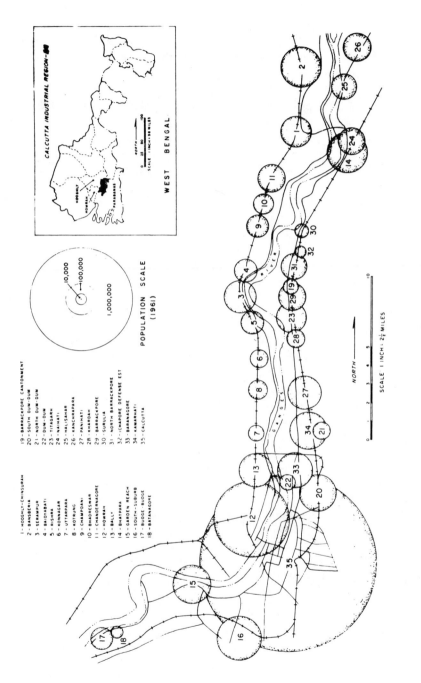

CALCUTTA INDUSTRIAL REGION—

1 - HOOGHLY-CHINSURAH
2 - BANSBERIA
3 - SERAMPUR
4 - BAIDYABATI
5 - RISHRA
6 - KONNAGAR
7 - UTTARPARA
8 - KOTRUNG
9 - CHAMPDANI
10 - BHADRESWAR
11 - CHANDERNAGORE
12 - HOWRAH
13 - BALLY
14 - BHATPARA
15 - GARDEN REACH
16 - SOUTH-SUBURB
17 - BUDGE-BUDGE
18 - BATANAGORE

19 - BARRACKPORE CANTONMENT
20 - SOUTH DUM-DUM
21 - NORTH DUM-DUM
22 - DUM-DUM
23 - TITAGARH
24 - NAIHATI
25 - HALISAHAR
26 - KANCHRAPARA
27 - PANIHATI
28 - KHARDAH
29 - BARRACKPORE
30 - GURULIA
31 - NORTH BARRACKPORE
32 - ICHAPORE DEFENSE EST
33 - BARANAGORE
34 - KAMARHATI
35 - CALCUTTA

POPULATION SCALE
(1961)

10,000
100,000
1,000,000

WEST BENGAL

NORTH

SCALE 1 INCH: 2½ MILES

Figure 1-1. Calcutta Industrial Region

towns in the metropolitan region and Calcutta City. Calcutta's problems are very much influenced by what is happening in these towns. For example, when we consider the transportation problem, the scheduling of trains and buses from these areas *to* Calcutta greatly contributes to the overcrowding in buses and trains *in* Calcutta. Anyone who lives in the area knows the nature and intensity of this correlation. The third linkage is between the CIR and other agricultural and industrial regions of West Bengal. Calcutta provides a classic challenge of development in a spatial framework.

This situation is symbolic for regions in countries in Asia, Africa, and Latin America. Indeed, the problem of development in all these countries is not only how to increase the total output but also how to distribute it fairly over space and geographic regions, particularly between urban and rural regions.

The role of space is not limited to economic variables. Historically, urbanization has acted as a strong factor in the social development of these countries. For example, it has been found that the rigidity of the caste system in India has lessened in urban centers, as compared with rural areas. The role of women has also changed. Liberal trends in society go hand in hand with urbanization. Political beliefs and ideologies are also dependent on urbanization. For example, political unrest and extremism in these countries tends to start in the urban centers. In fact, whatever wealth is generated is all concentrated in the urbanized area, leading to a serious urban-rural conflict in many countries.

The subsequent chapters will discuss how different techniques of management in regional science may be utilized for regional developments with conflicting goals in the framework of the economic, demographic, political, and social structure of the developing countries.

References

Isard, Walter. 1957. "Potential Contributions of Regional Science to Political Science." *Papers of the Regional Science Association* 3:29–34.

Isard, Walter, and Chatterji, Manas. 1968. "Potentialities of Regional Science Methods and Techniques in Attacking Indian Regional Problems." *Indian Journal of Regional Science* 1, no. i:1–23.

James, Preston F., and Jones, C. F. 1954. "Introduction." In Preston F. James and C. F. Jones, eds., *Inventory and Prospect.* Syracuse, N.Y.: Syracuse University Press.

Meier, Gerald. 1963. "The Problem of Limited Economic Development." In A. Agarwala and S. Singh, eds., *The Economics of Underdevelopment.* New York: Oxford University Press.

Park, R. L. 1962. "West Bengal with Special Attention to Calcutta." In Roy Turner, ed., *Indian Urban Future.* Berkeley: University of California Press.

Bibliography

Airov, Joseph. 1959. *The Location of the Synthetic Fiber Industry.* Cambridge, Mass.: MIT Press.

Fisher, Joseph. 1957. "Potential Contributions of Regional Science to the Field of Economics." *Papers of the Regional Science Association* 3:17–23.

Isard, Walter. 1956. *Location and Space Economics.* Cambridge, Mass.: MIT Press.

_____. 1960. *Methods of Regional Analysis.* Cambridge, Mass.: MIT Press; London: Wiley.

_____. 1969. *General Theory: Social, Political, Economic, and Regional.* Cambridge, Mass.: MIT Press.

Isard, Walter, and Liossatos, Panagis. 1979. *Spatial Dynamics and Optimal Space-Time Development.* Cambridge, Mass.: MIT Press.

Isard, Walter, and Reiner, Thomas A. 1966. "Regional Science: Retrospect and Prospect." *Papers of the Regional Science Association* 16:1–16.

Isard, Walter; Schooler, Eugene Walter; and Vietorisz, Thomas. 1959. *Industrial Complex Analysis and Regional Development.* Cambridge, Mass.: MIT Press.

Miller, Ronald E. 1963. *Domestic Airline Efficiency.* Cambridge, Mass.: MIT Press.

Smith, Thomas. 1957. "Potential Contribution of Regional Science to the Field of Geography." *Papers of the Regional Science Association* 3:13–15.

Viner, Jacob. 1963. "The Economics of Development." In A. Agarwala and S. Singh, eds., *The Economics of Underdevelopment.* New York Oxford University Press.

Wetmore, Louis. 1957. "Potential Contribution of Regional Science to the Field of City Planning." *Papers of the Regional Science Association* 3:16.

Whitney, V. H. 1957. "Potential Contributions of Regional Science to the Field of Sociology." *Papers of the Regional Science Association* 3:24–28.

2 ANALYSIS AND PROJECTION OF POPULATION AND INCOME

Definition of a Region

The starting point of any analysis of economic development is, of course, population. Before we discuss the issues involved with regional population growth and its projection, a region itself needs to be defined.

The fundamental argument of the discipline of regional science is that the problem of an open area is not the same as that of a nation. The area may be open from the point of view of geographic, economic, social, or political consideration. The definition of a region depends on the objective of the study in question. The determination of a geographic area within a country is well defined by the administration. A linguistic region is also obvious. A set of similar nations can also be taken as a region, such as the European Economic Community (EEC). For our purpose (although it is not appropriate in every case), a county/district, state or metropolitan region, and so on, as defined by the political authority, will be taken as the unit of operation. This is done to facilitate the use of existing data. We are not that concerned about the proper definition of a region in this book and assume that such a determination (through such methods as newspaper circulation, factor analysis, and the like) has already been made.

11

Demographic Indexes

After deciding at what level the problem has to be studied for the geographical unit of operation, the next important variable to consider is the population. Although the productivity of the people is more important than their total number, the aggregate number does matter from the point of view of total production, consumption, trade, and provision of services.

The treatment of population and its linkage with economic and social factors are crucial in the understanding of the functioning of the region. Before we start it will be worthwhile to discuss some of the indexes used to measure regional demographic force.

The total number of deaths in a community can be expressed mathematically as

$$D_x^t = (P_x^t - E_{x+1}^t) + (E_x^t - P_x^{t+1}), \tag{2.1}$$

where D_x^t = total number of deaths aged x during the calendar year t.

E_x^t = those who attain exact age x during the calendar year t.

P_x^t = population aged x (last birthday) at the beginning of the calendar year t.

From equation 2.1 the number of births E_0^t can be obtained by adding the appropriate number of deaths to the population in the later calendar years. Similarly, when the births are known, the population may be computed by subtracting deaths.

The index of death is the crude death rate, which is defined as the total number of deaths divided by the total population:

$$\text{Death rate} = \frac{D}{P} \times 1{,}000, \tag{2.2}$$

where D is the number of reported deaths, and P is the population. The death rate can also be disaggregated with respect to age, sex, region, urban/rural dichotomy, and so on. In line with the death rate, we can also construct morbidity and sickness rates.

Age-specific fertility rates are obtained by dividing the number of live births to married women of childbearing age in a specific age bracket by the total number of such women in that age bracket. Using these fertility rates, we can also compute what are known as the *gross* and *net reproduction rates*. The experience of the mortality and fertility rates is used for the construction of the so-called *life table*, which gives a vivid demographic picture of the region.

Although substantial theoretical and empirical work has been done in the construction and interpretation of the life tables, there have been few attempts to develop new theories involving the concept of space. Notwith-standing, in the following section, we shall present the characteristics of a national life table.

Life Tables

A life table is simply a portrayal of the demographic structure of a group of people born at the same time until each of its members dies.

The age-specific death rates, or the mortality rates, are used in the construction of the life table, which is then used for different purposes in actuarial work. A representative life table is shown in Table 2–1. The different columns in a complete life table give information about the following variables:

x = age.

m_x = mortality rates (death rates) obtained from census or other information.

q_x = probability of a person at age x dying during the next year. This can be computed by

$$q_x = \frac{2m_x}{2 + m_x}.$$ (2.3)

Table 2–1   A Sample Life Table

x Age in Years	$l_x =$ Number of Persons Living at Age x	d_x	m_x	q_x	P_x	M_x	L_x	T_x	e_x^0
7	100,000	152	.0015	.00152	.9984	.0014	99,923	5,806,862	
8	99,847	130	.0013	.00130	.9986	.0012	99,781	5,706,938	
9	99,716	116	.0011	.00116	.9988	.0011	99,658	5,607,157	
10	99,599	108	.0010	.00108	.9989	.0010	99,545	5,507,498	
11	99,491	106	.0010	.00106	.9989	.0010	99,438	5,407,953	
47	85,693	967	.0113	.0112	.9887	.0108	85,209	1,905,985	22
48	84,725	1,035	.0123	.0122	.9877	.0112	84,207	1,820,775	21
49	83,690	1,138	.0137	.0136	.9864	.0120	83,120	1,736,567	20
50	82,551								

$P_x = 1 - q_x$ = probability for survival for the next year.
l_x = the number of persons living at age x.
M_x = force of mortality:

$$\frac{l_{x-1} + l_{x+1}}{2l_x}.$$

L_x = number of years lived by L_0 persons between x and $x + 1$:

$$\int_0^1 l_{x+t} dt \cong \frac{l_x + l_{x+1}}{2} = l_x - 1/2 d_x.$$

T_x = number of years lived by the cohort after given age x; that is, $T_x = \int_0^\infty l_{x+t}\, dt = \Sigma_{i=x}^w L_i$, where w is last age for which any figure is available.

e_x^0 = complete expectation of life = T_x/l_x = number of years expected to be lived by a person at age x (without ignoring the fractional number of years lived).

Sometimes data are not available for each year. In those cases we construct what is known as the *abridged life table*. As mentioned before, a careful examination of a set of life tables constructed over a period of time can reveal population shifts over ages. These have grave implications for the production and consumption of resources and the provision of such services as health care. The key factor in the construction of a life table is a reliable estimate of the mortality rate m_x and, consequently, l_x. When reliable estimates are not readily available, they are usually estimated by mathematical formulations, as discussed later.

Makeham's and Gompertz's Formula for Smoothing Mortality Rates

Sometimes the l_x figures obtained from the census need to be smoothed. For this purpose we can use either the Gompertz curve or Makeham's formula. Which of the two we choose depends on the particular situation. Let us discuss the use of Makeham's formula to smooth l_x values for different ages x.

Makeham's formula is given by

$$l_x = K s^x \cdot g^{c^x}$$

or

$$\log l_x = \log K + x \log s + c^x \log g. \qquad (2.4)$$

$$\log l_{x+t} + \log K + (x + t) \log s + c^{x+t} \log g.$$

$$\log l_{x+2t} = \log K + (x + 2t) \log s + c^{x+2t} \log g.$$

Taking the second difference,

$$\Delta^2 \log l_x = c^x(c^t - 1) \log g. \qquad (2.5)$$

$$\Delta^2 \log l_{x+t} = c^{x+t}(c^t - 1)^2 \log g. \qquad (2.6)$$

Dividing equation 2.6 by 2.5, we get

$$\frac{\Delta^2 \log l_{x+t}}{\Delta^2 \log l_x} = c^t. \qquad (2.7)$$

Similarly,

$$\frac{\Delta^2 \log l_{x+2t}}{\Delta^2 \log l_{x+t}} = c^t. \qquad (2.8)$$

Thus, if we find that the ratio of consecutive second-order difference of log l_x values are consistent, a Makeham curve will fit well. To get the estimate of the parameters, we proceed by summing equation 2.6 for all t, as follows:

$$\Sigma \, \Delta^2 \log l_{x+t} = (c^t - 1)^2 \log g \sum_t c^{x+t}. \qquad (2.9)$$

From equation 2.9 we shall get the estimate of g. Again, considering the expression

$$\Delta \log l_x = t \log s + c^x(c^t - 1) \log g, \qquad (2.10)$$

we get an estimate of log s.

Finally, from the relation

$$\log l_x = \log K + x \log s + c^x \log g, \qquad (2.11)$$

the value of log K can be obtained. Once the parameters have been estimated, the graduated levels of l_x can be computed and compared to the observed values.

Population Forecasting

Extensive material is available in the literature regarding the projection of the population of an open area. Some of these techniques are as follows:

Historical Comparison

If we have two regions of the same size and age/sex composition, but one area is older than the other, then for the new region we can project the population by using the past growth pattern of the older area. This nonquantitative method has been found to be effective for crude estimation, but for refined analysis this is not good enough.

Ratio Method

In this method we assume that the ratio of a population of a small area (such as a county) to a larger-area unit (such as a state) will be the same as in the future. If we know the population of the state in the future, then multiplying this population figure with the ratio, we can obtain the population of the open area. Of course, we have to know the population of the benchmark area, namely the state. Alternatively, we can use the ratio of the number of schoolchildren to the total population, and multiply it by the number of schoolchildren in a future year, thus giving us the total population.

Population Register

A population register is a continuous census. It registers births, deaths, and migrations for a geographical area. Although it is being used in many European countries, it may not be practical or desirable in the United States.

Use of Census Registration Figures and Migration

When we have (1) population data from a decennial or middecade census, (2) complete birth and death registration, and (3) migration figures, we can simply get the population figures by addition and subtraction. However, migration figures are not usually available. As such, the problem of population projection is reduced to an estimation of the migration figures.

Growth-Component Method

This method focuses attention on the major components of population growth, namely, net natural increase, net migration, and annexation (or abandonment). The forecasting equation becomes

$$P_{t+\lambda} = P_t + N_\lambda + M_\lambda, \qquad (2.12a)$$

where N_λ is net natural increase during the period λ, and M_λ is net migration in the same period. Equation 2.12a can be written in its alternative form

$$P_{t+\lambda} = P_t + (\alpha P_t + \gamma) - (\beta P_t + \delta), \qquad (2.12b)$$

where α = birth rate during period λ.
β = death rate during period λ.
γ = in-migration during period λ.
δ = out-migration during period λ.
The problem of population projection then reduces to estimating the parameters α, β, γ, δ.

An extension of this growth component method is given by Rogers (1968). This formulation is

$$P(t + 1) = b + d - mP(t). \qquad (2.13)$$

Equation 2.13 simply states that the population in the next year depends on the current population, birth, death and migration. Of course, the equation can be disaggregated with respect to age, sex, and region. The model in terms of growth rate can be written in matrix form as follows:

$$P(t + \lambda) = GP(t), \qquad (2.14)$$

where $G = B + S - M$ denotes the growth rate of population, considering births, deaths, and migration.

The symbols in G are defined as follows:

$$S = \begin{bmatrix} 0 & 0 & \cdots & 0 \\ S_{21} & 0 & \cdots & 0 \\ 0 & S_{32} & \cdots & 0 \\ \cdots\cdots\cdots\cdots\cdots\cdots S_{RR-1} & 0 \end{bmatrix}$$

In this matrix, S_{RR-1} denotes the rate of survival of the age group $(R-1)$ population at t into population age R in the time period of t to $t+T$.

The rate of migration matrix is denoted by

$$M = \begin{bmatrix} 0 & 0 & \cdots & 0 \\ M_{21} & 0 & \cdots & 0 \\ 0 & M_{32} & \cdots & 0 \\ 0 & \cdots\cdots\cdots M_{RR-1} & 0 \end{bmatrix}$$

In the foregoing matrix the rate of net immigration of population in the age group $(R-1)$ to age group R between this year t and λ is denoted by M_{RR-1}; and $B = [0,0 \ldots B_\alpha, \ldots B_\beta, 0 \ldots 0]$, where the element b_k denotes the rates at which children are born to a population of age k.

The foregoing model can be generalized for multiregional cases by simply affixing appropriate subscripts and superscripts (Rees and Wilson 1974).

Correlation and Regression Technique

In this case population is related to such variables as employment income, exports investment, automobile registration, school enrollment, and so on through the framework of regression analysis of the form

$$Y = a + b_1 X_1 + b_2 X_2 + \ldots b_p X_p. \tag{2.15}$$

Here, Y is called the dependent variable (in this case, population); X_1, $X_2, \ldots X_p$ are termed independent variables, like those mentioned before. The parameters are $b_1, b_2 \ldots b_p$. They are known as regression coefficients, and a is known as the intercept. The parameter b_1, for example, measures unit change in Y (population) due to a unit change in X_1 (say, employment) when the other variables $X_2, X_3 \ldots X_p$ remain constant.

The parameters $a, b_1, b_2 \ldots b_p$ can be estimated by using time-series or cross-section data pertaining to the region. If the values of $X_1, X_2, \ldots X_p$ are known for a future date, then the projected value of Y can be obtained from equation 2.15 by plugging in these values.

For example, in a regression equation involving only one independent variable X (say, employment), the regression equation becomes

$$y = abx. \tag{2.16}$$

By using the method of least square, it can be shown that the best estimates of a and b are

$$a = \bar{y} - b\bar{x},$$

$$b = \frac{\Sigma(x - \bar{x})(y - \bar{y})}{\Sigma(x - \bar{x})^2}, \qquad (2.17)$$

where $\bar{x}$ and $\bar{y}$ are the sample means of x and y, respectively. Given the empirical data, a and b can be computed and inserted in equation 2.16. The effectiveness of a regression equation depends on the correct sign of the regression coefficient b (in this case it should be positive), low standard error of b, and high value of the coefficient of determination. This coefficient is the square of the correlation coefficient between the variables x and y. The nearer the coefficient to 1, the better the fit.

Of course, the relationship between y and x need not be linear. Investigators have used different types of mathematical functions. One such formulation, involving the population (P) and time period (t) most commonly used in the literature is the logistic curve.

Logistic Curve

The equation of the logistic curve is given by

$$P_t = \frac{L}{1 + e^{r(\beta - t)}} \qquad (2.18)$$

for time period t, where P_t is the population value and L, r, and β are constants. For the estimation of the parameters, we consider the population at two points in time, t and $t + h$.

From equation 2.18 we have

$$\frac{1}{P_t} = \frac{1 + e^{r(\beta - t)}}{L}. \qquad (2.19)$$

$$\frac{1}{P_{t+h}} = \frac{1 + e^{r(\beta - t - h)}}{L}. \qquad (2.20)$$

That is,

$$\frac{1}{P_{t+h}} = \frac{1 - e^{-rh}}{L} + e^{-rh} P_t. \qquad (2.21)$$

If we substitute

$$\frac{1}{P_t} = x \text{ and } \frac{1}{P_{t+h}} = y$$

as our new variables, then, from equation 2.21, the relationship between x and y will be linear:

$$y = a + bx. \tag{2.22}$$

Since both the variable y and x are subject to error, we do not use the least-squares method for estimation. Instead, we use the Rhodes estimate, namely,

$$\hat{b} = \frac{\Sigma(y - \bar{y})^2}{\Sigma(x - \bar{x})^2}, \tag{2.23}$$

and

$$\hat{a} = \bar{y} - b\bar{x}. \tag{2.24}$$

Noting from equation 2.22 that

$$b = e^{-rh}, \tag{2.25}$$

we can estimate the value of r. Again, from equation 2.22

$$a = 1 - \frac{e^{rh}}{L}. \tag{2.26}$$

From equation 2.26 we can compute the value of L easily. From the equation of the logistic curve (2.16), it follows that

$$r(\beta - t) \log_{10}e = \log_{10}(L/P_t - 1), \tag{2.27}$$

or

$$r\beta \log e = \log_{10}. \tag{2.28}$$

Thus all the parameters of the logistic curve are known. It now can be used for projecting population P_t for any value of t in the future.

Spatial Regularity and Population Modeling

The population and its growth rate over space are not random variables. Spatial regularities of population growth over time can be mathematically modeled. Given the knowledge of present population of a center, if the future rate of growth of the population is known, then the population at a future data can be estimated. However, rate of growth of population in cities of different size is not constant for every decade. It is a stochastic variate, and it will be useful if the probability distribution of such a variate is obtained. Here we will show how such probability distributions can be obtained by using a class of distribution functions, known as the Pearsonian system, for central cities in the United States with population of 100,000 or more in 1960 (see Elderton and Johnson 1969).

For each ten-year period (1900–1910, 1910–1920, 1920–1930, 1930–1940, 1940–1950, 1950–1960), the frequency distribution of the growth rates of all U.S. cities has been considered.

We can now follow very closely the procedures given by Elderton and Johnson (1969). For any given decade, let x denote the growth rate and $y = f(x)$ the density of probability. For most variates, the probability generally starts at zero, rises to a maximum and then falls asymptotically to the x axis. Mathematically, this means that there exists a series of functions, $y = \Phi_1(x)_1$, $y = \Phi_2(x)$ . . . for which

$$\frac{dy}{dx} = 0$$

for some values of x, namely at $y = 0$ and $x = -a$, where the maximum of y appears at $x = -a$. The foregoing argument suggests that we should have the relation

$$\frac{dy}{dx} = y(x + a). \tag{2.29}$$

To make this relation more general, we can write equation 2.29 as

$$\frac{dy}{dx} = \frac{y(x + a)}{F(x)}. \tag{2.30}$$

Expanding $F(x)$ by Maclaurin's theorem in ascending powers of x, we get

$$\frac{dy}{dx} = \frac{y(x + a)}{b_0 + b_1 x + b_2 x^2}. \tag{2.31}$$

For the sake of simplicity and accuracy in graduation, we stop at x^2. Equation 2.31 can be written as

$$(b_0 + b_1 x + b_2 x^2)\frac{dy}{dx} = y(x + a). \tag{2.32}$$

Multiplying each side by x^n and integrating with respect to x for its appropriate limits gives us

$$\int x^n(b_0 + b_1 x + b_2 x^2)\frac{dy}{dx}\,dx = \int y(x + a)x^n\,dx. \tag{2.33}$$

Depending on the value of b_1, b_2, the exact nature of the frequency density function (y) will change. The criteria used for the determination of the type of function is determined by β_1 and β_3, where $\beta_1 = u_3{}^2/u_2{}^3$, $\beta_2 = u_4/u_2{}^2$.

Coming to the differential equation 2.31, we see

$$\frac{1}{y}\frac{dy}{dx} = \frac{x + a}{b_0 + b_1 x + b_2 x^2}. \tag{2.34}$$

The solution of the foregoing equation will depend on the roots of the quadratic equation $b_0 + b_1 x + b_2 x^2 = 0$, or on the discriminant $\kappa = b_1{}^2/4b_0 b_2$. Substituting the values of the constants, the criterion is then

$$\kappa = \frac{\beta_1(\beta_2 + 3)^2}{4(2\beta_2 - 3\beta_1 - 6)\,(4\beta_2 - 3\beta_1)}. \tag{2.35}$$

If κ is negative, the roots are real and of different signs, and the frequency density function we obtain is known as Pearsonian type 1 (main). Assuming that $-A_1$ and A_2 are the two roots, the equation of the type 1 curve can be obtained from

$$\log y = \int \frac{x + a}{b_2(x + A_1)\,(x - A_2)}\,dx. \tag{2.36}$$

After appropriate substitutions and integration, we get

$$y = y_0\left(1 + \frac{x}{a_1}\right)^{m_1}\left(1 - \frac{x}{a_2}\right)^{m_2}, \tag{2.37}$$

where

$$\frac{m_1}{m_2} = \frac{a_1}{a_2}.$$

The four parameters involved in equation 2.37 can be estimated by the method of moments. This method consists in equating the moments obtained from the frequency distribution to those obtained from the frequency function (equation 2.37). For nth-order moment it will be

$$\Sigma f(x)x^n = \int x^n y_0\left(1 + \frac{x}{a_1}\right)^{m_1}\left(1 - \frac{x}{a_2}\right)^{m_2}dx. \tag{2.38}$$

The left-hand side of equation 2.38 can be obtained from descriptive statistics. The right-hand side of equation 2.38 will be algebraic, involving m_1, m_2, a_1, a_2. Putting

$$y_e = y'\,x^{m_1}(a - x)^{m_2},$$

where ms are given as in type 1 (main), so that

$$y' = \frac{N}{a^{m_1+m_2+1}} \frac{\Gamma(m_1 + m_2 + 2)}{\Gamma(m_1 + 1)\,\Gamma(m_2 + 1)} , \qquad (2.39)$$

and $a = a_1 + a_2$. These parameters can be estimated by the method of moments.

To see whether a type 1 (main) or a type 1 (J-shaped) curve can be fitted to a skewed frequency distribution, we have to calculate the value of κ in equation 2.35 and see whether it is negative. We have found that for all the decades under consideration, this is the case. If in addition, m_1 is negative, then a type 1 (J-shaped) curve is the one to fit. Although a main type 1 curve is appropriate for 1900–1910, for all other decades a J-shaped one is relevant. The frequency functions can be written as follows:

1900–1910:

$$y = 2.4480\left(1 + \frac{x}{37.4738}\right)^{.6232}\left(1 - \frac{x}{67.9962}\right)^{1.9506} \qquad (2.40)$$

1920–1930:

$$y = .1343\,x^{-.2941}(94.8250 - x)^{.7967} \qquad (2.41)$$

1930–1940:

$$y = .004559\,x^{-.3486}(108.661 - x)^{1.5446} \qquad (2.42)$$

1940–1950:

$$y = .04283\,x^{-.3551}(87.9690 - x)^{1.1229} \qquad (2.43)$$

1950–1960:

$$y = .01434\,x^{-.3348}(100.4510 - x)^{1.1905} \qquad (2.44)$$

Once the frequency functions of the rate of growth are known, we can apply them to estimate the population of 1990 on the basis of the population of the current year. For an example of an application of the foregoing model, see Chatterji (1972).

Estimation of Migration

It is clear that for population projection the crucial variate estimate is the migration. There are various ways of projecting the migration. It can be based on historical trends, ratio, and correlation methods (Isard 1960). Other models often used are known as the gravity and interaction models. Following Wilson (1974), we can explain the model as follows.

Let U_i be the propensity to migrate per 1,000 population from region i, where γ denotes the national propensity. Let the push factor of region i be characterized by a set of k variates (such as unemployment), and let T_j denote the k variables for attraction.

Then we may write

$$U_i = \gamma + \sum_T a^k X^k.$$

O_i = No. of migrants leaving i.

= $U_i P_i$, where P_i is he population of the ith region   (2.45)

The attractiveness of each region can be defined by

$$W_j = \sum_P b^p T^p. \tag{2.46}$$

When the difference between U_i and γ is known, the a coefficients can be estimated by regression analysis. We can assume

$$W_j = KM \cdot j$$

for the same period and estimate the coefficients b^p by regression analysis. Then the migration function can be specified as

$$M_{ij} = A_i O_i W_j e^{-\beta c_{ij}}, \tag{2.47}$$

where

$$A_i = \frac{1}{\sum_j W_j e^{-\beta c_{ij}}}$$

and c_{ij} is the cost of migration from i to j. The coefficient β can be estimated by different techniques.

Estimation of Regional Income

After the analysis and projection of population and migration in different regions for a country—say, India—are made, the next task is to estimate regional income. Although the state income figures are not readily available, it is possible to estimate the regional variations from data on agriculture. (The land area cultivated per capita in 1951 ranged from 0.6 acres in Kerala and 0.8 acres in Bihar to 2.4 acres in the state of Bombay and 3.1 acres in Rajasthan. The annual income of families engaged in agricultural labor was estimated to vary from a low of 340 rupees in Orissa to 622 rupees in West

Bengal.) Over the years many methods of regional income accounting have been developed in regional science. Although most of these methods were constructed to suit the conditions in the developed countries, they can be easily modified and combined with other accounting frameworks specifically designed for developing countries. One such method is by Deane (1953).

In her study Deane aims at the development of a meaningful triple-column income-output expenditure table. The first column of this table would show the groups of individuals or institutions by which income is earned; the second column, in what industries the income is earned; and the third column, how the income is consumed or invested. In this table each transaction would appear three times—first as it becomes part of income received, next as it represents the value of a particular kind of good or service produced, and finally as it enters into some form of consumption or investment. Deane's system permits the effective utilization of every scrap of economic information by providing a considerable number of cross-checks. It thereby reduces the area of unconfirmed estimate to the smallest possible range and presents the sum of both the available data and the deductions that can be drawn from the material.

The specific form of the table may vary significantly from study to study, not only because of variations among basic characteristics of regions and available data, but also because of differences in study objectives and meaningful conceptual frameworks. In a country like India, a considerable portion of economic activity is concentrated on subsistence agriculture and handicraft; and there is a significant volume of barter transactions that do not pass through a formal market. Thus the standard Western-world functional classification (wages, rent, interest, and profit) should be replaced in many cases by a more meaningful classification related to a subsistence economy or by a combination of these classifications with a standard Western-world set of categories. Such a combination may be desirable when an under-developed region has an important export sector tied to the industrialized sector within the country or abroad. Otherwise, imposing on an under-developed region a set of social accounts appropriate for industrialized regions will lead to overstating the importance of money transactions and thus destroy the measure of welfare. This is an area in which Indian regional scientists can contribute significantly by developing new definitions, ideas, and techniques that will be appropriate for income accounting not only in underdeveloped areas of India but also in similar countries (Choudhury 1966).

When we come to the question of income accounting for developed open regions in India, the applicability of the tools of regional science becomes easier. The industrial economy of India is concentrated in a few urban centers like Calcutta, Bombay, and Ahmedabad, and a number of other centers such as Durgapur, Bangalore, Bhilai, and Rourkela, which have developed in recent years. In this sense, income accounting in India is not too difficult. If we have a set of regional accounts for these industrial regions, then what remains is to account for the agricultural sector, for which we can use the area and output figures for different agricultural crops. The income accounting of urban areas is useful not only for income accounting for India as a whole but also for urban planning. Consider, for example, the case for the Calcutta Industrial Region. One of the prerequisites for planning in Calcutta (which is presently being considered under the auspices of the Calcutta Metropolitan Development Authority) is to prepare a regional social accounting of this region: (1) the income coming into this region and going out, (2) the incomes and expenditures of different constituent municipalities (which may help us to determine investment outlays in supplying different civic amenities at a future date), and (3) the import-export relation of this region with the rest of India and abroad (see Chatterji 1968). For the construction of such an interregional accounting system, the framework

Table 2-2 Rest-of-the-World Account

Value added in the production of goods for export.	Net investment in the private sector of the rest of the world.
Out-commuters wages over in-commuters wages.	
Net receipts of interest, rent, and dividend from abroad.	
Profits of outside branches of local firms over profits of local branches of outside firms.	
Minus import of final and intermediate goods for corporation.	
Minus import of final and capital formation.	
Net current payments due to the area on private account.	
Minus: Direct and indirect nonlocal tax and nontop payments over transfer payments from nonload government.	Less: Net contribution to the nonlocal government.
Net current payments due to this area.	Net investment in the rest of the world.

Table 2-3 Local Capital Formation Account

Value added in the production of goods for local capital formation.	Purchases of capital goods by businesses.
Charges against local capital formation product.	Less: Imports of final and intermediate goods for capital formation.
	Local capital formation product.

suggested by Leven (1958) in Tables 2-2 through 2-7 can be of much help. See also Hirsch (1964) and Hochwald (1961).

Income accounting for Calcutta may reveal many interesting facts that are not now apparent. For the construction of such accounts it may be necessary to conduct special surveys and refashion some of the existing materials. Again, using the data on costs and revenues of different civic amenities provided by the municipalities, we can construct a regional model for projection of these items at a future date. This model will be extremely useful for deciding the optimum size of each of the municipalities.

Regional income accounting can be supplemented and its value greatly enhanced by the analysis of interregional commodity flow. Such analysis points out the manner and extent to which any region (1) can and does avail itself of the natural advantages of other regions through imports, and (2) can and does compete with other regions in the disposal of its products in the several regional and subregional markets. The money flow counterpart of it can provide us with a rupee tag and a common denominator for the exchange of goods and transfer of assets. Thus flow analysis can help formulate monetary and fiscal policies both within a region and in India as a whole. When commodity flow and money flow studies are completed, regional balance-of-payment studies can be undertaken to assess the current financial position of a region's economy and its general economic health. The interregional commodity flow data for India are reasonably good, but no significant use has yet been made of this material. The flow data can give a

Table 2-4 Local Consumption Account

Value added in the production of goods for local consumption.	Purchases of goods by consumers.
Charges against local consumption service.	Less: Imports of final and intermediate goods for consumption.
	Equals: Local consumption product.

Table 2-5   Savings and Investment Account

Purchases of capital goods by business.	Undistributed profits of local corporation.
	Personal saving.
	Capital consumption allowances and statistical discrepancy.
	Less: Net investment in the rest of the world.
Equals: Gross investment.	Equals: Gross saving.

clear picture of spatial movements and how they affect regional activities, but they have more than mere descriptive value. They can be very helpful in future transportation planning. When commodity flows are tied to interregional money flows, they are extremely useful. The same is true for money flow analysis.

The Indian economy is mostly agricultural and thus depends on the vagaries of nature. The level of total economic activity fluctuated greatly over the years depending on agricultural population. This fluctuation took different forms in different regions. Even in the industrial sector, total industrial activity depended on such big industries as jute, textiles, and tea. The ups and downs of these industries in a few regions influenced national cycles. Industrial location policies should consider the implications of such regional cycles. Other things being equal, it is generally more desirable to develop an industrial mix in a region whose cyclical tendencies tend to balance or at least not to intensify each other. Thus one valuable avenue of inquiry has been concerned with the industrial composition of regions and the cyclical fluctuations of different types of industries as they may offset each other. We discover that in the short run at least certain industries are basic, particularly

Table 2-6   Sources and Uses of Funds for Local Saving and Investment

Sources of locally used funds.	Uses of locally generated funds.
Locally financed imports of goods.	Locally used area savings.
Outside financed imports of goods for capital formation.	Outside placement of local savings.
Equals: Imports for capital formation.	Equals: Local savings.

Table 2-7   Gross Product Account

Value added in the production of goods for export.	Sale of goods for the rest of the world.
	Purchase of goods by consumers.
Value added in the production of goods for local capital function.	Purchases of capital goods by business.
Value added in the production of goods for local consumption.	Less: Imports of intermediate goods for production of goods for export.
Charges against gross area product.	Less: Imports of final and intermediate goods for capital formation.
	Less: Imports of final and intermediate goods for consumption.
	Equals: Gross area product.
Equals: Charges against gross area product.	

those that serve national markets. Their fluctuation leads to changes in local income, which in turn influence retail sales and various service trades. In short, the fluctuations of basic industry have a multiplier effect. In India there are many regions that depend solely on the export of one commodity. When there is a change in the export of this product, the direct and indirect impact of this change is considerable. Regional and interregional multipliers can be devised for evaluating this impact. For regional scientists there is considerable opportunity to develop the theoretical basis of such regional cycle and multiplier analysis (Airov 1963).

References

Airov, Joseph. 1963. "The Construction of Interregional Business Cycle Models." *Journal of Regional Science* 5, no. 1:1–20.

Chatterji, Manas. 1972. "The Future of Regional Science." *Northeast Regional Science Review* 2:1–4.

Choudhury, M. D. 1966. *Regional Income Accounting in an Underdeveloped Economy.* Calcutta: Asia Publishing House.

Deane, Phyllis. 1953. *Colonial Social Accounting.* Cambridge: Cambridge University Press.

Elderton, William D., and Johnson, N. L. 1969. *Systems of Frequency Curves.* Cambridge: Cambridge University Press.

Hirsch, Werner, ed. 1964. *Regional Accounts for Policy Decisions.* Baltimore, Md.: Johns Hopkins University Press.

Hochwald, Werner, ed. 1961. *Design of Regional Accounts.* Baltimore, Md.: Johns Hopkins University Press.

Isard, Walter. 1960. *Methods of Regional Analysis.* Cambridge, Mass.: MIT Press; London: Wiley.

Leven, Charles L. 1958. "Theory and Method of Income and Product Accounts for Metropolitan Areas." Mimeographed, Iowa State College, Ames.

Rees, P. H., and Wilson, Alan G. 1974. *Spatial Demographic Analysis.* New York: Wiley Interscience.

Rogers, Andrei. 1968. *Matrix Analysis of Interregional Population Growth and Distribution.* Berkeley: University of California Press.

Wilson, Alan G. 1974. *Urban and Regional Models in Geography and Planning.* New York: Wiley.

Bibliography

Bourland, D. D. 1950. "The Distribution of Progressions within Cities in the United States." *American Journal of Psychology* 63:244–249.

Champernowne, D. G. 1953. "A Model of Income Distribution." *Economic Journal* 63:318–351.

Chatterji, Manas. 1963. "Studies in the Structure of the Calcutta Economy." Docterol dissertation, University of Pennsylvania, Philadelphia.

———. 1966. "Municipal Costs and Revenues in the Calcutta Industrial Region." *Quarterly Journal of Local Self-Government Institute* (Bombay) 36, no. 3, issue 143 (January–March).

———. 1969. "A Model of Resolution of Conflict between India and Pakistan." *Papers of the Peace Research Society* 12 (November): 87–102.

Committee on National Statistics. 1980. *Estimating Population and Income of Small Areas.* Washington, D.C.: National Academy Press.

Hirsch, Werner, ed. 1962. *Elements of Regional Accounts.* Baltimore, Md.: Johns Hopkins University Press.

Mandelbrot, B. 1965. "A Class of Long-Tailed Probability Distributions and the Empirical Distribution of City Sizes in Mathematical Explorations in Behavioral Sciences." In Fred Massarik and Philburn Ratosh, eds., *Mathematical Explorations in Behavioral Science.* Homewood, Ill.: Irwin.

Simon, H. A. 1955. "On a Class of Skew Distribution Functions." *Biometrika* 42: 425–440.

Wolfenden, Hugh H. 1954. *Population Statistics and Their Compilation.* Chicago: University of Chicago Press.

Zipf, George Kingsley. 1949. *Human Behavior and the Principle of Least Effort.* Cambridge, Mass.: Academy-Wesley Press.

3 Regional Activity Analysis

Location and Measurement of Economic Activity

After the analysis and projection of population and migration in different regions are done, the next task for economic development is to decide its optimal location, measurement, and projection.

Most of the classical scholars in location theory come under the influence of German thought. The first attempt at a general location theory began with Alfred Weber (Friedrich 1929), although Von Thünen (1856), the father of location theorists, far in advance of his time, did make progress toward a general locational analysis. Launhardt (1885), a major predecessor of Weber, treated the location theory with narrower sets of circumstances than were encompassed in Von Thünen's isolated state. Weber was also influenced by Roscher (1878) and Schaffle (1873). Predohl (1925) extended the partial equilibrium analysis of Weber to a more general equilibrium case. The more recent theory of location starts with the modification and extension of the classical system. The basic reference begins with Isard (1956), Hoover (1937, 1948), Lösch (1959), Alonso (1964), and Greenhut (1956). They focus on the total transportation cost but introduce variations in labor, power cost, and the like, as well as internal and external economies. Kuhn and

Keunne (1962), Cooper (1968), and others have proposed algorithms for this extended version.

Let us briefly state Isard's model. Like Weber, he assumes constant-coefficient production functions and uses a general spatial transformation function such as

$$\Phi(Y_1, \ldots, Y_k, M_A S_A, M_B S_B, \ldots, M_j S_j, X_{K+1}, X_{K+2}, \ldots, X_n) = 0,$$

where $Y_1, \ldots Y_K$ represents quantities of various inputs other than transport; $M_A S_A \ldots M_L S_L$ represent quantities of various transport inputs; $X_{K+1} \ldots X_N$ represent quantities of various outputs; M_A, M_B, $\ldots M_L$ represent the weights of various raw materials; and S_A, S_B, $\ldots S_L$ represent the distances products and raw materials moved. Assuming that total revenue and costs on all inputs are fixed, the firm's customary problem is to maximize profits.

$$V = -P_1 Y_1 - P_2 Y_2 \ldots - P_K Y_K - r_A M_A S_A - r_B M_B S_B - r_L M_L S_L + P_{K+1} \ldots + P_n X_n,$$

where $P_1, P_2 \ldots P_n$ are prices and $r_A, r_B \ldots r_L$ are transport rates. This maximization leads to the conditions

$$\frac{r_I}{r_J} = -\frac{d(M_J S_J)}{d(M_I S_I)} (M_c S_c) = \text{constant},$$

$$\frac{r_I}{r_C} = -\frac{d(M_C S_C)}{d(M_I S_I)} (M_J S_J) = \text{constant},$$

$$\frac{r_J}{r_C} = -\frac{d(M_C S_C)}{d(M_J S_J)} (M_I S_I) = \text{constant},$$

which can be interpreted as substitution principles of marginal analysis of economics. Isard's conditions were relaxed by Moses (1958). Lefeber (1955) reformulated them for a more realistic situation with respect to discrete points. Samuelson (1952) extended this problem within a linear programming framework. An interesting formulation of the problem is that of Stevens (1961), who discusses the implications of the dual variables in transportation programs for the classical theory of location rent.

Lösch's formulation of location theory is both spatial and multiregional. He considers a broad, homogeneous plane with uniform transport facilities in all directions where raw materials are uniformly available in sufficient quantities. Under this condition, he deduces that the market area of an individual producer will be a hexagon. For each commodity the plane is dissected into a honeycomb of hexagonal market areas.

Closely related to the Lösch theory of market areas is Christaller's (1933) central place theory. According to Christaller, a large homogeneous territory may be conceived as patterned and structured. For a given number of villages, there is a township. For a given number of townships in the second-order hierarchy, we might have a city, and so forth. The whole plane may be thought of as a hierarchical system of central places. For each member of the central place we have an allocation of broad categories of functions. For example, the first-order place (say, household) may perform only one function (say, consumption). The second-order central place may be a retail trade center for a given number of first-order central places. Christaller's central place theory gives a framework of location and allocation of services within such a hierarchical system.

Most of the literature in location theory is based on the assumption of certainty. Webber (1972) injects the concepts of uncertainty into location economics. According to Webber, economic activities take place in terms of spatial context under uncertainty. The recent trend in geography and regional science is from deterministic to more and more stochastic or probabilistic models. In deterministic models, once we have stipulated the initial conditions (for example, transport cost, population density, and so on, in the Lösch system of hexagonal nets), the system is automatically determined. The uncertainty for location decisions may arise for different reasons. One may be due to interpersonal difference in human behavior; for example, it is not true that human beings *always* maximize their profit. In a stochastic model, the existence of individual values as well as of those small factors that cannot be explicitly incorporated to the model can be considered. Morill (1963, 1967), Cherry (1961), Goldman (1953), Danskin (1962), Tiebout (1957), and others give examples of the implications of uncertainty in location decisions.

Another direction in which location theory has expanded relates to the competitive element. Hotelling (1929) first introduced the location game. He gives an example of a location game for a given quantity of a commodity under constant cost conditions for two firms, each competing for a market stretched along a line of length l. Corresponding to each unit length of time, one unit quantity of commodity is consumed during each unit of time. The demand from each unit of the line is infinitely elastic. Customers' purchases are influenced only by price at the factory plus transport cost. Hotelling determines the set of equilibrium factory prices for A and B in terms of $a, b, l,$ and c, where a and b are the locations of firms A and B, and c is transport cost.

Stevens (1961) gives an interesting example of a locational game. There are three service franchises for sale along a turnpike, and two buyers with equal funds make sealed bids. The sites are sold to the highest bidder. To avoid a non-zero-sum game, Stevens assumes that each seller attempts to maximize his advantage over his competitor. The players can bid for one, two, or three of the locations, and any combination of bids uses up all the funds. It turns out that an optimum strategy for each player is to make a random choice of any two of the three locations and to bid for those two. The game is fair in that one player will obtain one location and the second player another location, whereas the third location is allocated to a player on the basis of a device that gives each player a probability of one-half of gaining that location.

Isard (1969) also presents an example of gamelike decision models for interdependent firms. In his model, participants wish to locate one or more activities, whereas his optimal location depends on the location decisions of the other participants. At first, he considers economic location games that involve decisions regarding production plants, retail stores, and so on, so that profits are maximized. The interdependence in these location decisions derives from spatial market competition, agglomeration possibilities, and the like in a general political, social, economic equilibrium system that he extends to a gaming framework.

The general conclusion reached by studying location theory under uncertainty (from the viewpoint of both interindustry interdependence and within-industry interdependence) is that the existing town, especially a large one, will grow. Uncertainty will also force the location in larger towns even though the cost of production may be higher there.

The location theory has been developed to great perfection by statistical geographers and regional scientists. For example, multiobjective location allocation, in a hierarchical system, and stochastic location can be mentioned in passing.

However, location-allocation modeling can be improved in several ways. For example, new theories related to locating plants for disposing of nuclear waste and dangerous chemicals need to be developed. There is a need for a new approach to location theory for reindustrialization purposes, as in the Northeast region of the United States. The most promising avenue of research seems to be the integration of the theory of conflict management with location theory.

The operational aspect of location theory is embodied in the procedure of cost-benefit analysis. In the field of political science and public policy research, this method is fully developed. The central theme of this method is to take a number of possible location points in space, compute the net benefit (monetary or otherwise), and choose that location for which the net benefit is maximum.

Crucial to any decision about the location of economic activity is its measurement. The activity level can be measured by total employment or by output. Care should be taken when employment is used as an index, since it is easy to disregard part-time and seasonal employment. For some activities, such as petrochemicals or the electronic industry, the employment level does not reveal the level of its true dimension. For these industries the total output level per employee is much higher than in such industries as iron and steel. The output can be measured either in terms of physical units or in monetary terms. In the latter case, care should be taken to deflate the time-series data by appropriate indexes. The total output of an open region is measured by the gross domestic product (GDP), analogous to the gross national product (GNP).

The output figures for the computation of the GDP are taken in terms of *value added*, which is defined as total output minus all raw materials and fuel input. Value added is then composed of two things: wages and salaries, and nonwage income. Usually there can be three types of output: (1) primary, such as agriculture and forestry; (2) manufacturing, such as iron and steel, chemicals, and so on; and (3) tertiary, or service, activities such as retail sales, transportation, and the like. In most countries each of these activities is denoted by number code, usually called the Standard Industrial Classification Number (SIC). On the international level there is also the system of international industrial classification (ISIC).

Projecting Economic Activity:
Use of Econometric Models

Unfortunately, little work has been done in several potential fields. Only three will be mentioned here. The first may be termed the *regional history approach*. In this approach, we look into the economic, social, and political history of a region and identify the general pattern of its responses in the past when faced with new forces of change (Buchanan and Ellis 1955). If exogenous changes in the future can be foreseen, then the region's responses can be predicted on the basis of past experience. It is true that this method is quite subjective and qualitative; but such a historical study, together with a quantitative analysis, can lead to more valid conclusions than the latter method alone.

A more quantitative form of the historical study may be termed the *regional economic development approach*. This emphasizes such concepts as capital-output ratio, saving-income ratio, population growth, resource and factor availability, levels of investment, allocation of resources, productivity changes, and other economic and demographic indexes pertaining to the economic development of a region. Mathematical formulations involving these indexes can be developed, and conditions for an optimum growth path can be determined (Chakroborty 1959). Such models increasingly appear in the literature, but most of them are on the national level. There are few attempts to develop what can be termed regional and interregional growth models. The best of such model to my knowledge is that of Rahman (1963). Sakashita's (1967) effort in this respect can also be mentioned. If such a regional and interregional growth theory can be developed, it can be integrated with input-output analysis. This will be a major contribution to regional science theory. Without this integration and synthesis, such growth models will remain theories rather than tools of developmental planning despite their mathematical elegance and sophistication.

Another potentially significant avenue of research in which there has been little work is the *regional econometric model*. An econometric model tries to relate several variables of an economy, such as GNP, consumption, investment, export, and import, by means of a system of regression equations. The variables are classified into two types: endogenous and exogenous. An endogenous variable is one that, if changed, can affect the whole system and that in turn is affected itself. For example, consumption is an endogenous variable that can affect GNP and other variables in an economic system and then in turn be affected. On the other hand, the exogenous variable can affect the system without itself being affected; an example is the investment variable.

An example of a simple macroeconomic model can be given as follows:

Endogenous variables (all in real terms)

1. Consumption C
2. Gross private domestic investment I
3. Disposable personal income Y
4. Business gross product X_b
5. Labor income in business W_b
6. Property income P
7. Corporate saving S_c

The exogenous variables (in real terms)

1. Government purchases G
2. Government wage bill W_g
3. Personal taxes T_p
4. Business taxes T_b
5. Depreciation D

The static model is:

1. Consumption: $C = \alpha Y + \beta$.
   Consumption depends on personal income investment.
2. Investment: $I = \delta X_b + \varepsilon$.
   Investment depends on business gross product.
3. Labor: $W = \gamma X_b + \eta$.
   Labor income depends on the business gross product.
4. Corporate saving: $S_c = \theta P + \lambda$
   Corporate saving depends on property income since property income $\rightarrow$ corporate profit $\rightarrow$ corporate saving.
5. GNP = expenditure: $X_b + W_g = C + I + G$.
6. GNP = income: $X + W_g = Y + T_p + S_c + T_b + D$.
7. Income distribution: $P + W_b + W_g = Y + T_p + S_c$
   Property income is defined as residual.
   Slopes: $(\alpha, \delta, \gamma, \theta)$ have positive signs and < 1.

There are seven endogenous variables and seven equations.

If we start with a system of linear equation interelating all the endogenous, exognous, and lagged variables, we can in general solve for each of the endogenous variables in terms of predetermined (exogenous and lagged endogenous) variables alone. This form of equation is known as a *reduced-form equation*. For example, the reduced-form equation of X_b:

$$X_b = (g - W_g) + \alpha W_g - \alpha t_p - \delta(1 - \theta)(T_b + D) + U,$$

where $M = 1 - \delta - a [1 - \theta(1 - \gamma)]$.
$U = \beta + \varepsilon - \alpha\lambda + \alpha\theta\eta$.

For real GNP the reduced-form equation is

$$X_b + W_g = (g - W_g) + (\alpha + \Delta)W_g - \alpha t_p - \alpha(1 - \theta)(t_b + d) + U,$$

where M is a positive multiplier.

Although the regression relationships are formulated on the basis of macroeconomic theory, the "usual procedure is to develop an aggregative model from a more global and less closely reasoned argument" (Klein, 1965). The coefficients of the regression equations are estimated from time-series data, using such models as single-stage least square, two-stage least square, limited information, and maximum likelihood methods. In recent years national econometric models have been increasingly available since the publication of the Klein-Goldberger model (1955). In the field of regional science there are few such econometric models. The work of Maki and Tu (1962) cannot be termed an econometric model, although their growth model for rural areas development is an important contribution to regional science. It is identical to a national model except that a smaller area has been substituted for a nation. The same is true for Niedercorn and Kain's model, which is "used first in an attempt to describe the structure of metropolitan development, and later it is used to evaluate changes in spatial structure of large urban complexes" (Niedercorn and Kain 1963). This model is definitely an outstanding contribution to the field of urban complex analysis; but, as mentioned before, this model has few spatial characteristics. The article by Ichimura (1966) seems to me a significant contribution in this field. For more recent work, see Glickman (1978) and Brown et al. (1978).

Some Examples of Regional Econometric Modeling

A regional growth model, unlike a national model, should take into account sociological and political variables such as age structure, sex ratios, migration characteristics, and political opinions, since these are very important factors on the regional level. The model can be made an intraregional one that will predict economic activity in subareas of a region as well. Generally, areas within a region (for example, the towns in Calcutta's metropolitan region) are not uniform with respect to economic and other activities. Some areas are so-called bedroom communities in which people live but do not work; others are industrial areas specializing in certain industries; still others are business districts; and so on. Some subareas contain a concentration of people whose demographic, cultural, and political outlook may be quite different from that of those in nearby areas. The central city influences these subareas with varying degrees of intensity through different types of transportation, social, and political interactions. In short, a dichotomy is suggested, with the central city and the rest of the metropolitan district as distinct units. Then an intraregional model may be constructed, taking into consideration the influence of the central city on meaningful subareas in the metropolitan districts. This model can be used for projection purposes for these subareas; for the center city; and, consequently, for the whole region.

This model will take into account the fact that growth in any area depends on the location of that area with respect to the center city, the type of people living in that area, the type of activities pursued, the history of development of that area, and many other characteristics that depend on the distance of the subarea from the center city. Again, most growth models are based on either time-series or cross-section data. There have been few efforts to combine the two to obtain more reliable estimates, although this can be done with little trouble. For example, in the case of the central city (say, Calcutta) a time-series procedure can be used, whereas the cross-sectional data (for this case, of towns) may be used to estimate the growth of the subareas. Then they can be combined to get better estimates for the region as a whole. This will also avoid difficulty caused by the absence of data about the subareas on a time-series basis.

Let us now outline four models to bring out some of the points I am trying to make. The four situations considered are these:

1. Industrial region in a developing country (Calcutta).
2. Highly urbanized area in a developed country (Philadelphia).
3. Depressed area in a developed country (Nova Scotia).
4. Agricultural region in a developed country (North Atlantic region, United States).

Industrial Region in a Developing Country:
Calcutta Industrial Region

The greatest difficulty in constructing regional econometric models is the unavailability of data. Even if, in the case of the United States, we were to take the states (or a combination of states) or the standard metropolitan statistical areas (SMSAs) as the areal units, data regarding income, consumption, or investment are difficult to obtain for a single year, let alone a time series. Until adequate data are available, research will be limited to partial studies. For example, instead of studying the whole economy, we can focus on the one most important industry or all the manufacturing industries for which reliable data are usually available on a time-series basis. This will be particularly useful for industrial regions in an underdeveloped country. Many such countries have a few basic manufacturing industries that account for a considerable proportion of the total economic activity of a region. Other activities are closely linked to these industries. If a satisfactory model can be constructed for these major sectors, then the projection for the total economy can be made by means of base theory or other more refined techniques.

The Calcutta Industrial Region (CIR) includes Calcutta City and thirty-four adjoining urban centers. It covers a major portion of the Calcutta Metropolitan District as defined by the Calcutta Metropolitan Planning organization. The towns lie on both sides of the Hooghly River. Administratively, twenty-two towns belong to the district of 24-Paraganas, all lying to the east of the Hooghly. Eleven towns belong to the district of Hooghly and two to the district of Howrah; all thirteen of these towns are on the western side of the Hooghly River. Most of the towns grew with the development of the jute industry in this region. The CIR covers an area of 164 square miles and had a population of nearly 10 million in 1981.

Primarily starting as a jute-manufacturing region, the CIR was until recently one of the leading centers of business and economic activity in India. Since India gained independence in 1947, however, its importance has declined, although it still holds a leading position in the country in terms of international trade, bank deposits, corporate headquarters, and the like.

The region, however, once a prosperous center of economic activity, is facing serious problems. After the partition of India, millions of refugees poured into this congested region, which already suffered from various other problems. With its chronic unemployment and refugee problems, this region has become a nightmare for the troubled state of West Bengal. One Calcutta household in every four has one or more unemployed persons: at least 20 percent of the labor force is unemployed. Paradoxically, unemployment is severe among the educated. Nearly 8 percent of the illiterate labor force is unemployed (illiterates constitute 24 percent of the CIR labor force). Of high school graduates belonging to the labor force, 26 percent are unemployed, as are 15–20 percent of college graduates. Perhaps even more serious are the environmental conditions, notably poor housing and inadequate transportation. Finally, it is noteworthy that single individuals form more than one-half of all households (Chatterji 1963).

For determining the economic development of such a depressed region, regional econometric models can be effectively used. However, the data requirement precludes the development of such a comprehensive model. Alternatively, we can construct a partial model of a dominant industry (in this case, the jute industry) and project the global economic condition on the basis of the prospects of this industry.

Jute is a soft fiber derived from the leaves of jute plants. It can replace hard fibers in more uses than any other soft fiber. The principal of jute is for manufacturing the fabrics from which jute bags, used for packaging, are made. Jute fabric is also a component of many other industrial and commercial products.

Jute is grown in a small portion of the world—in four Indian states (West Bengal, Bihar, Orissa, and Assam) and in Bangladesh. Before World War II, Bengal accounted for 2.25 million acres out of a world total of 2.70 million acres of jute. Most of this was in East Bengal, which is now in Bangladesh. Ironically, however, almost all the jute mills in undivided India were in the CIR. Therefore, after the partition of the counry, India was left with the jute mills in the CIR without any supply of raw jute; Pakistan, with an abundance of raw jute, found itself with no mills.

To feed the ready market for raw jute, rice fields were increasingly used for jute cultivation in the state of West Bengal. This transition was very rapid in the agricultural districts of Hooghly, Howrah, and 24-Paraganas surounding the CIR, where transportation costs were low. Neighboring states like Assam and Bihar also started to cultivate jute, although they are at a disadvantage because of the high transport cost. As a result, of the total of 4,065,000 acres under jute civiliation in the world, India's share was 43%, Pakistan's 40%, and the rest of the world's 17%.

Despite the upward trend in the area under jute cultivation, there have been fluctuations over the past years. The most important determining factor has been the demand for jute goods in the world market. Any change in the world market has affected the output of jute mills, which in turn has influenced the decision whether to cultivate jute or rice. The prices of raw jute and rice and the cost of production have also played important parts. Other factors, no less significant in determining the acreage, are the import of raw jute from Pakistan, the purchase of raw jute by the mills, the stock of raw jute with the mills, and the area under cultivation of mesta (a substitute crop).

Any change in the level of these exogenous factors will affect the endogenous acreage variables, which again will influence production of jute goods. The major purpose of this model is to estimate the change in the endogenous variables related to the jute industry in the CIR, following a stipulated change in the level of exogenous variables. Variables are listed in Table 3–1.

The variables on the left side of the regression equations in Table 3–2 are endogenous variables; the remaining variables are exogenous. The regression equations were estimated by the single-stage least-square method, using time-series data over the years 1947–1957. It can be seen from each equation that the test for identification is satisfied. From the first equation (3.1), it is seen that A_j^R, the area under jute cultivation in West Bengal, has a negative relationship to imports from Pakistan in the previous period. If there have been many imports in the previous year, the cultivated area in the current period is less. This negative relationship has clearly held even though imports from Pakistan stopped in 1951. The area under jute cultivation in the adjoining districts of the CIR is positively related with A_j^R. This is understandable since the diffusion of information from the CIR to the rest of West Bengal takes little time, and the farmers in West Bengal are aware of what farmers near the region are doing (since the latter are more adequately informed). Although jute and rice cultivation in West Bengal are negatively related, the regression coefficient is not statistically significant. This is so because in West Bengal as a whole, jute and rice cultivation are not competitive, since large amounts of land are involved. The area under the substitute crop, mesta A_m^R, is positively related with A_j^R, since there has

Table 3-1   List of Variables, Econometric Model of the Jute Industry

1. Area under jute cultivation in the state of West Bengal (in thousand acres). A_j^B

2. Area under rice cultivation in the state of West Bengal (in thousand acres). A_r^B

3. Area under jute cultivation in the adjoining districts of the CIR (Calcutta Industrial Region) (in thousand acres). A_j^R

4. Area under rice cultivation in the adjoining districts of the CIR (in thousand acres). A_r^R

5. Area under jute cultivation in the state of Assam (in thousand acres). A_j^{AS}

6. Area under jute cultivation in the state of Bihar (in thousand acres). A_j^{BI}

7. Area under mesta (substitute for jute) cultivation in the state of West Bengal (in thousand acres). A_m^B

8. Net area sown in the adjoining districts of the CIR (in thousand acres). A_t^R

9. Area under jute cultivation in the state of West Bengal in the previous year (in thousand acres). $(A_j^B)_{-1}$

10. Total production of raw jute in the adjoining districts of the CIR (in thousand bales of 400 pounds each). Y_j^R

11. Total production of rice in the adjoining districts of the CIR (in thousand tons). Y_r^R

12. Total production of Hessian jute goods in the mills of the CIR (in thousand tons). Q_{hj}^R

13. Total production of sacking jute goods in the mills of the CIR (in thousand tons). Q_{sj}^R

14. Total production of other jute goods in the mills of the CIR (in thousand tons). Q_{oj}^R

15. Total number of looms at work. N_j^R

16. Average daily numbers of workers employed in the jute mills of the CIR. L_j^R

17. Total value of jute goods produced by the mills in the CIR (in 10^5 rupees). V_j^R

18. Consumption of sacking goods in India (in thousand tons). C_{sj}^I

(Continued)

19.	Consumption of other jute goods in India (in thousand tons).	C_{oj}^{I}
20.	Consumption of raw jute in United Kingdom (in thousand tons)	C_{rj}^{UK}
21.	Consumption of Hessian goods in the United States (in million yards)	C_{hj}^{US}
22.	Previous year's stock of raw jute in the mills of the CIR (in 10^5 bales of 400 pounds each).	$(I_{rj}^{R})_{-1}$
23.	Previous year's import of raw jute from Pakistan to India (in 10^5 bales of 400 pounds each).	$(M_{rj}^{PK \rightarrow 1})_{-1}$
24.	Previous year's purchase of raw jute by the mills of the CIR (in 10^5 bales of 400 pounds each).	$(B_{rj}^{R})_{-1}$
25.	Import of raw jute by United Kingdom, mainly from Pakistan (in thousand tons).	$M_{rj}^{PK \rightarrow UK}$
26.	Export of Hessian jute goods to the United States from the CIR (in thousand tons).	$E_{hj}^{R \rightarrow US}$
27.	Export of sacking jute goods to the United States from the CIR (in thousand tons).	$E_{sj}^{R \rightarrow US}$
28.	Price of cotton (100 pounds of flour bag in cents per bag yard) in the United States.	P_{c}^{US}
29.	Price of paper (100 pounds of flour bag in cents per bag yard) in the United States.	P_{p}^{US}

Note: Time period covered 1947–1957.

been an increasing trend in mesta production and since land used for its production cannot easily be used for growing jute.

The second equation shows that the area under jute cultivation near the region has a negative relationship with the purchasing behavior of the jute mills in the previous period. If in the previous period purchases were high, then the farmers employed less land for cultivation of jute. Since the total amount of arable land near the region is limited, and since it faces competition from different types of land use, the area under jute (A_{j}^{R}) and the area under rice (A_{r}^{R}) have a significant negative correlation; see equations 3.2 and 3.3. It can be seen from equations 3.4 and 3.5 that areas under jute in Assam and Bihar states are positively related with purchases of raw jute in the previous period. This is so because alternative land uses are limited, cost of production of jute is low, heavy rainfall (at least in Assam) is assured, and the quality of jute is good. However, the stock variable in the previous period

Table 3-2 List of Equations, Econometric Model of the Jute Industry

$$A_j^B = 134.9222 - 2.4771(M_{rj}^{PK-I})_{-1} + 1.5569 A_j^R - .0044 A_r^B + .2942 A_m^B \qquad [3.1]$$
$$\qquad\qquad\quad (.9390) \qquad\qquad\quad (.1122) \qquad\quad (.0035) \qquad (.1028)$$
$$R^2 = .9882$$

$$A_j^R = 1879.6975 - .0506(B_{rj}^R)_{-1} - .5132 A_r^R + .5353(A_j^B)_{-1} \qquad [3.2]$$
$$\qquad\qquad\quad (.0412) \qquad\quad (.1471) \qquad (.1072)$$
$$R^2 = .7926$$

$$A_r^R = -370.5015 + .9778 A_t^R - .8697 A_j^R \qquad [3.3]$$
$$\qquad\qquad\quad (.1609) \qquad (.2435)$$
$$R^2 = .8240$$

$$A_j^{AS} = 138.7192 + .0420(B_{rj}^R)_{-1} - 4.4951 (I_{rj}^R)_{-1} - 1.5763(M_{rj}^{PK-I})_{-1} \qquad [3.4]$$
$$\qquad\qquad\quad (.0184) \qquad\quad (3.6022) \qquad\quad (.7750)$$
$$R^2 = .8053$$

$$A_j^{BI} = -281.5638 + .1593(B_{rj}^R)_{-1} - 24.0981 (I_{rj}^R)_{-1} \qquad [3.5]$$
$$\qquad\qquad\quad (.0462) \qquad\quad (6.8778)$$
$$R^2 = .7795$$

$$Y_j^R = 11.6950 + 2.4888 A_j^R \qquad [3.6]$$
$$\qquad\qquad\quad (.2432)$$
$$R^2 = .9209$$

$$Y_r^R = -1950.0607 + 1.0327 A_r^R \qquad [3.7]$$
$$\qquad\qquad\qquad (.2339)$$
$$r^2 = .6841$$

$$Q_{hj}^R = 88.0685 + .9903 E_{hj}^{R-US} \qquad [3.8]$$
$$\qquad\qquad\quad (.1980)$$

$$Q_{sj}^R = 314.3570 + .2703 E_{sj}^{R-US} + 1.4662\, C_{sj}^I \qquad R^2 = .7355 \qquad [3.9]$$
$$(.3586) \qquad (.4889)$$

$$Q_{oj}^R = -18.7551 + 3.3263 C_{oj}^J \qquad R^2 = .5409 \qquad [3.10]$$
$$(.7244)$$

$$L_j^R = -227631.2090 + 8.6217 N_j^R \qquad R^2 = .7008 \qquad [3.11]$$
$$(2.0370)$$

$$V_j^R = -2263.1511 + .0649 L_j^R \qquad R^2 = .6656 \qquad [3.12]$$
$$(.0284)$$

$$E_{hj}^{R-US} = -658.6108 + .5194 C_{hj}^{US} + 8.6578\, P_c^{US} + 27.9589\, P_p^{US} \qquad R^2 = .3672 \qquad [3.13]$$
$$(.1078) \qquad (4.2555) \qquad (12.2811)$$

$$M_{rj}^{PK \to UK} = -16.9861 + 1.1378 C_{rj}^{UK} \qquad R^2 = .7746 \qquad [3.14]$$
$$(.3164)$$

$$Q_j^R = Q_{hj}^R + Q_{sj}^R + Q_{oj}^R \qquad R^2 = .5897 \qquad [3.15]$$

Source: M. Chatterji, "A Regional Econometric Model of the World Jute Industry, *Papers of the Regional Science Association* 18 (1966): 127–137. Reprinted with the kind permission of the Regional Science Association.

$(I_{rj}^R) - 1$ is negatively related to the area variables in both cases. In equation 3.4 imports from Pakistan $(M_{rj}^{PK-1}) - 1$ were included, since the transportation network from Assam to the CIR is very bad and, consequently, imports from Pakistan are a potential competitor. This is not the case with areas under jute in Bihar.

It is generally assumed that the harvest prices of raw jute and rice are also important factors in determining land use decisions. If the ratio of prices of raw jute to rice was high in the previous year, then the area under jute in the current year is expected to be high also. However, the observed correlation was never greater than .30 and, as such, cannot support the foregoing hypothesis. No significant correlation was found between the harvest price of rice and the area variables. Other important factors that determine the acreage are rainfall and humidity at the time of sowing. No correlation was found between such variables and acreage variables. This was expected, however, since an annual model cannot take into account seasonal rainfall factors.

Equations 3.6 and 3.7 are the production functions of jute and rice cultivation, respectively, in the surrounding districts of the CIR. As before, efforts to include rainfall and humidity variables in the equations did not result in any significant improvement. It is true that outputs of rice and jute depend on average plot size. Because of the paucity of data, however, this could not be taken into account. Input of labor was not included for the same reason. Some crude estimates were made of production costs, but no significant relationships with production variables were obtained. In all fairness, it must be said that the most important predictive variables for jute and rice production are the areas under these crops. The raw jute from the fields is transported to the mills of the CIR. The cost of transportation is an important factor in determining the competitive ability of different raw jute supplying areas. Without time-series data, however, the present model could not take these into account.

For the time period under consideration, there were nearly 100 jute mills in the CIR, employing about 200,000 persons. These mills had nearly 1 million spindles and more than 50,000 looms. They produced 1 million tons of manufactured jute goods, which can be divided into three categories: hessian, sacking, and other jute goods. Nearly 80 percent of the manufactured jute goods are exported, mainly to the United States and Europe. Hessian goods constitute nearly two-thirds of the export. As far as the United States is concerned, the export is mainly hessian, although the amount of sacking export is not small. The domestic demand for sacking is much higher than that for hessian, and the demand for other jute goods comes from domestic sources. Thus the level of production of three types of jute goods depends on the export and domestic demand. Equations 3.8, 3.9, and 3.10 relate the production variables with these demand variables. As can be seen from these equations, the regression coefficients are statistically significant. Besides export and domestic demand, prices of jute goods in the domestic, as well as international, markets also influence production. Several price variables were considered (such as prices of hessian at Calcutta, Dundee prices, mill first, Dundee hessian prices, and so on); but in all cases the correlation coefficients were statistically insignificant.

Equation 3.11 shows that the employment in the jute mills depends on the number of looms at work. Since many of the jute mills are improving the quality of the looms, and since in many cases the mills have to shut some looms for the lack of demand, the number of looms working in a mill is exogenously determined and agreed on by the employer, the employee, and the government. From that equation, the total employment can be determined, given the number of looms at work. From equation 3.12 the total value of jute goods can be estimated from the number of people employed. This estimating equation has not been found satisfactory, however, since there has been a great deal of change in the technology of the jute industry in the CIR, and the number of workers is no longer the determining factor of jute goods production.

Productive capital employed in the production function was not found to be statistically significant. The capital figures are available only in historical value.

Equation 3.13 shows how hessian exports to the United States from the CIR are dependent on consumption of hessian in the United States, prices of cotton cloth, and prices of paper bags. When the prices of these substitute items are high, then the export is also high; the same is true of the consumption variable. The last equation (3.14) shows how the import of raw jute from Pakistan to the United Kingdom depends on the consumption of jute. Thus if the future values of the exogenous variables are known, the values of the endogenous variables can be projected. For example, if the prices of substitute items and the consumption of jute goods in the United States are known, then exports to the United States at a future date can be estimated. This export figure will determine the level of jute production, total number of persons employed in the jute mills, and so on. Then the area under jute and rice cultivation can be predicted on the basis of raw jute demand by the jute mills. For purposes of direct estimation from the knowledge of the exogenous variables, the equations can be expressed in a reduced form. When the level of the jute industry in the CIR is estimated, other activity levels can be estimated. The jute industry is important not only in the CIR, but also in West Bengal and India. The total employment and gross product in West Bengal can be predicted on the basis of information about the future of the jute industry. As the jute industry earns substantial foreign exchange for India, the implications brought about by a change in the level of this industry can be evaluated.

It is true that the model is based on too few observations. Furthermore, variables (particularly prices) should be involved in this model; and this model should be linked with other industrial activities in the CIR and West Bengal. Even if all this were done, there would still be room for improvement. The CIR is not the only place where the jute industry is important. Other areas, such as Bangladesh, should also be taken into account. New markets and new competitors are emerging in different parts of the world, particularly in Asia and Africa. What is really needed is an interregional model through which the levels of endogenous variables in all regions can be projected simultaneously with the knowledge of the exogenous variables.

We acknowledge that the situation has changed dramatically from the 1960s to the 1980s. For example, the engineering industries are now probably more important than jute. The objective here, however, was to point out the need to link partial models to global variables to avoid data difficulties. Again, it is not necessary to follow exactly the procedures of national econometric models. A distinct methodology for regional econometric models can be developed consistent with location and space economics, guided by the ideas and methods recently developed in the field of regional science. I hope such an effort will soon be forthcoming.

This global model for Calcutta can be developed in three stages. First, we have to construct an intraregional model for Calcutta City. Then we link it to a model developed for the remaining part of the metropolitan area. The third dimension of analysis will be to relate other regions of West Bengal with Calcutta. Consider, for example, the agricultural sector in the West Bengal, the Durgapur-Asansol region, the Jalpaiguri area, and Calcutta Industrial Region—that is, areas that basically determine what is going to happen in West Bengal. For each of these regions, we define a set of variables and collect data on them on a time-series or cross-section basis. These variables need not always be economic. Social and political variables such as age structure, sex ratio, death rate, birth rate, social mobility, community participation, and political opinion should also be considered. It will be extremely difficult to find data. In that event, we need to collect data for a basic commodity (say, rice) in the agricultural sector, coal and steel in the Durgapur-Asansol area, tea in Jalpaiguri, and engineering and jute goods in Calcutta. For each of these regions, an econometric model with several production, supply, and consumption functions can be constructed. These submodels are linked through transportation or some other variable. Ultimately, these models should be linked with a national model.

Highly Urbanized Area in a Developed Country:
Philadelphia Standard Metropolitan Statistical Area.

The Philadelphia standard metropolitan statistical area (henceforth known as Phila SMSA) consists of eight counties or districts. Five of these counties—namely Philadelphia, Chester, Montgomery, Delaware, and Bucks—are in the state of Pennsylvania; the remaining three counties— Gloucester, Burlington, and Camden—are in the state of New Jersey. Each of these counties consists of a number of townships or municipalities. These townships are the lowest levels of administrative area in the Phila SMSA. These subregional areal units have a unique economic structure and spatial interrelationships. This intra-areal differentiation developed for different social, economic, and political reasons. The forces of regional economic history also played an important part.

The importance of political factors can be realized from the fact that Gloucester, Burlington, and Camden counties are within the boundary of the state of New Jersey and, as such, are governed by different tax laws and other public policies. The pattern of public expenditure and the planning objectives in these areas may be quite different, despite their linkage with Philadelphia through spatial interaction. Other areas in the Phila SMSA are favorably located in the eastern megalopolis of the United States and, consequently, are better able to share in the growth of this highly industrialized region. On the other hand, western counties have easier access to the resource areas of Pennsylvania and the rest of the United States and have a definite comparative advantage for transport-cost-oriented industries.

Other areas are located in such a way that good transportation networks through highways and waterways are available, so that movement from and to the city of Philadelphia can be realized quickly and economically. Some areas are specifically reserved for residential purposes, with severe zoning restrictions. The people in these areas work in Philadelphia, and what is happening in the city is extremely important to them. Some areas in the Phila SMSA are dependent to a large extent on defense and space contracts; thus any cut in these expenditures by the federal government is bound to affect the economy of these areas.

When we consider the city of Philadelphia in particular, the problem becomes more complicated; such factors as intracity transportation, housing conditions, distribution of population by different ethnic and economic classes, demographic features, zoning restrictions, labor force participation, and availability of social and health benefits become important variables to be considered in our model.

The foregoing statements were made to emphasize that intraregional differences are important in the Phila SMSA, and that any effort to construct a global growth model (such as the input-output model) that ignores these differences is sure to lead to inconsistent and inaccurate projection. Besides, a micro approach to projection will be extremely useful for planning purposes with respect to such civic amenities as water supply, drainage, and the like in a township or county. A sketch of such a model follows. (For a more detailed model, see Glickman (1978).

For the local industries, we have the following equation:

$$E_L^S = f(p^s, A^s) \qquad (3.16)$$

where E_L^s = local employment in Sth subarea.
$\quad S = 1, 2, \ldots n$. In our case, $n = 8$.
$\quad p^s$ = the population of Sth subarea.
$\quad A^s$ = an index of accessibility of Sth subarea to Philadelphia City.
$\quad\quad$ where

$$A^s = \sum_{j=i}^{K} \frac{w_j(m_j^s)^a}{d_{S_p}^b} \qquad (3.17)$$

Here, m_j^S is the magnitude of local service facilities in Sth subarea for jth service and d_{S_p} is the time-distance between Philadelphia and Sth area. W_j is a weight for jth service, and a, b are the parameters; w_j, a, b are to be derived from other information. The value of these parameters will change for different SMSAs. Similarly, the sum

$$I^j = \sum_{S=1}^{n} \frac{w_j(m_j^s)^a}{d_{S_p}^b} \qquad (3.18)$$

can be taken as our index of accessibility of jth activity to Philadelphia for all the subareas in Phila SMSA. Finally, the sum

$$I = \sum_{j=i}^{k} \sum_{S=1}^{n} \frac{w_j(m_j^s)^a}{d_{S_p}^b} \qquad (3.19)$$

can be taken as an index of accessibility for Phila SMSA. We can calculate the same thing for other cities and make a comparison.

The accessibility factor A^s will change over time. Since intrametropolitan highway construction will change d_{S_p} and diseconomies of scale in the city of Philadelphia, its high land values, zoning regulations, and so on will also change m_j^s. In equation 3.16, instead of taking the population p^s as the only demographic variable, we can take the rate of growth of population, migration, age structure, and so forth. Another important variable will be the per capita income for which data are not available on smaller areal units.

The equation for national industries can be written as

$$E_N^S(t) = f\{E_N^{US}(t),\ E_i^{US}(t),\ E_A^{US}(t),\ H_T^{PH}(t)\} \qquad (3.20)$$

where $E_N^S(t)$ = employment of the Sth subarea in national industries in the time period t.

$E_i^{US}(t)$ = U.S. employment in iron and steel industries in time period t.

$E_A^{US}(t)$ = the employment in the automobile industry in the United States for the time period t.

$H_T^{PH}(t)$ = the share of Philadelphia SMSA's employment to U.S. total in the time period t.

If from some other services the values of the variables on the right-hand side of equation 3.20 can be predicted, a projection for $E_N^S(t)$ can be made for 1985, for example.

Instead of taking such a gross variable on national industries, we can break them into the following groups

1. Industries whose locational factors are such that they can be handled with the comparative cost approach.
2. Industries that can be handled with the industrial complex approach.
3. Complementary and ancillary industries.

The defense and space industries can be treated as

$$E_D^S(t) = (t)f[D^{US}(t),\ D_P^{US}(t),\ Q_D^S(t)] \qquad (3.21)$$

where $E_D^S(t)$ is the employment in space and defense industries in Sth subarea in the time period t, $D^{US}(t)$ is the U.S. defense spending in the time period t, D_P^{US} is the U.S. defense contract to Philadelphia in the time period t, and $Q_D^S(t)$ is the location quotient of Sth subarea, and tth time period. If, from other sources, the values of the variables on the R.H.S. of 3.21 can be predicted, then the projection for $E^S_D(t)$ for a future period—say, 1985—can be made.

For Philadelphia-oriented manufacturing employment, we have

$$E_{PM}^S(t) = f[E_M^P(t),\ C_p(t),\ F_m^{US \to P}(t)], \qquad (3.22)$$

where $E_{PM}^S(t)$ is the employment in the Philadelphia-oriented manufacturing employment in the Sth area at the time period t; $E_M^P(t)$ is the manufacturing employment in the city of Philadelphia for the time period t; $C_p(t)$ is the consumption expenditure in Philadelphia in the time period t; and $F_M^{US \to P}(t)$ is the flow of manufactured goods from the rest of the United States to Philadelphia in the time period t. If, from other sources, the nature of a functional relationship is known, then, for given values of the variables in the R.H.S. of equation 3.22, the employment for Philadelphia-oriented manufacturing industries can be found from equation 3.22:

$$E_{PNM}^S(t) = f[E_M^P(t), T^{S \to P}, P^p(t), E_W^{US}], \qquad (3.23)$$

where $E_{PNM}^S(t)$ represents employment in nonmanufacturing Philadelphia-oriented industries in Sth area at time period t, and $E_M^P(t)$ is the employment in the manufacturing industries of Philadelphia in the time period t. $T^{s \to p}$ is the time-distance from Sth area to Philadelphia; $P^p(t)$ is the population of Philadelphia at the time period t; and $E_W^{US}(t)$ is the U.S. employment in white-collar jobs in the time period t. If the nature of the relationship and also the values of the variables on the R.H.S. of equation 3.23 can be known, $E_{PNM}^S(t)$ can be predicted from equation 3.23.

When the employment figures for each one of the categories is known for a future date, the total employment

$$E^S(t) = E_L^S(t) + E_N^S(t) + E_{PM}^S(t) + E_D^S(t) + E_{PNM}^S(t). \qquad (3.24)$$

Summing $E^s(t)$ for all S, we can find out the total employment figure of the Philadelphia SMSA. We can compare the employment figures with those obtained from equation 3.16, using the employment-output ratio for the economy as a whole.

If there is any discrepancy between these two figures, we have to adjust the final demand figures so that there is a balance between what is required as final demand and what the region can produce. Then, following Isard and Czamanski's (1966) paper, the investment figures in each of the sectors (I_{cc}, I_t, I_a, I_v, I_h) can be obtained.

When the employment figures for each of the subareas have been obtained, the population figures can be derived from

$$P^s = f(E^S); \qquad (3.25)$$

when the population figures are known, the required demand for housing units can be obtained from

$$H^s = f(p^s). \qquad (3.26)$$

Similarly, we can find out the requirement of water resources, open space, hospital facilities, school enrollment, and so on for each of the subareas in the future, by means of suitable regression relations.

The foregoing discussion is only a sketch. Each equation may include other variables that are thought appropriate at the time of operation of the model and for which the data are available. An important distinction between this model and Isard and Czamanski's model (1966) may be noted. Their model contains many variables, such as regional income, investment in different sectors, number of households, average construction costs, and so on, for which the data for smaller areas are practically impossible to obtain. In that sense our model is more operational than theirs. The foregoing model has not been empirically estimated. For an estimated model on the same lines, see Putman (1975).

Depressed Area in a Developed Country: Nova Scotia, Canada

In recent years there has emerged a new kind of underdevelopment in the midst of the affluence of highly industrial countries, pockets of poverty that could not compete against other areas because of locational or other disadvantages.

The province of Nova Scotia in Canada is a good example. It was once a prosperous area, but now it can definitely be termed a declining region, in which the per capita income is much below the national average. Much of the income generated in the region is the result of central and provincial subsidies. The problem is to identify a set of policy variables and determine their levels so that the values of some target variables can be achieved. This has to be done by taking into consideration the rate of growth of the economy in Nova Scotia, its interindustry connection, and its relation to the rest of the world.

This model should be a bit different from the normal econometric type of model, wherein short-run cyclical functions are of prime importance. In contrast, this can be termed a *planning model,* wherein the objective is to find the values of instrument variables that would maximize the welfare function or attain some targets. For this purpose, given the dimension of some target variables, the required value of the instrument variables and intermediate variables through which the instrument variables will act to achieve the targets has to be discovered. For such a model, see Czamanski and Chatterji (1967).

Agricultural Region in a Developed Country:
North Atlantic Region in the United States

Most of the techniques of regional science have been devised to attack problems of an industrial region, particularly for a Western country. If we want to apply them to agricultural countries or agricultural regions, they must be properly modified. New techniques for agricultural regional planning can be developed. Such factors as quality of the soil, pattern of ownership, fertilizers, irrigation facilities, market size, transportation network, weather conditions, and so on become quite important.

The case for an agricultural region in the midst of a highly urbanized region, as in the North Atlantic region of the United States, presents an interesting problem. The North Atlantic region of the United States is unique in at least one sense. Agriculture is becoming less important in this area, and there is a tendency for subregional specialization—namely, dairy products in New England, poultry in Delaware and Maryland, and so on. On the other hand, the region is becoming more and more urbanized. Although agriculture still occupies a considerable amount of land, it is competing with the ever growing demand of the exploding urban centers for new housing, industry, highways, roads, recreational facilities, and other urban amenities. To the farmer, the spreading urban centers present a vast market with immense purchasing power. He faces a dilemma of whether to sell the land as real estate or use it for agricultural purposes.

The growth of urbanization poses a serious problem not only to agriculturists but also to the urbanized areas themselves. When the empty spaces between cities are filled, the problems of housing, transportation and other urban amenities will be greatly increased. The problem here is to project agricultural economic activity and land use in the face of increasing urbanization and competition against highly efficient agricultural regions in other parts of the country (Chatterji 1969). The following model is proposed for such a purpose. The North Atlantic region includes the following states:

1. Maine
2. Vermont
3. New Hampshire
4. Massachusets
5. Rhode Island
6. Connecticut
7. New York
8. Pennsylvania
9. New Jersey

10. Delaware
11. Maryland (including Washington, D.C.)
12. Virginia
13. West Virginia

To discern the impact of urbanization on agricultural activities, land use, population, and so on, we propose the following model structure. This proposed model can be divided into the following submodels, which shall be discussed in that order.

1. Population submodel
2. Supply submodel
3. Land use submodel

A graphic sketch of the models will be found in Figures 3–1 through 3–3. The list of variables used in the model is listed in Table 3–3.

Population—and related variables such as migration, birthrate, death rate, and age structure—is extremely important for a planning model, particularly at the regional level. When it comes to urban planning, other socioeconomic and political variables are of crucial importance (Chatterji 1969).

The population of the North-Atlantic region can be divided into two categories: rural farm and nonfarm. The term *farm population* includes the population living on farms, regardless of occupation. Farm residents are persons residing on places of ten acres or more from which at least $50 worth of farm products were sold in the preceding year. Persons are also included if they live on places of less than ten acres from which at least $250 worth of products were sold. *Nonfarm population* is the total population minus the rural farm population.

From the foregoing definitions, it is clear that a person may belong to the nonfarm category but still commute to do agricultural work, and vice versa. The farm population in any year is composed of additions to the population from natural increase and net migration. The natural increase will depend on the growth rate of the farm population in the previous year. However, time-series data of the growth rate are not available. Instead, we can calculate the median growth rate in each of the river basin areas and estimate the population for the next period. Adding these population figures of twenty-one river basin areas, we get the total population due to natural increase only.

Again, migration figures are not available on a time-series basis either. The estimates of migration can be computed for the standard metropolitan statistical area (SMSA) and non-SMSA level for each of the river basin areas for the 1956–1960 period only. It is emphasized that non-SMSA

Table 3–3 List of Variables

		ENDOGENOUS
1.	P_t	= total population (in millions)
2.	P_t^{NF}	= Non-farm population (in millions)
3.	P_t^F	= Rural farm population (in thousands)
4.	E_t^T	= Total agricultural employment (in thousands)
5.	E_t^H	= Hired employees (in thousands)
6.	E_t^F	= Family employees (in thousands)
7.	Q_t^{Ap}	= Supply of apples (in million dollars).
8.	Q_t^{Gr}	= Supply of grapes (in million dollars)
9.	Q_t^{Ph}	= Supply of peaches (in million dollars)
10.	Q_t^{Pr}	= Supply of pears (in million dollars)
11.	Q_t^R	= Supply of red meat (beef, veal, hogs, sheep, and lambs) (in million dollars)
12.	Q_t^M	= Supply of milk and other dairy products (in million dollars)
13.	Q_t^P	= Supply of poultry products (chicken and turkey) (in million dollars)
14.	Q_t^E	= Supply of eggs (in million dollars)
15.	Q_t^G	= Supply of grains (in million dollars)
16.	q_t^W	= Supply of wheat (in million bushels)
17.	q_t^N	= Supply of corn (in million bushels)
18.	q_t^Y	= Supply of rye (in million bushels)
19.	q_t^B	= Supply of barley (in million bushels)
20.	Q_t^F	= Supply of fruits (in million dollars)
21.	q_t^{VF}	= Supply of fresh vegetables (in million tons)
22.	q_t^{VC}	= Supply of vegetables for processing (in million tons)
23.	q_t^{Po}	= Supply of potatoes (in million cwt.)
24.	q_t^{To}	= Supply of Connecticut tobacco (in million pounds)
25.	Q_t^V	= Supply of vegetables (in million dollars)
26.	Q_t^T	= Total agricultural output (in million dollars)
27.	A_{it}^U	= Amount of urban land in i^{th} county (in thousand acres)
28.	$\dfrac{\Delta M_{ti}^F}{P_{ti}^F}$	= Rate of outmigration for i^{th} (non-SMSA) areal unit between two successive time periods (percentage)

(Continued)

29. $\dfrac{\Delta A^T_{it}}{A^T_{it}}$ = Change in road mileage for the ith areal unit between two successive time periods (percentage)

30. A^U_t = Urban land area (in thousand acres)

31. A^T_t = Total road mileage (transformed to thousand acres)

32. q^{cc}_t = Supply of cattle and calves (in million pounds)

33. q^h_t = Supply of hogs (in million pounds)

34. q^{SL}_t = Supply of sheep and lambs (in million pounds)

35. q^E_t = Supply of eggs (in billions)

36. q^M_t = Supply of milk (in billion pounds)

37. Q^O_t = Supply of oats (in million dollars)

38. q^R_t = Total amount of red meat (beef, hogs, sheep and lamb) (in million pounds)

39. Q^{Po}_t = Total supply of potatoes (in million dollars)

40. Q^{TO}_t = Total supply of tobacco (in million dollars)

41. A^r_t = Land used for recreational purposes (in thousand acres)

42. F_t = Number of farms

43. A^F_t = Land in farms (in thousand acres)

44. W^r_t = Agricultural wage rate (index, 1950=100)

45. P^R_t = Price received by the farmer (U.S. index 1957-59=100)

46. M^F_t = Total non-SMSA migration (in thousands)

47. P^F_{Nti} = Farm population through natural increase only for i^{th} areal unit (in millions)

48. P^F_{Nt} = Farm population through natural increase only (in millions)

EXOGENOUS

1. p^{-E}_t = Price of eggs (cents per dozen)

2. p^{-M}_t = Price of milk (cents per quart)

3. p^{-c}_t = Price of poultry product (cents per pound)

4. p^{-vc}_t = Price of processed variables (dollars per ton)

5. p^{VF}_t = Price of fresh vegetables (index, 1950=100)

6. p^{-W}_t = Price of wheat (dollars per bushel)

7. p^{-N}_t = Price of corn (dollars per bushel)

8. p^{-Y}_t = Price of rye (dollars per bushel)

(Continued next page)

Table 3–3 (continued)

9. p_t^{-B} = Price of barley (dollars per bushel)

10. p_t^{-Po} = Price of potatoes (dollars per pound)

11. p_t^{-To} = Price of Connecticut tobacco (dollars per pound)

12. p_t^{-O} = Price of oats (dollars per bushel)

13. $A_{(t-1)}^{SW}$ = Area seeded for wheat in the previous period (in thousand acres)

14. $A_{(t-1)}^{Po}$ = Acres harvested for potatoes (in thousand acres)

15. $q_{(t-1)}^{R}$ = Supply of red meat in the previous period (in million pounds)

16. $q_{(t-1)}^{M}$ = Supply of milk in the previous period (in million pounds)

17. E_{ti}^{U} = Non-agricultural employment for the ith areal unit (percentage)

18. E_{it}^{T} = Total employment in the ith county (percentage)

19. P_{it}^{NF} = Non-farm population in i^{th} areal unit (percentage)

20. $\dfrac{\Delta H_{it}}{H_{it}}$ = Change in the number of houses for the ith county between two consecutive periods (percentage)

21. $\dfrac{\Delta P_{it}^{NF}}{P_{it}^{NF}}$ = Change in the non-farm population for the ith state between two consecutive periods (percentage)

22. $\dfrac{\Delta C_{it}}{C_{it}}$ = Change in the number of registered automobiles for the ith state between two consecutive periods (percentage)

23. A_t^{W} = Water area (thousand acres)

24. L = Total land area of the region (thousand acres)

25. A_t^{P} = Pasture land (thousand acres)

26. A_t^{FO} = Forest and miscellaneous area (thousand acres)

27. E_t^{U} = Non-agricultural employment (in millions)

28. T = Time (1950=1)

29. $E_{(t-1)}^{F}$ = Number of family workers in the previous period (in thousands)

30. P_t^{-cc} = Price of beef received by the farmer (cents per pound)

31. p_t^{-h} = Price of hogs received by the farmer (cents per pound)

32. p_t^{-SL} = Price of sheep and lamb received by the farmer (cents per pound)

33. $p_{(t-1)}^{-Pr}$ = Price received by the farmer for pears in the previous period (dollars per bushel)

34. $p^{-Ph}_{(t-1)}$ = Price received by the farmer for peaches in the previous period (dollars per bushel)

35. $p^{-Gr}_{(t-1)}$ = Price received by the farmers for grapes in the previous period (dollars per ton)

36. p_t^{-Ap} = Price received by farmer for apples (dollars per bushel)

37. $(W^U/W^R)_t$ = Ratio of manufacturing to agricultural wages (index, 1950=100)

38. W_t^U = Manufacturing wage rate (index, 1950=100)

39. $A_{(t-1)}^V$ = Area under vegetable production in the previous period (thousand acres)

40. M_t = Index of machinery and mechanical power used in agriculture (U.S. index, 1957-59=100)

41. $A^{To}_{(t-1)}$ = Acreage harvested of tobacco (Connecticut) in the previous period (in thousands)

42. Q_t^X = Supply of all agricultural products (in million dollars)

43. E_{it}^M = Manufacturing employment for the ith areal unit (percentage)

44. $\dfrac{\Delta A_{it}^F}{A_{it}^F}$ = Decrease in land in farms for i^{th} areal unit between two successive periods (percentage)

---

migration is *not* rural migration. However, the non-SMSA migration with a large outward migration can be taken as a good indicator for rural migration. For the river basin areas where this is the case, we can hypothesize that migration depends on the growth of cities, urban unemployment, unsatisfied demand for workers, the percentage of young people among the population, the attraction of the nearest urban centers, and so on. If a satisfactory relationship between the migration and some of the foregoing variables can be made, the future migration can be predicted. This, together with the population from natural increase, will give the estimated population for each river basin area. Summing all river basic areas, we will get the total population of the region at a future time period. The submodel is sketched in Figure 3–1. The population submodel is connected to a supply submodel through farm population and total agricultural employment. The total employment in agriculture is composed of hired employment and family employment. Rural and urban wage rates, family employment, the price received by farmers in the previous period, machinery used, and time trends determine hired employment. The number of farms and land under

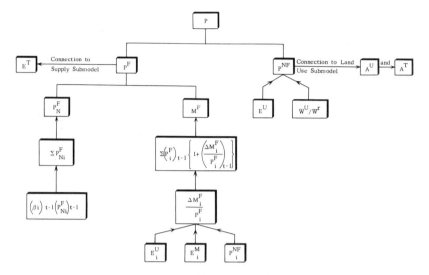

Figure 3–1. Population Submodel

cultivation determine family employment. The total agricultural output is obtained from the employment figure, taking into consideration the changes in productivity.

The total output is assumed to originate in the following sector:

1. Red meat (beef, hogs, sheep, and lamb).
2. Milk and dairy products.
3. Eggs.
4. Poultry (chicken and turkey).
5. Fruits (apples, peaches, pears, and grapes).
6. Vegetables (fresh and processed).
8. Tobacco (Connecticut only).
9. Potatoes.
10. All others.

For each of these sectors we have a supply function with lag price as the independent variable. The supply submodel has been sketched in Figure 3–2. The supply functions may involve other variables like the price of the substitute commodity or the price of feed. For this model, however, only the price with a one-year lag has been taken as the independent variable.

The total amount of land in the North Atlantic region can be classified as

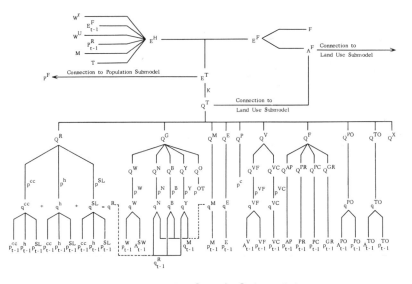

Figure 3-2. Supply Submodel

follows:

1. Land in farms.
2. Urban land.
3. Land under roads, highways, and the like.
4. Water area.
5. Pastureland.
6. Forest land.
7. Other.

If the estimate of the agricultural production in any year in the future is known from the supply submodel, then the land requirement for this purpose can be estimated (taking into consideration the change in productivity). The urban land area will depend on the number of houses, the nonfarm population, and the manufacturing and nonagricultural employment. The land under roads and highways will depend on the urban land, the nonfarm population, and the number of cars. The land use submodel is sketched in Figure 3-3.

Various other forms of supply functions have been considered and reported elsewhere. For a critical discussion on agricultural supply functions, see Chatterji (1969). The relationships between the variables in Figures 3-1 through 3-3 are expressed as regression equations. They are reported in Table 3-4.

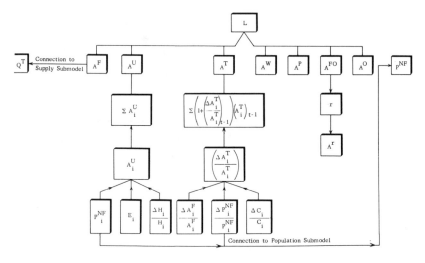

Figure 3–3. Land Use Submodel

These variables have been estimated by ordinary least-square method using the time-series data for the period 1950–1965. The migration equation (3.6) has been estimated on the basis of river basin areas. The urban land equation (3.44) has been estimated on the basis of thirty-two counties contiguous to the New York–Philadelphia and Washington–Baltimore areas. The land under transportation equation (3.45) has been estimated on the basis of the thirteen states constituting the region. The period for the percentage change variables is from 1950 to 1960. In the regression equation, the figures in brackets under the regression coefficient denote the standard errors. The value of R^2 gives the percentage of the dependent variables explained by the independent variables; and, as such, R^2 can be taken as an index for judging the efficiency of each equation.

It is not suggested that the model presented herein is complete. In order for this model to be used for decision making, further work will be necessary. As mentioned before, the population submodel can be enlarged, and age-specific birth- and death rates should be used. Admittedly, the migration portion of the model is not satisfactory. Time-series data for migration do not exist. Even for the cross-section method, no data for rural farm migration exist. Again, for a satisfactory migration model, qualitative aspects of the behavior of migrants are to be considered. In fact, these factors are more important than, say, higher wages in the city. These qualitative aspects can only be considered on a micro basis through a sample survey.

Table 3-4 Estimated (Single-Stage Least-Square) Equations

1. $P_t = P_t^F + P_t^{NF}$

2. $P_t^F = P_{Nt}^F + M_T^F$

3. $P_{Nti}^F = (1 + B_{(t-1)i}) P_{i(t-1)}^F$

4. $M_t^F = \sum_{i=1}^{n} (\Delta M_{it}^F / P_{it}^F) p_{i(t-1)}^F$

5. $P_{Nt}^F = \sum_{i=1}^{21} P_{Nti}^F$

6. $\dfrac{\Delta M_{ti}^F}{P_{ti}^F} = -66.6738 + .8044\, E_{ti}^U - .3628\, E_{ti}^M$
    $\phantom{\dfrac{\Delta M_{ti}^F}{P_{ti}^F} = -66.6738 + .}(.1672)(.0964)$
    $\phantom{\dfrac{\Delta M_{ti}^F}{P_{ti}^F} = -66.67}- .0005\, P_{ti}^{NF}$
    $\phantom{\dfrac{\Delta M_{ti}^F}{P_{ti}^F} = -66.6738}(.0013)R^2 = .8357$

7. $E_{Tt}^F = E_{Ht}^F + E_{FT}^F$

8. $P_t^F = -713.9491 + 4.1228\, E_t^T R^2 = .9240$
    $(.3156)$

9. $P_t^{NF} = -53.9493 + 2.1395\, E_t^U + .6233\,(W^U / W^R)_t R^2 = .9688$
    $\phantom{P_t^{NF} = -53.9493 + }(.3364)(.0778)$

10. $E_t^F = -873.0428 - .00050\, F_t + .0275\, A_t^F R^2 = .9853$
    $(.00024)(.0041)$

11. $E_t^H = 680.5988 - 3.7815\, W_t^R - .6185\, P_t^R + 3.6427\, M_t$
    $(3.1847)(1.0641)(4.1992)$

    $- 2.0022\, T - .2407\, E_{(t-1)}^F R^2 = .9128$
    $(11.8164)(.3445)$

12. $Q^T = Q_t^R + Q_t^M + Q_t^E + Q_t^P + Q_t^G + Q_t^F + Q_t^V + Q_t^{PO} + Q_t^{TO} + Q_t^X$

13. $q_t^R = q_t^{cc} + q_t^h + q_t^{SL}$

14. $Q_t^R = p_t^{-cc}\, q_t^{cc} + p_t^{-h}\, q_t^h + p_t^{-SL}\, q_t^{SL}$

15. $q_t^{cc} = 883.6440 + 2.5873\, p_{(t-1)}^{-cc} + 7.9456\, p_{(t-1)}^{-h}$
    $\phantom{q_t^{cc} = 883.6440 + }(2.6548)(3.3639)$

    $- 8.8275\, p_{(t-1)}^{-SL} R^2 = .4537$
    (3.9073)

(Continued next page)

Table 3–4 (continued)

16. $q_t^h = 88.0657 - 3.8161\, p_{(t-1)}^{-cc} + 6.4133\, p^{-h}_{(t-1)}$
         (2.6336)   (3.3371)

    $+ 11.0503\, p^{-SL}_{(t-1)}$ $R^2 = .7298$
    (3.8762)

17. $q_t^{SL} = 26.6226 - .5581\, p^{-cc}_{(t-1)} + .2348\, p^{-h}_{(t-1)}$
          (.2311)   (.2929)

    $+ .4937\, p^{-SL}_{(t-1)}$ $R^2 = .4706$
    (.3402)

18. $q_t^M = 4.1661 + .8023\, p^{-M}_{(t-1)}$ $R^2 = .8940$
                (.0767)

19. $Q_t^M = q_t^M\, p_t^{-M}$

20. $q_t^E = 5.4177 + .1377\, p^{-E}_{(t-1)}$ $R^2 = .6749$
             (.0265)

21. $Q_t^E = q_t^E\, p_t^E$

22. $Q_t^P = 126.9627 + 7.9452\, p_t^{-c}$ $R^2 = .7898$
            (1.0957)

23. $Q_t^G = q_t^W\, p_t^{-W} + q_t^N\, p_t^{-N} + q_t^B\, p_t^{-B} + q_t^O\, p_t^{-O} + q_t^Y\, p_t^{-Y}$

24. $q_t^W = 17.2234 + 2.2154\, p^{-W}_{(t-1)} + .0103\, A^{SW}_{(t-1)}$ $R^2 = .6090$
            (5.9701)   (.0037)

25. $q_t^N = 305.2929 - .0084\, q^M_{(t-1)} + .0505\, q^R_{(t-1)}$ $R^2 = .2896$
            (.0040)   (.1624)

26. $q_t^Y = -5.0347 + .0002\, q^M_{(t-1)} + .0022\, q^R_{(t-1)}$ $R^2 = .6468$
            (.00004)   (.0016)

27. $q_t^B = -28.4442 + .0005\, q^M_{(t-1)} + .0267\, q^R_{(t-1)}$ $R^2 = .3454$
            (.0003)   (.0125)

28. $Q_t^O = -7.9067 + .7318\, p_t^{-O}$ $R^2 = .5890$
            (.1634)

29. $Q_t^V = q_t^{VF}\, p_t^{VF} + q_t^{VC}\, p_t^{VC}$

30. $q_t^{VF} = 640.2926 + 1.2874\, p^{VF}_{(t-1)} + 1.1099\, A^V_{(t-1)}$ $R^2 = .5964$
            (2.4261)   (.2777)

31. $q_t^{VC} = -1450.4893 + 69.91\, p^{VC}_{(t-1)}$ $R^2 = .7100$
             (26.00)

32. $\quad q_t^{Po} = 124.2730 - 3.4717\, p^{-Po}_{(t-1)} - .1197\, A^{Po}_{(t-1)}$ $\qquad\qquad R^2 = .3506$
$\qquad\qquad (2.4923) \qquad\qquad (.0551)$

33. $\quad Q_t^{Po} = q_t^{Po}\, p_t^{Po}$

34. $\quad q_t^{To} = -14.0911 + 7.6982\, p^{-To}_{(t-1)} + 1.6937\, A^{To}_{(t-1)}$ $\qquad R^2 = .9080$
$\qquad\qquad (2.1388) \qquad\qquad (.2298)$

35. $\quad Q_t^{To} = q_t^{To}\, p_t^{To}$

36. $\quad Q_t^{F} = Q_t^{Ap} + Q_t^{Pr} + Q_t^{Ph} + Q_t^{GR}$

37. $\quad Q_t^{Ap} = 71.4140 + 14.3880\, p^{-Ap}_{(t-1)}$ $\qquad\qquad\qquad R^2 = .0399$
$\qquad\qquad (19.5685)$

38. $\quad Q_t^{Pr} = .5209 + .6705\, p^{-Pr}_{(t-1)}$ $\qquad\qquad\qquad\qquad R^2 = .2500$
$\qquad\qquad (.3189)$

39. $\quad Q_t^{Ph} = 1.0677 + 6.9198\, p^{-Ph}_{(t-1)}$ $\qquad\qquad\qquad R^2 = .5333$
$\qquad\qquad (1.8217)$

40. $\quad Q_t^{GR} = -26.1683 - 35.5739\, p^{-GR}_{(t-1)}$ $\qquad\qquad R^2 = .5613$
$\qquad\qquad (8.7225)$

41. $\quad A_t^{F} = \bar{h}_t\, Q_t^{T}$ For time series values of $\bar{h}$ see Appendix B.

42. $\quad Q_t^{T} = \bar{K}_t\, E_{Tt}^{F}$

43. $\quad L = A_t^{F} + A_t^{U} + A_t^{T} + A_t^{W} + A_t^{P} + A_t^{FO} + A_t^{O}$

44. $\quad A_{it}^{U} = -2.4398 + .0106\, p_{it}^{NF} + .2628\, E_{it}^{T} + .3248\, \dfrac{\Delta H_{it}}{H_{it}}$ $\qquad R^2 = .9325$
$\qquad\qquad\qquad (.0459) \qquad (.1084) \qquad (.0733)$

45. $\quad \dfrac{\Delta A_{it}^{T}}{A_{it}^{T}} = -50.1364 + .1452\, \dfrac{\Delta A_{it}^{F}}{A_{it}^{F}} - 4.4710\, \dfrac{\Delta p_{it}^{NF}}{P_{it}^{NF}} + 3.2921\, \dfrac{\Delta C_{it}}{C_{it}}$
$\qquad\qquad\qquad\qquad (.2132) \qquad\quad (1.4567) \qquad\quad (1.3251)$
$\qquad\qquad\qquad\qquad\qquad\qquad\qquad\qquad\qquad\qquad\qquad\qquad R^2 = .6400$

46. $\quad A_t^{U} = \displaystyle\sum_{i=1}^{n} A_{it}^{U}$

47. $\quad A_t^{T} = \displaystyle\sum_{i=1}^{13} \left(1 + \dfrac{\Delta A_t}{A_{it}^{T}}\right) A_{i(t-1)}^{T}$

48. $\quad A_t^{r} = r(L_t - A_t^{F} - A_t^{U} - A_t^{T})$

Source: M. Chatterji, "Regional Econometric Model Building: A Case for Agriculture in the North Atlantic Region of the United States," *Pacific Regional Science Association* 1 (1972): 95–105. Reprinted with the kind permission of the Regional Science Association.

The area that can be largely extended is the supply submodel. In the supply equations, besides the lagged price, the prices of other variables can be considered. For example, in the cases of red meat and poultry, feed price should be taken into consideration. Again, interregional competition can also be compared. For example, the surplus or deficit of the product in the region in the preceding year may determine the output in the current year. However, care should be taken to see that we are talking about the same commodity. For example, imported red meat from the Midwest is used for steak and other prime beef, whereas most of the meat produced in the region is used for hamburger, hot dogs, and so on. Since no citrus fruits are grown here, competition in the field of fruits is meaningless. In the case of vegetables, this is possible; but the seasonality of the production has to be kept in mind. Another important aspect missing in the model is the price equation. The model has been constructed in such a way that the previous year's price determines the output in the current year. However, price equations can be constructed on the basis of output, income, price of the competing product, feed price, and so on. Similarly, demand equations are absent. The model implies that whatever output is presented in the market, it will be used up, since the population is quite large. This is, however, a reasonable assumption. In that sense the model is partial. Again, in most of the equations a lag of one year is taken, but this need not be the case. Different lags can be tested and the appropriate one taken. To obtain the elasticities directly, a logarithm formulation can be taken.

The same holds for a land use submodel. Here different types of land use can be taken into account, and meaningful relations with other variables can be formulated. It is suggested that the relations be tested on the micro level, such as for the New York–Philadelphia area, and so on. A more comprehensive land use model will not only be useful in relating urban areas to agricultural sectors, but will also help us in recreational and water resource planning. A recreational submodel can be added to the foregoing model, and it is possible for a comprehensive agro-urban-environmental model to be constructed involving a large number of policy variables designed to achieve stipulated goals.

An econometric model can be developed on different levels—national, state, regional, and local—or it can be a sectoral model. In the extreme case, it can be a combination of all of these.

A hierarchical system of national and regional econometric models can efficiently project optimum decision making with respect to national and regional policies, so that goals at various levels can be achieved. Such a model for Belgium can be sketched in Figure 3–4 (Van Rompuy et al. 1975).

Attention will be given only to the determination of output, investment,

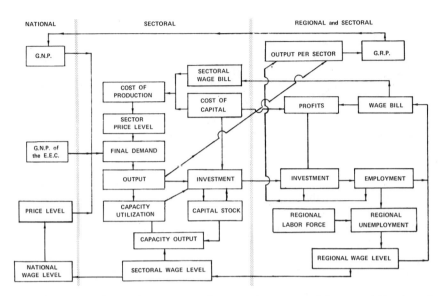

Figure 3–4. Simplified Flow Chart of National-Sectoral-Regional Relations in Belgium

and employment at the regional and sectoral level. The model outlined here constitutes the embryo of a potential regional sectoral model.

The RENA model, actually used by the Belgian Planning Office for its medium-term forecasts and planning, lacks a sectoral treatment. Moreover, only three regions (Flanders, Wallonia, and Brussels) are considered. These three regions are constitutionally determined, but from an economic point of view they cover heterogeneous spatial units. Brussels has been circumscribed as the metropolitan area, including the suburbs, and contrasts sharply with the two other regions, which display a much more diversified spatial economic structure.

Furthermore, the RENA model contains only a few spatial features that appear mainly in the labor market block. In fact, RENA belongs to the disaggregated national models containing a national block, in which a large part of final demand is determined, and a regional block in which labor market variables and investment are treated. Consequently, the regional blocks depend heavily on the variables determined nationally (Glickman 1978), as is the case with most first-generation regional models.

The backbone of the model outlined in this chapter has several features that distinguish it from RENA. First, the model describes the economic medium-term behavior of nine regions that coincide with the nine provinces.

These regions differ significantly with regard to economic activity, degree of urbanization, and accessibility; but each of them is more homogeneous than the three regions covered by RENA.

Second, manufacturing has been split up into six sectors at the regional level. Further, the services sector and a "residual" sector are taken into account. Third, an effort has been made to introduce more spatial features into the model—for example, in the regional allocation of sectoral investments. The specification of the labor supply equations will also offer an opportunity to focus more intensively on spatial aspects as compared with RENA.

The basic assumptions that characterize this model have been introduced to a large extent by the availability of data. Ideally, one would like to specify at the regional level as much as possible spatially determined behavior or technical relations and their links with nationally determined activities. An example of a regional model that has been built up from below is offered by the regional-national econometric model of Italy, constructed by Brown, Di Palma, and Ferrara (1972) and by the IRIS model for Belgium.

Since no reliable data on interregional trade, regional consumption, and capital subsidies per sector and per region are available for Belgium, a compromise must be sought between the disaggregation of national variables and the construction of aggregates starting from the regional level.

The sector has been adopted as an operational concept at the macroeconomic level. It is assumed that final demand of each sector and the sector price level are determined at the national level. In this respect, the model can be linked with international models such as Comet (Barten and D'Alcantara 1974) and Desmos.

Capacity output per sector as well as the total amount of investment are also determined nationally. The allocation of total investment per sector across the regions is a crucial part of the model, since specific regional attractivity features play a role. It is furthermore assumed that regional production functions differ from the sectoral aggregate production function by a shift variable that is supposed to depend on the relative concentration of past private investment in a particular region. As such, regional features influence regional output and employment not only through the location decision dealing with *new investment,* but also through the specific *regional productivity* that can be attributed to agglomeration economies and/or regional specialization.

Interregional dynamics shows up in the regional labor markets where the regional and the regional-sectoral wage rates are determined. Product prices have so far been treated at the national level. It may be argued, as has been done in the Macedoine model that the regional price level relative to that of competing regions reflects the comparative advantage of the region. In the Mississippi model, the ratio of the regional cost of production in manufacturing to the national one forms a key variable in the regional allocation of output.

The regional relative cost of production will show up here, though only indirectly, in the investment allocation function, where the elasticity of regional sectoral investment with respect to regional sectoral profits appears as a weight. Regional differences in consumer prices have not yet been taken into account. Although these differences are relatively small in Belgium, they may influence migration patterns and commuting flows. It is intended to incorporate these price differences in future work, together with a simultaneous analysis of environmental quality.

In order to explicate the mechanics of the model, a simplified flow chart follows. It appears from this chart that relevant variables can be classified as national, regional, sectoral, and regional sectoral. The GNP of Belgium and of the EEC, together with the relative price level, determine the sectoral final demand that will be translated into sectoral value added. Sectoral value added explains sectoral investment, which will be allocated regionally. Employment at the regional sectoral level depends on investment. Regional sectoral employment leads to regional employment and unemployment and consequently to regional wages. Regional sectoral output is derived from regional employment and investment.

Feedbacks from regions to sectors are manifold. The regional sectoral wage bill will, among other things, determine regional sectoral profits, which will influence the regional allocation of sectoral investment. Regional sectoral wages can be aggregated into the sectoral wage bill—which plays a role in the determination of the sectoral cost of production and hence in the sectoral price level and final demand. Feedbacks from regions to the national level are also present. GNP at factor cost is the sum of the regional wage levels and influences the general price level.

The income determination at the regional level is still incomplete, since regional property income is missing. It will, however, be introduced at a later stage, together with labor supply, land use, and land price equations. For a detailed discussion of the model, see Van Rompuy et al. (1975).

References

Alonso, W. 1964. *Location and Land Use: Toward a General Theory of Land Rent.* Cambridge, Mass.: Harvard University Press.

Barten, A., and D'Alcantara, G. (1974) "The Linking of Models of the E.E.C. Countries." C.O.R.E. Louvain. (Multilith).

Brown, Murray, Maurizio DiPalma and Bruno Ferrara 1978. *Regional-National Econometric Modeling.* London: Pion.

Buchanan, Norman S., and Ellis, Howard S. 1955. *Approaches to Economic Development* New York: Twentieth Century Fund.

Chakroborty, S. 1959. *The Logic of Investment Planning.* Amsterdam: North-Holland.

Chatterji, Manas. 1963. "Regional Economic Planning—Importance for India." *Economic Weekly* (India), March 20.

_____. 1969. "Improved Techniques of Projection of Economic Activity and Land Use of Agriculture in North Atlantic Region." Report prepared for U.S. Department of Agriculture, June.

Cherry, C. 1961 *On Human Communication.* Cambridge, Mass.: MIT Press.

Christaller, Walter. 1933. *Central Places in Southern Germany,* trans. C.W. Baskin. Englewood Cliffs, N.J.: Prentice-Hall.

Cooper, L. 1968. "An Extension of the Generalized Weber Problem." *Journal of Regional Science* 8: 181–197.

Czamanski, Stanislaw, and Chatterji, Manas. 1967. "Regional Planning Model of Nova Scotia." Institute of Public Affairs, Dalhousie University, Halifax.

Danskin, J. M. 1962. "A Game Theory Model of Convoy Routing." *Operations Research* 10:774–785.

Friedrich, C. J. 1929. *Alfred Weber's Theory of the Location of Industry.* Chicago.

Glickman, Norman. 1978. *Regional Econometric Model.* New York: Academic Press.

Goldman, Stanford. 1953. *Information Theory.* Englewood Cliffs, N.J.: Prentice-Hall.

Greenhut, M. L. 1956. *Plant Location in Theory and Practice: The Economics of Space.* Chapel Hill: University of North Carolina.

Hoover, Edgar Malons. 1937. *Location Theory and the Shoe and Leather Industries.* Cambridge, Mass.: Harvard University Press.

_____. 1948. *The Location of Economic Activity.* New York: McGraw-Hill.

Hotelling, H. 1929. "Stability in Competition." *Econometric Journal* 39:41–57.

Ichimura, S. 1966. "An Economic Analysis of Domestic Migrations and Regional Economy." *Papers of the Regional Science Association* 16:67–76.

Isard, Walter. 1956. *Location and Space-Economy.* Cambridge, Mass.: MIT Press.

Isard, Walter, and Czamanski, Stanislaw. 1966. "A Model for the Projection of Regional Industrial Structure, Land Use Patterns and Conversion Potentialities." *Papers of the Peace Research Society (International)* 5:1–14.

_____. 1969. *General Theory: Social, Political, Economic, and Regional.* Cambridge, Mass.: MIT Press.

Klein, Lawrence Robert. 1965. *An Introduction to Econometrics.* Englewood Cliffs, N.J.: Prentice-Hall.

Klein, Lawrence Robert, and Goldberger, A. 1955. *An Econometric Model of the United States.* Amsterdam: North-Holland.

Kuhn, H. W., and Kuenne, R. E. 1962. "An Efficient Algorithm for the Numerical Solution of the Generalized Weber Problem in Spatial Economics." *Journal of Regional Science* 4:21–33.

Launhardt, W. 1885. *Mathematische Begründung der Volkwirtschaftlehre.* Leipzig: Aalen Scientia Verlag, Reprinted 1963.

Lefeber, Louis. 1955. *Allocation in Space.* Amsterdam: North-Holland.

Lösch, A. 1959. *The Economics of Location,* trans. W. F. Stolper and W. H. Woglom. New Haven: Yale University Press.

Maki, Wilbur R., and Tu, Tien-I. 1962. "Regional Growth Models for Rural Areas," *Papers of the Regional Science Association* 9:235–244.

Morrill, R. L. 1963. "The Development of Spatial Distribution of Towns in Sweden: An Historical-Predictive Approach." *Annals of the Association of American Geographers* 53:1–14.

_____. 1967. "The Movement of Persons and the Transportation Problem." In W. L. Garrison and D. Marble, eds., *Quantitative Geography I: Economic and Cultural Topics.* Evanston, Ill.: Northwestern.

Moses, L. N. 1958. "Location and the Theory of Production." *Quarterly Journal of Economics* 72:259–272.

Niederkorn, John H., and Kain, John F. 1963. "An Econometric Model of Metropolitan Development." *Papers of the Regional Science Association* 11:123–143.

Predohl, Andrew. 1925. "Das Standorts Problem in der Wirtschaftstheorie." *Weltwirtschaftliches Archiv.* 21.

Putman, Stephen H. 1975. *An Empirical Model of Regional Growth with an Application to the Northeast Metropolis.* Monograph Series no. 6. Philadelphia: Regional Science Research Institute.

Rahman, Anisur. 1963. "Regional Allocation of Investment." *Quarterly Journal of Economics* 77(February):26–39

Roscher, Wilhelm. 1878. *Studien uber Naturgesetze Welche den zweckmässigen Standort der Industriezweige Bestimmen. Ansichten der Volkswirtschaft aus dem geschichtlichen Standpunkte.* 3rd ed.

Sakashita, Noburu. (1967). "Regional Allocation of Investment," Papers of the Regional Science Association 19:161–182.

Samuelson, P. A. 1952. "Spatial Price Equilibrium and Linear Programing." *American Economic Review* 42:283–303.

Schäffle, A. 1873. *Das Gesellschaftliche System der Menschlichen Wirtschaft.* 3rd ed. Tübingen.

Stevens, B. H. 1961. "An Application of Game Theory to a Problem in Location Strategy." *Regional Science Association, Papers and Proceedings* 7:143–57.

Tiebout, C. M. 1957. "Location Theory, Empirical Evidence and Economic Evolution." *Regional Science Association, Papers and Proceedings* 3:74–86.

Van Rompuy, Paul, et al. (1975). Output, Investment and Employment in a Regionɛ ᶜ Sectoral Model for Belgium. XVth European Congress of Regional Science Association, Budapest, Hungary, August.

Von Thünen, Johan Heinrich. 1826. *Isolated State,* trans. Carla M. Wartenberg. Oxford: Pergamon Press. Reprinted 1966.

Webber, Michael J. 1972. *Impact of Uncertainty on Location.* Cambridge, Mass.: MIT Press.

Bibliography

Artle, Ronald. 1965. "Planning and Growth: A Simple Model of an Island Economy." *Papers of the Regional Science Association* 15:29–44.
Blumenfeld, Hans. 1955. "The Economic Base of the Metropolis." *Journal of the American Institute of Planners* 21 (Fall):114–132.
Chatterji, Manas. 1970. "A Scheme of Decentralized Decision Making for India." *Indian Journal of Public Administration* (October–December).
Czamanski, Stanislaw. 1965. "A Method of Forecasting Metropolitan Growth by Means of Distribution Lag Analysis." *Journal of Regional Science* 6, no. 1 (Summer):35–49.
_____. "A Model of Urban Growth." Ph.D. dissertation, University of Pennsylvania, Philadelphia.
Isard, Walter. 1959. *Industrial Complex Analysis.* New York: Wiley.
_____. 1960. *Methods of Regional Analysis.* New York: Wiley.
Park, R. L. 1962. "West Bengal with Special Attention to Calcutta." In Roy Turner, ed., *Indian Urban Future.* Berkeley: University of California.

4 REGIONAL AND INTERREGIONAL INPUT-OUTPUT AND PROGRAMMING MODELS

Economic Base Theory

From the point of view of data requirements and the cost of operation, regional econometric models, as described in the previous chapter, fall between two other techniques—namely, the economic base theory and input-output analysis.

The population of a region can be projected on the basis of employment, particularly that part of employment related to export, which brings income into the region and consequently attracts more people. This is the basic principle of *economic base theory*, which is extensively used for planning purposes. It is postulated that the total employment in any region depends on the employment in the basic industries. So if the employment in the basic industries for the future is known, the total employment can be estimated. Symbolically, let

$$E_t = E_B + E_{NB}, \qquad (4.1)$$

where E_t = total employment.

E_B = employment in the basic industries.

E_{NB} = employment in the nonbasic industries.

From equation 4.1,

$$E_t = \frac{(1 + E_{NB}) E_B}{E_B}.$$

Assuming

$$\frac{E_{NB}}{E_B} = a = \text{constant},$$

we have

$$E_t = (1 + a)E_b. \tag{4.2}$$

So if the value of basic employment at a future date is available from, say, national projection or otherwise and if we assume that the value of a is approximately constant over the year, then equation 4.2 can be used to project total employment and, consequently, population, land use, and so on. It is obvious that the assumptions made by the base theory are often unrealistic, and it is difficult to implement it when the industrial structure is complex. It often becomes a subjective task to identify basic and nonbasic industries. Again, a region may well grow without exporting. The question of import and internal investment has not been taken into account (Blumenfeld 1955). Although this theory is quite inexpensive to use, it is too simple to be of any practical use in complex situations.

An important direction of research has been to divide the activities into three groups, as contrasted with two in the base theory. The first group includes the geographically oriented industries, whose locational factors are environmental. The second group includes the complementary industries, for which the existence of the city is the main locational factor. Regression relations of the following kind are formulated between the population variable, total employment variable, and three categories of employment.

$$\begin{aligned}
p &= a_1 + b_1 E. \\
E &= E_g + E_c + E_u. \\
E_c &= a_2 + b_2 E_g. \\
E_u &= a_3 + b_3 P.
\end{aligned} \tag{4.3}$$

Here P means population of the city; E means total employment in the city; and E_g, E_c, and E_u mean empoyment in geographically oriented, complementary, and urban-oriented industries, respectively. This formulation is very aggregative and abstracts from many factors, such as size of the city, type of city, and so on. It is an improvement over base theory, however, since it takes into account, at least partially, the effect of location and space economics. This model (Czamanski 1963) was applied to cross-section data for cities of different sizes in the United States. Later on this method was extended for lagged time series with some modifications.

One of the basic deficiencies of base theory is that it completely neglects interindustry and interregional connections. For example, if we want to increase the output of the steel industry, then we have to think about providing for the inputs, such as coal, iron, ore, and so on. Steel needs coal, and coal production needs steel (for coal-mining machines); thus we have to think in terms of direct and indirect requirements for producing more steel. Activities in each region are dependent on those in other regions. For example, when steel production in Pittsburgh rises, the shipment of coal from West Virginia may also change. Interregional input-output analysis takes note of these interactions in very efficient ways.

Input-Output Analysis

The first task in input-output analysis is to construct an input-output table, as shown in Table 4-1. Here the activities are aggregated under a number of homogeneous groups, and a flow matrix is constructed to trace the source of inputs coming from all industries to every industry. This matrix, as shown in Table 4-1, is called an input-output matrix. The sectors are generally divided into two categories: (1) the sectors that may be termed the final demand, bill of goods, or exogenous sectors; and (2) the other sectors, which may be termed endogenous or processing sectors whose outputs (we judge) can be reliably approximated by a set of coefficients that we assume to be constant over time.

The endogenous or processing sectors constitute the structural matrix, from which are excluded the columns and rows referring to the final-demand sectors. If we read along the rows, this table gives us the sales of each sector to every other sector; if we read along the columns, it gives us the purchases of one sector from other sectors. Obviously, the sum of the sales (or output) must be equal to the sum of the purchases (or input).

Input-output analysis has two advantages. First, it is an excellent accounting method, which brings out a clear picture of the economy and points out the sources of data inadequacy. Second, and more important, it is used in deciding planning strategy—that is, to find out the required output levels of

Table 4–1 Input-Output Table

Industry Producing	Industry Purchasing 1 2 3 . . . 10	Final Demand Sector				Total Output
		Consumption	Investment	Change in Inventory	Exports	
1. Agriculture						
2. Heavy manufacturing						
3. Light manufacturing						
10.						
Total input						

the sectors so that the stipulated final demands can be satisfied. To do so from the input-output table, the input-output coefficients are first estimated as

$$a_{ij} = \frac{X_{ij}}{X_j},$$

where X_{ij} = total amount of input coming from ith sector to the jth sector.

X_j = output of the jth sector.

If a stands for the input-output matrix, then the fundamental equation is

$$X = (1 - a)^{-1}F, \qquad (4.4)$$

where X = the vector of output.

F = the vector for final demand.

$a = (a_{ij})$ input-output matrix.

If the final demand vectors at a future date are stipulated consistent with national goals and resource limitations, and if we have a satisfactory input-output coefficient table, then from equation 4.4 the required output level can be estimated. Input-output analysis has found wide application in national planning. In recent years it has been used more and more in the field of regional planning. When the question arises of the impact of major government spending—that is, reduction in defense expenditures—on the regional economy in an industrial country, what is needed is to adjust the final demand sector correspondingly and to find out the corresponding output figures (Isard and Schooler 1964). We can also decide what is the best offset program to compensate for the decrease in employment. An interregional input-output table similar to the national input-output table can be constructed, as shown in Table 4–2.

For the interregional framework, equation 4.4 can be reformulated as

$$X^K = (1 - a^{LK})^{-1}Y^L. \qquad (4.5)$$

The Construction of an Input-Output Table

It is not easy to construct an input-output (I-O) table, and for the developing countries it is even more difficult. Regional and interregional output tables demand a data base that does not exist. There are two principal ways to construct an I-O table. The first is to use the already published data; the second is the survey method, aided by engineering information. Since detailed instruction necessary for the construction of an I-O table is available elsewhere, it will not be repeated here. I shall only explain the construction

Table 4–2 Interregional Input-Output Table

	East	West	North	South	Total Output
East Ind. 1 Agriculture	1 . . . 30	1 . . . 40	1 . . . 50	1 . . . 60	
2 Light manufacturing					
30 Household					
West Ind. 1 Agriculture					
2 Light manufacturing					
40 Household					
North Ind. 1 Mining					
2 Heavy manufacturing					
50 Household					
South Ind. 1 Light manufacturing					
2 Recreation					
60 Household					
Total input					

and use of an input-output table. For more information, see my previous study (Chatterji 1963).

As a first step, a regional input-output table for the CIR has been constructed for the year 1957. The total number of sectors is thirty-two. These sectors are also divided into a large number of subsectors. Theoretically, sectors should be chosen in such a way that, with respect to cost structure and flow aspect, each is homogeneous within itself and heterogeneous outside; but here such considerations could not govern in all cases because the sectors had to be nearly identical with those of the all-India input-output table.

Production Sectors in CIR.   These include (1) large-scale industry, (2) small-scale industry, and (3) tertiary activities. In the case of some small-scale industries, separate sectors have been constructed for Calcutta City and for the remainder of the region. This has been done in an attempt to trace the intraregional commodity flow. Nonprofit concerns such as educational institutions have been treated along with professions and services.

Imports from the Sectors outside CIR.   Sectors such as agriculture, of which there is little or no activity in this region, have been treated as import sectors. In the construction of the table, it has been assumed that if an input is available in CIR, it is used in the region and not imported from outside.

Household Sectors.   Since the household sector in CIR is highly heterogeneous with respect to consumption and saving behavior, I thought it desirable to divide the household sector into the following homogeneous groups: (1) directly employed male workers, (2) directly employed female workers, (3) contractors' workers, (4) other workers, and (5) self-employed persons.

In the case of nonwage income, I have also distinguished the following classes: (1) rent, (2) interest, (3) managing agents' remuneration, (4) dividends, (5) taxes, (6) retained earning, and (7) depreciation.

Public Authorities Sector.   This sector includes a portion of the central government of India, a portion of the state government of West Bengal, the Calcutta City Council, municipalities in the remaining towns, the Calcutta Improvement Trust (an organization devoted to improving civic conditions in Calcutta), and the Calcutta Port Trust.

Data are available for the different sectors in terms of purchasers' value, which includes, besides the producers' value, transportation costs, commodity taxes, and trade margins. Following existing practice, I have constructed the table in producers' value because it renders clearly the financial flow interpretation. For this purpose a deduction was made for commodity taxes and trade-cum-rail-cum-other-transport costs. For this, I have followed in most cases the procedure of the all-India table. Whenever this led to difficulties, I have freely used the all-India coefficients; my coefficients do not differ markedly from them. A detailed description of the definitional and computational procedures has been presented elsewhere (Chatterji 1963).

Sectoral Interdependence in the CIR Economy

The input-output table constructed for the region gives both the total import required by each sector and imports under different categories. However, these imports are direct imports and do not depict the true import content of any sector. Most sectors in the input-output table purchase their inputs from other sectors and thus depend indirectly on the imports of the latter sectors. For example, the jute textile industry depends on electricity, which imports coal from outside the CIR; thus the jute industry depends indirectly on the coal required by the electricity sector. This dependence of import must be added to the total import directly required by the jute industry, along with its dependence on the import of other sectors. The elements of the inverse matrix give us the amount of dependence of any sector on all sectors, after taking into account the infinite number of chain effects. These coefficients were used to calculate the direct-plus-indirect import requirement for each of the sectors.

Let us denote the rest of the world sector by r and the total import of jth sector from the rest of the world as

$$X_{rj} \qquad j = 1, \ldots, 32.$$

Next, I define

$$a_{rj} = \frac{X_{rj}}{X_j} = \text{direct import coefficient.} \qquad (4.6)$$

Thus a_{rj} is the average amount of direct imports absorbed by the jth sector per unit output of the jth sector.

Then the total amount of import that has been absorbed directly and indirectly by the production sector j will be given by

$$_r X_j = X_j \sum_{i=1}^{32} a_{rj} a_{ij}. \qquad (4.7)$$

The numbers a_{ij} are the elements of the inverse matrix, and they can be interpreted as the average amount of supply from sector i that is needed to enable sector j to produce one unit of output.

If we are interested in the direct and indirect import content of a particular sector, then equation 4.7 can be used fruitfully. However, if we are interested in a group of sectors such as textiles, then the use of equation 4.7 will involve double counting, since the indirect import of one will be the direct import of another at the same time. To avoid this difficulty and to obtain results that are additive, we shall use

$$r^{X_j^F} = X_j \sum_{i=1}^{32} a_{rj} a_{ij}.$$ (4.8)

In this case, instead of taking the total delivery X_j, I take X_j^F, the delivery to the final demand sectors.

Thus $r^{X_j^F}$ can be described as the direct and indirect import content of the commodities absorbed by the final demand sectors from sector j. The final demand sector has been divided into two parts: (1) export sector and (2) other than export sector.

The second sector consists mainly of consumption. I have calculated $r^{X_j^F}$ separately for sectors (1) and (2) and then by adding the two, obtained the corresponding figure for the total final demand sector. We can denote the corresponding $r^{X_j^X}$ for (1) and (2) as $r^{X_j^{F1}}$ and $r^{X_j^{F2}}$, respectively, where $r^{X_j^F} = r^{X_j^{F1}} + r^{X_j^{F2}}$.

Column 3 in Table 4–3 gives the total import of each of the sectors. Column 4 gives the direct import coefficient obtained from equation 4.1. Column 5 gives the direct-plus-indirect import coefficents defined as

$$\sum_{i=1}^{32} a_{rj} a_{ij} \qquad j = 1, 2, \ldots, 32.$$ (4.9)

Columns 6, 7, and 8 give r^{X_j}, r^{X_j}, and r^{X_j}, respectively.

It will be seen that the total of direct and indirect imports as given by the total of column 8 equals the total of direct imports. It is interesting to note that although sector 1 has imported directly 227 lakh rupees, the total value of its direct and indirect imports contained in its deliveries to the final demand categories was 50 lakh rupees. The reduction is due to the fact that a major portion of its output was used up by the processing sectors. The same is true for sectors 2 and 12.

The commodity balance of each sector is defined as the difference between export and direct import. To have a real picture, however, we should take as

Table 4–3 Direct Plus Indirect Import Incorporated in Deliveries to Final Demand in 1957

1	2	3	4	5
Sector Number	Sector Name	Direct Total Import (in Lakh of Rupees)	Direct Import per Unit Output	Direct-Plus-Indirect Import per Unit of Output
1	Iron and steel	227	.24278	.27245
2	Nonferrous metals	123	.12094	.17864
3	Engineering	1386	.14488	.18359
4	Chemicals and chemical products	428	.12176	.18474
5	Food, drink, and tobacco	2589	.54874	.62582
6	Cotton textiles	556	.24322	.33741
7	Other textiles	58	.07703	.12788
8	Jute textiles	4731	.37304	.38969
9	Glass and ceramics	118	.23600	.27691
10	Leather and rubber	812	.21799	.29923
11	Paper, printing, and stationery	236	.10621	.15800
12	Electricity and gas	200	.17953	.21426
13	Plywood and furniture	13	.05556	.10818
14	Metalware and metalworking (Calcutta)	69	.09544	.17986
15	Metalware and metalworking (C.I.R. except Calcutta)	28	.10000	.19032
16	Building materials and wood (Calcutta)	275	.47169	.54727
17	Building materials and wood (C.I.R. except Calcutta)	52	.38235	.43392
18	Textiles and textile products (Calcutta)	301	.26450	.37302
19	Textiles and textile products (C.I.R. except Calcutta)	35	.13060	.24084
20	Food, drink, and tobacco (Calcutta)	793	.56522	.61150
21	Food, drink, and tobacco (C.I.R. except Calcutta)	408	.58119	.62968
22	Glass and ceramics	8	.16000	.24621

(Continued)

6	7	8	9	10	11
Direct-Plus-Indirect Import Incorporated in Deliveries to Export (in Lakh of Rupees)	Direct-Plus-Indirect Import Incorporated in Deliveries to Consumption (in Lakh of Rupees)	Direct-Plus-Indirect Import Incorporated in Deliveries to Total Final Demand (in Lakh of Rupees) Col. (6) + (7)	Direct-Plus-Indirect Effect on Itself per Unit Change of Final Demand (Using A Matrix)	Direct-Plus-Indirect Effect on Itself per Unit Change of Final Demand (Using A* Matrix)	Total Activity Generated per Unit Change in Final Demand
42	8	50	1.0727	1.0753	1.2207
4	13	17	1.2186	1.2199	1.5981
1521	64	1585	1.0389	1.0430	1.3125
288	133	421	1.1422	1.1525	1.3791
—	2304	2304	1.1030	1.1333	1.3162
168	208	376	1.2729	1.2878	1.5348
7	24	31	1.2120	1.2150	1.5380
4831	—	4831	1.0017	1.0034	1.1448
100	14	114	1.0208	1.0220	1.2730
921	57	978	1.0435	1.0465	1.4922
243	37	280	1.1152	1.1194	1.4546
—	123	123	1.0453	1.0500	1.2367
9	3	12	1.2724	1.2729	1.6856
59	7	66	1.0336	1.0367	1.6538
28	4	32	1.0221	1.0234	1.6888
219	67	286	1.0877	1.0886	1.3397
4	20	24	1.0709	1.0714	1.2904
334	78	412	1.0107	1.0142	1.6306
25	21	46	1.0000	1.0018	1.5134
592	248	840	1.0000	1.0040	1.1542
163	273	436	1.0086	1.1101	1.1662
—	4	4	1.0003	1.0024	1.5006

(Continued next page)

Table 4–3 *(continued)*

1	2	3	4	5
Sector Number	Sector Name	Direct Total Import (in Lakh of Rupees)	Direct Import per Unit Output	Direct-Plus-Indirect Import per Unit of Output
23	Leather and rubber	44	.09322	.24031
24	Other small-scale industries	191	.31939	.37018
25	Railways and communication	179	.09054	.11567
26	Other transportation	580	.19870	.25589
27	Trade and distribution	430	.03146	.04431
28	Banking insurance co-operatives	5	.00269	.02247
29	Professions and services	68	.02703	.06227
30	Construction	122	.10304	.16414
31	Residential property	35	.01244	.01756
32	Public administration	—	—	—
	Total	15100	—	—

Source: M. Chatterji, "An Input-Output Study of the Calcutta Industrial Region," *Papers of the Regional Science Association* 13 (1964): 93–102. Reprinted with the kind permission of the Regional Science Association.

the commodity balance for the jth sector the difference between the direct export of the jth sector and its direct-plus-indirect import, or

$$j^{X_r} - j^{X_r^F}, \qquad j = 1, 2, \ldots, 32, \qquad (4.10)$$

where j^{X_r} denotes the export of the jth sector to the rest of the world.

The direct-plus-indirect export has been calculated in Table 4–4. Similarly, the direct-plus-indirect capital requirements have been worked out for different sectors; and the estimates of capital in each sector have been made as shown in Table 4–5.

Use of I-O Table to Protect the CIR Economy

In the next step, specific goals of employment for the year 1970 have been formulated. These goals are consistent with national goals and with the

6	7	8	9	10	11
Direct-Plus-Indirect Import Incorporated in Deliveries to Export (in Lakh of Rupees)	Direct-Plus-Indirect Import Incorporated in Deliveries to Consumption (in Lakh of Rupees)	Direct-Plus-Indirect Import Incorporated in Deliveries to Total Final Demand (in Lakh of Rupees) Col. (6) + (7)	Direct-Plus-Indirect Effect on Itself per Unit Change of Final Demand (Using A Matrix)	Direct-Plus-Indirect Effect on Itself per Unit Change of Final Demand (Using A* Matrix)	Total Activity Generated per Unit Change in Final Demand
74	38	112	1.0161	1.0195	1.8313
4	147	151	1.0530	1.0671	1.3945
9	109	118	1.0095	1.0564	1.1731
415	215	630	1.0043	1.0350	1.5002
200	210	410	1.0189	1.1512	1.0832
31	4	35	1.0078	1.0270	1.2358
38	95	133	1.0036	1.0417	1.2423
—	194	194	1.0000	1.0000	1.5144
—	49	49	1.0000	1.0040	1.0417
—	—	—	1.0000	1.0007	1.0000
10329	4771	15100	—	—	—

present industrial structure of the economy. In formulating these goals, the social, economic, and political conditions existing in the region have also been taken into acount (Chatterji 1970). The following two cases have been considered.

Case 1.   A goal of a 2 percent increase in export to the rest of the world has been stipulated. In the case of the jute industry, I assume no such increase because the jute industry is still in a bad state. Employment in jute mills has fluctuated widely in recent years. The machinery of the jute mills is old and needs replacement; in the world market, it faces much competition from countries with modern jute mills. Thus it is well to be satisfied with the 1957 export level, if this can be maintained. Household consumption in 1970 has been based on the increase in population. Corrections have been made for the expected increase in the standard of living. Expenditure by public authorities has been projected on the basis of the trend witnessed in the past years. Adding up the individual components of the final demand, I obtain the goal of final demand in 1970. Then, multiplying this vector of desired formal demand by the inverse matrix, I obtained the required output.

Table 4–4 Direct Plus Indirect Export and Commodity Balance of Sectors of the Calcutta Industrial Region in 1957

Sector Number	Direct Export (in Lakh of Rupees)	Direct Export as Percentage of Total Output	Direct-Plus-Indirect Export (in Lakh of Rupees)	Direct-Plus-Indirect Export as Percentage of Total Output	Direct Commodity Balance (in Lakh of Rupees)	Direct-Plus-Indirect Commodity Balance-Direct Export-Direct-Plus-Indirect Import (in Lakh of Rupees)
1	154	16.5	735	78.6	− 73	+ 104
2	22	2.0	792	77.9	− 101	+ 5
3	8284	86.6	8901	93.0	+6898	+6699
4	1558	44.3	2453	69.7	+1130	+1137
5	—	—	477	10.1	−2589	−2304
6	498	21.8	1356	59.3	− 58	+ 122
7	52	6.9	304	40.3	− 6	+ 21
8	12419	97.9	12516	99.1	+7688	+7588
9	361	72.2	401	80.2	+ 243	+ 247
10	3079	82.6	3441	92.3	+2267	+2101
11	1541	69.3	1872	84.2	+1305	+1261
12	—	—	412	37.0	− 200	− 123
13	81	34.6	167	71.3	+ 68	+ 69
14	330	45.6	523	72.3	+ 261	+ 264

15	145	51.7	208	74.2	+ 117	+ 113
16	400	68.6	—	—	+ 125	+ 114
17	9	.1	21	15.4	− 43	− 15
18	896	78.7	910	80.0	+ 595	+ 484
19	103	38.4	104	38.8	+ 68	+ 57
20	968	69.0	977	69.6	+ 175	+ 128
21	259	36.8	273	38.8	− 149	− 177
22	—	—	21	42.0	8	4
23	296	62.7	311	65.8	+ 252	+ 184
24	12	—	107	17.8	− 179	− 139
25	77	—	1339	67.7	− 102	− 41
26	1621	55.5	1929	66.0	+1041	+ 991
27	4514	33.0	7606	55.6	+4084	+4104
28	1383	74.3	1553	83.4	+1378	+1348
29	606	24.1	833	33.1	+ 538	+ 473
30	—	—	—	—	− 122	− 194
31	—	—	—	—	− 35	− 194
32	—	—	20	.8	—	—
Total	39668	—	24568	—	24568	24568

Source: M. Chatterji, "An Input-Output Study of the Calcutta Industrial Region," *Papers of the Regional Science Association* 13 (1964): 93–102. Reprinted with the kind permission of the Regional Science Association.

Table 4–5   Direct Plus Indirect Capital Output Ratios for Different Sectors of the Calcutta Industrial Region in 1957

Sector Number	Capital Coefficient- Amount of Capital Needed Per Unit Output	Net Value-Added by Manufacture Per Unit Output	Direct Capital Output Ratio	Direct-Plus- Indirect Capital Output Ratio Per Unit Output	Estimate of Total Capital Employed (in Lakh of Rupees)	Capital Employed Per Worker (in Rupees)
1	.9517	.5594	1.7013	1.4290	890	3467
2	.7480	.2291	3.2649	1.6431	761	21412
3	.6683	.3263	2.0481	1.1196	6393	5605
4	.6366	.3710	1.7159	1.0552	2238	9277
5	.2025	.1895	1.0686	.5876	955	7053
6	.7788	.2887	2.6941	1.4113	1780	3709
7	.5085	.2829	1.7975	1.0999	383	1662
8	.6650	.2694	2.4684	.8772	8434	3660
9	.7780	.4440	1.7523	1.0829	389	2786
10	.1823	.2215	.8230	.7292	679	2953
11	.8642	.4631	1.8661	1.5080	1920	5148
12	2.5554	.3223	7.9286	2.8996	2847	26007
13	.6544	.3419	1.9140	1.7194	153	4081
14	.3599	.4205	.8464	1.3114	260	1364

15	.3599	92	.9247	1.3750	101	1218
16	.2495	.2573	.9697	.9287	145	1378
17	.2495	.3824	.6525	.8999	34	986
18	.3087	.3111	.9923	.9216	351	2080
19	.3087	.4851	.6364	.7706	83	799
20	.0930	.3122	.2979	.2781	130	495
21	.0930	.2849	.3264	.2756	65	516
22	.2308	.4400	.5245	.8730	12	380
23	.1483	.3263	.4545	.7440	70	654
24	.1450	.3578	.4053	.6614	87	457
25	6.5782	.7739	8.5000	6.7970	11025	18756
26	3.5824	.5207	6.8800	4.0970	10381	8383
27	1.2231	.9001	1.3700	1.3731	16855	3673
28	1.1413	.8152	1.4000	1.4999	2124	5861
29	.2516	.7862	.3200	.5575	633	223
30	6.5617	.5076	12.9269	7.0208	7769	13495
31	13.6660	.9527	14.3381	13.7134	37506	—
32	6.5617	1.0000	6.5617	6.5617	15840	10612

Source: M. Chatterji, "An Input-Output Study of the Calcutta Industrial Region," *Papers of the Regional Science Association* 13 (1964): 93–102. Reprinted with the kind permission of the Regional Science Association.

Case 2. I next considered another alternate design, similar to case 1 but mainly concerned with investment. Let us assume that the capacity K_h^t, when fully used, stands in a certain proportion to the total production in sector h, or

$$K_h^t = b_h X_h^t, \qquad (4.11)$$

for all h, where b_h is a constant. The depreciation D_h^t stands in a certain proportion to the total production in sector h, or

$$D_h^t = d_h X_h^t, \qquad (4.12)$$

for all h, where d_h is constant.

Finally, our assumption is that the labor requirement N_h^t stands in a certain proportion to the total production sector h, or

$$N_h = n_h X_h^t, \qquad (4.13)$$

for all h where n_h is constant. Now I denote the total investment goods delivered to sector h in year t from all the thirty-two sectors as

$$J_{.h}^t = \sum_{i=1}^{32} J_{ih}^t. \qquad (4.14)$$

The way in which the capacity in any sector evolves over time is given by

$$K_h^t = K_h^{t-1} + J_{.h}^t - D_h^{t-1}, \qquad (4.15)$$

where s_h is the maturity lag of sector h. Substituting equations 4.11, 4.12, and 4.13 in equation 4.15,

$$J_{.h}^t = \frac{b_h}{N_h} \cdot N_h^{t+s_h+1} \frac{b_h - d_h N_h^{t+3}}{N_h}. \qquad (4.16)$$

From equation 4.6, it is clear that if we have the coefficients b_h, n_h, and d_h, then the requirement of capital for each sector can be calculated year by year so as to attain the goal of an employment set for each sector in future years.

I then calculated the constants b_h, d_h, and n_h for all thirty-two sectors of the CIR. The constants b_h have been estimated from the capacity estimates given in the *Monthly Bulletin on Production of Selected Industries in India*. Except for the large industries, the coefficients have been assumed to be unity for every sector. The constants n_h have been estimated using census-derived employment figures and output figures obtained from the input-output table. The constants for depreciation are calculated from the information available in the input-output table. In the next step, I formulated the goals of employment in future years. For that, I estimated the employment

figures in 1966 in different sectors, assuming that the past trend of employment increase will hold up to 1966.

Beginning with 1967, I set the goals of a 5 percent increase per year in
large and small industries and a 2 percent increase per year in tertiary
activities. These goals are consistent with the national goal of a 5 percent
increase. So that these goals can be achieved, the required employment
figures for each sector in different years have been calculated. From equation
4.16, the required investment is estimated so that the employment targets can
be attained.

It is noteworthy that in the construction of a regional input-output model,
one faces serious data difficulties. This is particularly so in the case of a
region in an underdeveloped country like India. So the example given here
serves only for demonstration purposes, particularly since this study is quite
outdated. So far, the input-output model has been based on econmic sectors.
However, other types of sectors (social, political, and environmental) can be
added (Isard 1969). One commonly used variation is the inclusion of the
environmental and pollution-abatement sectors. A practical example of such
an input-output model involving environmental sectors can be given for a
small country such as Belgium, as follows.

Interindustry Linkage and Pollution in Belgium

The pollution coefficients can be defined as the amount of air/water pollution
of a given type generated from the production of a unit level of activity of a
given sector. The activity level can be measured by a physical or monetary
unit. Satisfactory pollution coefficients do not exist for Belgium, but such
data for the Netherlands are given by Den Hartog and Houweling (1974).
For the United States the data are given by Leontief and Ford (1972).

On the other hand, Belgium has a reasonably good input-output table
prepared by the National Institute of Statistics (NIS) of the Belgium
government (NIS 1970). It will not be too inappropriate to use these
coefficients and combine them with the input-output table to calculate the
direct and indirect pollution generation per unit activity in different sectors. It
is true that the industrial mixes in the Netherlands, Belgium, and the United
States are not the same and the states of technology are different, but the
alternative would be to invest considerable money and time to gather data.
To get some crude estimates, we chose the first approach.

Belgium is a small country, with about 10 million people. Its per capita
income is little higher than that of the Netherlands. Compared with the
Netherlands, Belgium has more polluting industries (particularly iron and
steel), as reflected in the output of high polluting industries at a % of GNP

given in Table 4–6. The pattern of urbanization, population density, industrial structure, and climate are about the same, indicating that comparisons with respect to environmental pollution between the two countries are justified.

Let us consider the pollution generated in different sectors of the Belgian economy. The sectors to be considered are those given in the input-output table for Belgium (1965) published in NIS (1970). It consisted of ninety-three industrial classifications. Tejano and Brauer (1974) reduced the table to fifty-three classifications. Pollution coefficients are obtained by using U.S. figures for similar sectors given by Leontief and Ford (1972).

These coefficients were properly adjusted with respect to monetary units, changes in price level, and difference in time period. Five types of pollutants were identified: particulates, sulfur oxides, hydrocarbons, carbon monoxide, and nitrogen oxides. The pollution matrix has been designated by P, with the elements denoted by P_{ij}. These direct pollution coefficients tell us the amount of pollution generated from the production of a unit level of output. To produce iron and steel, however, we need to produce coal, which again contributes to pollution. We also need electricity, the production of which leads to pollution. Thus it is necessary to consider not only the direct pollution generated for production of iron and steel, but also the direct and indirect pollution generated by the inputs needed to produce them. This direct and indirect amount can be obtained by using the input-output model (Isard 1960). The fundamental equation is given by

$$X = (1 - A)^{-1}F$$

where X is the vector of output, F is the vector of final demand, $A = a_j$ is the interindustry coefficient matrix, and I is the identity matrix; that is,

$$X = \begin{bmatrix} x_1 \\ x_2 \\ \cdot \\ \cdot \\ \cdot \\ x_n \end{bmatrix} \quad F = \begin{bmatrix} F_1 \\ F_2 \\ \cdot \\ \cdot \\ \cdot \\ F_n \end{bmatrix} \quad A = \begin{bmatrix} a_{11} & a_{12} & \cdots & a_{1n} \\ \cdot & & & \\ \cdot & & & \\ \cdot & & & \\ a_{n1} & a_{n2} & \cdots & a_{nn} \end{bmatrix}$$

$$I = \begin{bmatrix} 1 & 0 & 0 & & 0 \\ 0 & 1 & 0 & & 0 \\ \cdot & & & & \\ \cdot & & & & \\ 0 & 0 & 0 & 0 & 1 \end{bmatrix}$$

Table 4-6 Some Basic Environmental Indicators

	Per Capital GNP at 1970 market prices in U.S. dollars (1970 exch. rates)	Output of high polluting industries in % of GDP	Average rainfall (1000 m³ per capita)	Population Density (Persons per Km)	Urbanization ratio
United States	$4,816	14.9%	—	22	0.752
Germany	3,089	18.6	3.4	240	0.824
Sweden	4,055	13.1	39.2	18	0.661
Netherlands	2,410	14.5	2.3	319	0.772
United Kingdom	2,120	12.4	4.6	228	0.801
Italy	1,794	16.5	5.6	178	0.515
Japan	1,921	14.8	—	280	0.844
Belgium	2,659	18.75	2.29	316	—

Source: M. Chatterji, "Interindustry Linkage and Pollution in Belgium," *Environmental Management* 2, no. 4 (1978). Original source: Organization for Economic Cooperation and Development, *Economic Implications of Pollution Control* (Paris: OECD, 1974), pp. 28–29. Reprinted with permission.

$$a_{ij} = \frac{x_{ij}}{x_j} = \frac{\text{flow of inputs from } i\text{th to } j\text{th sector}}{\text{output of } j\text{th sector}}$$

From the input-output economics we know that the inverse $(1-A)^{-1}$ describes the total (that is, direct and indirect) effect of an increase of 1 million BF (Belgian francs) in final demand for the products of any given industry on the total output of that and every other industry. Accordingly, the amount of pollution generated directly and indirectly from delivery to final demand will be given by $P(I-A)^{-1}$. The results are shown in Table 4–7. Note that the input-output coefficients are based on nationally produced inputs only. The figures in parentheses are for the United States.

One may want to know the amount of pollution generated directly and indirectly from all sectors owing to the delivery of a \$1 million U.S. ouput to final demand (say, for additional \$1 million U.S. consumption). This can easily be obtained from Table 4–7. Referring to column 4 of Table 4–7 for the electricity sector (no. 11), we see that 13.1 additional tons of carbon monoxide would be generated by all industries, contributing to the delivery to final users of an additional \$1 million worth of electricity. Multiplying this figure by the total final demand for electricity, we get the amount of pollution of that type generated by the delivery of that amount of final demand. In mathematical notation, the complete set of such multiplication is given by $P(I-A)^{-1}Y_k$, where Y_k is the column vector of deliveries to final customers of kth type of final demand. For any one of the five types of pollution, the sum is taken for all sectors, and the pollution is expressed per unit final demand.

Table 4–8 gives this information for eight types of final demand. The figures are given in dollars, so they can be compared with the U.S. figures. It is seen that the U.S. figures are consistently higher. The figures in the table are important since pollution levels can be precisely estimated when we plan to project the final demand in a particular fashion. Table 4–9 gives the pollution content of import for different types of final demand.

This study presents some empirical results that, though crude, can be used for policy decisions. It is true that the technological structure and pollution-emission pattern in Belgium are not the same as those in the United States and the Netherlands. I have freely used the average exchange-rate price indexes to modify my observation for international comparison. In the absence of any data, however, this is probably the best one can do. In the future, when more comprehensive data are available, sophisticated analysis should be applied.

Table Table 4-7 Direct and Indirect Air Pollution Coefficients, Matrix (P'_i)

	Particulates	SO_x	HC	CO	NO_x
1. Agriculture & Forestry	0.0068 (0.01024)	0.07754 (0.07768)	0.0036 (0.00526)	0.0087 (0.01608)	0.0034 (0.00457)
2. Iron ore	0 (0.01697)	0 (0.03603)	0 (0.00379)	0 (0.04038)	0 (0.00908)
3. Fishery	0.0038 (0.00683)	0.0362 (0.04856)	0.0023 (0.00296)	0.0209 (0.01748)	0.0012 (0.00209)
4. Food	0.0068 (0.02086)	0.0414 (0.03991)	0.0022 (0.00454)	0.0076 (0.02286)	0.0032 (0.00523)
5. Drinks	0.0066 (0.02086)	0.0198 (0.03991)	0.0017 (0.00454)	0.0068 (0.02286)	0.0031 (0.00523)
6. Tobacco	0.0032 (0.0053)	0.0049 (0.02226)	0.0003 (0.00186)	0.0016 (0.00757)	0.0009 (0.00244)
7. Oils	0.0060 (0.02086)	0.0160 (0.03991)	0.0009 (0.00454)	0.0034 (0.02286)	0.0027 (0.00523)
8. Coal mines	0.0824 (0.0754)	0.0478 (0.0340)	0.0029 (0.0026)	0.0332 (0.0316)	0.0111 (0.0076)
9. Cokes, gas, & petrol	0.0367 (0.00748)	0.0452 (0.02718)	0.0034 (0.00164)	0.0233 (0.01098)	0.0099 (0.0046)
10. Refining (kerosine)	0.0055 (0.0139)	0.0963 (0.1277)	0.0414 (0.0468)	0.0896 (0.1086)	0.0008 (0.0058)
11. Electricity	0.3032 (0.29552)	0.7949 (0.78882)	0.0039 (0.00305)	0.0131 (0.01145)	0.1357 (0.18516)
12. Water	0.2781 (0.2541)	0.0310 (0.0320)	0.2887 (0.2904)	0.6045 (0.5730)	0.1002 (0.1530)

(Continued next page)

Table 4–7 (continued)

13. Textile	0.0084 (0.01523)	0.0201 (0.04246)	0.0013 (0.00516)	0.0050 (0.01464)	0.0042 (0.00617)
14. Clothing & footwear	0.0049 (0.01157)	0.0104 (0.03285)	0.0007 (0.00443)	0.0033 (0.01216)	0.0022 (0.00529)
15. Saw mills	0.0488 (0.07393)	0.0417 (0.04918)	0.0016 (0.00578)	0.0072 (0.01803)	0.0049 (0.00786)
16. Furniture & bedding	0.0134 (0.01175)	0.0178 (0.03114)	0.0011 (0.00360)	0.0330 (0.04602)	0.0034 (0.00497)
17. Paper	0.0590 (0.07393)	0.0444 (0.04918)	0.0022 (0.00578)	0.0116 (0.01803)	0.0066 (0.00786)
18. Printing & publishing	0.0116 (0.01844)	0.0197 (0.02659)	0.0010 (0.00281)	0.0046 (0.00919)	0.0031 (0.00477)
19. Non-metalliferous minerals	0.0440 (0.0585)	0.7441 (1.0386)	0.0017 (0.0049)	0.0167 (0.0233)	0.0071 (0.0136)
20. Iron & steel	0.1283 (0.0835)	0.0417 (0.0467)	0.0026 (0.0045)	1.4894 (0.9724)	0.0100 (0.0084)
21. Non-ferrous	0.0562 (0.0592)	0.0170 (0.1276)	0.0007 (0.0063)	0.0056 (0.0132)	0.0037 (0.0089)
22. Construction materials	1.0205 (1.03489)	0.0860 (0.06245)	0.0018 (0.01726)	0.02696 (0.04029)	0.0078 (0.00841)
23. Glass	0.0132 (0.0167)	0.0378 (0.02926)	0.0017 (0.00318)	0.0088 (0.01418)	0.0063 (0.00559)
24. Chemicals & related activities	0.0263 (0.0248)	0.0820 (0.1064)	0.0021 (0.0076)	0.0103 (0.0454)	0.0082 (0.0081)
25. Metal products	0.0188 (0.02576)	0.0223 (0.07516)	0.0009 (0.00321)	0.1431 (0.17625)	0.0035 (0.00563)

26. Industrial machinery	0.0144 (0.01818)	0.0148 (0.04633)	0.0009 (0.00289)	0.1009 (0.07850)	0.0031 (0.00442)
27. Electrical machinery	0.0111 (0.01632)	0.0208 (0.06227)	0.0006 (0.00297)	0.0511 (0.08174)	0.0026 (0.00465)
28. Shipyards	0.0166 (0.01582)	0.0153 (0.03802)	0.0009 (0.00322)	0.0822 (0.12062)	0.0032 (0.00487)
29. Rolling rail material	0.0229 (0.01582)	0.0175 (0.03802)	0.0009 (0.00322)	0.2187 (0.12062)	0.0036 (0.0032)
30. Cars & Motorbikes	0.0040 (0.01582)	0.0076 (0.03802)	0.0003 (0.00322)	0.0150 (0.12062)	0.0014 (0.0032)
31. Aircraft construction	0.0042 (0.01047)	0.0164 (0.04527)	0.0009 (0.00322)	0.0045 (0.12062)	0.0020 (0.0032)
32. Remaining industries	0.0048	0.0071	0.0005 (0.00240)	0.0092 (0.03943)	0.0012 (0.00392)
33. Construction industry	0.1141 (0.02914)	0.0445 (0.05157)	0.0014 (0.00426)	0.0773 (0.06876)	0.0029 (0.0051)
34. Garages	0.00065	0.0126	0.0009	0.0072	0.0028
35. Railway transportation	0.0324 (0.02156)	0.0446 (0.02219)	0.0215 (0.02473)	0.0519 (0.02844)	0.0355 (0.03115)
36. Road transporation	0.0136 (0.01650)	0.0139 (0.01952)	0.0170 (0.01919)	0.0142 (0.01653)	0.0158 (0.01927)
37. Sea Freight traffic	0.0280 (0.03508)	0.0890 (0.10337)	0.0302 (0.03272)	0.0911 (0.10373)	0.0503 (0.06085)
38. Inland navigation	0.0268 (0.03508)	0.0783 (0.10337)	0.0262 (0.03272)	0.0835 (0.10373)	0.0492 (0.06085)
39. Airborne freight traffic	0.0079 (0.00496)	0.0127 (0.02171)	0.0396 (0.04306)	0.2987 (0.31263)	0.0014 (0.00287)
40. Subsidiary activities of transportation	0.0052	0.0128	0.0002	0.0006	0.0029

(Continued next page)

Table 4–7 (continued)

41. Traffic	0.0155 (0.02156)	0.0110 (0.02219)	0.0159 (0.02473)	0.0127 (0.02844)	0.0172 (0.03115)
42. Credit banks	0.0035 (0.00897)	0.0083 (0.02513)	0.0007 (0.0021)	0.0021 (0.00605)	0.0019 (0.00604)
43. Insurance business	0.0060 (0.00897)	0.0126 (0.02513)	0.0020 (0.0021)	0.0053 (0.00605)	0.0037 (0.00604)
44. Commercial transactions	0.0060 (0.00843)	0.0174 (0.02797)	0.0014 (0.00182)	0.0045 (0.00523)	0.0016 (0.00527)
45. Hotel and catering industry	0.0086 (0.01090)	0.0226 (0.02941)	0.0019 (0.00269)	0.0057 (0.01268)	0.0087 (0.01038)
46. Private houses	0.0123 (0.02914)	0.0199 (0.05157)	0.0001 (0.00426)	0.0083 (0.06876)	0.0003 (0.00501)
47. Free education	0.0109	0.0122	0.0017	0.0089	0.0029
48. Services concerning sanitation	0.2543 (0.2541)	0.0158 (0.0320)	0.2911 (0.2904)	0.05703 (0.5730)	0.1474 (0.1530)
49. Remaining private services	0.00116 (0.019090)	0.00204 (0.02941)	0.00029 (0.00269)	0.00072 (0.01268)	0.00087 (0.01038)
50. Services by public bodies	0.00142 (0.01909)	0.00271 (0.02941)	0.00026 (0.00269)	0.00104 (0.01268)	0.00104 (0.01038)
51. Non-ferrous ores	0. (0.01833)	0 (0.04101)	0 (0.00356)	0	0
52. Official education	0.00093	0.00096	0.00023	0.00085	0.00028
53. Household appliances	0 (0.01923)	0 (0.0501)	0 (0.00355)	0 (0.10927)	0 (0.00535)

Source: M. Chatterji, "Interindustry Linkage and Pollution in Belgium," *Environmental Management* 2, no. 4 (1978).

Table 4–8 Thousands of Tons of Pollutants per Million (1965) U.S. Dollars of Final Demand of the Belgian Economy

	Particulates	SO_x	HC	CO	NO_x
1. Private consumption	0.0306	0.0399	0.0196	0.0455	0.0153
	(0.019)	(0.045)	(0.007)	(0.025)	(0.011)
2. Public consumption	0.0137	0.0230	0.0026	0.0106	0.083
	(0.014)	(0.026)	(0.005)	(0.049)	(0.003)
	(0.028)	(0.051)	(0.003)	(0.053)	(0.008)
3. Total investment	0.0917	0.0396	0.0015	0.0783	0.0032
	(0.023)	(0.046)	(0.004)	(0.075)	(0.005)
4. Inventory changes	0.1135	0.0576	0.0079	0.0886	0.0077
	(0.023)	(0.046)	(0.007)	(0.070)	(0.006)
5. Exports to EEC countr.	0.0464	0.0383	0.0034	0.1929	0.0062
6. Exports to non-EeC countr.	0.0456	0.0394	0.0054	0.2974	0.0082
7. Total exports	0.0461	0.0385	0.0041	0.2318	0.0069
	(0.023)	(0.065)	(0.010)	(0.071)	(0.0011)
Net	(0.0358)**	(−0.0010)**	(0.0080)**	(0.1105)**	(0.0122)**
8. Total final demand	0.0423	0.0373	0.0103	0.1036	0.0101

Source: M. Chatterji, ''Interindustry Linkage and Pollution in Belgium,'' *Environmental Management* 2, no. 4 (1978). The figures were obtained by multiplying the pollution vector by the national inverse matrix and different components of final demand vector. The sum of the pollution generated by all sectors was then expressed as per unit of final demand.

*The figures in parentheses are comparable results for the United States.

**The third item is given by Anthony Koo (1974).

Table 4-9 Thousands of Tons of Pollutants per Million (1963) U.S. Dollars of Import by Belgium (1965) for Different Items of Final Demand, Using U.S. Pollution Coefficients

	Particulates	SO_x	HC	CO	NO_x
1. Import for total consumption	0.0365	0.0695	0.0050	0.0600	0.0070
2. Import for investment	0.0310	0.0340	0.0015	0.1590	0.0055
3. Inventory change (import)	−0.0110	0.0900	0.0035	−0.1805	0.0025
4. Export to EEC (Import for)	0.0210	0.0660	0.0045	0.0425	0.0080
5. Export to non-EEC (Import for)	0.0200	0.0480	0.0020	0.0480	0.0050
6. Total export (Import for)	0.0220	0.0504	0.0030	0.0450	0.0060
7. Total import	0.0321	0.0557	0.0040	0.0852	0.0065
	(0.0699)	(0.1357)	(0.0127)	(0.0885)	(0.0129)

Source: M. Chatterji, "Interindustry Linkage and Pollution in Belgium," *Environmental Management* 2, no. 4 (1978). Figures in parentheses are for United States (Koo 1974).

These direct and indirect pollution figures are given per \$1 million U.S. The direct and indirect pollution coefficients for Belgium and the United States are quite different, and the figures for the United States are almost always higher. Assuming that U.S. technology is more advanced and pollution-efficient, this might imply that the interindustry linkage in the United States is much stronger and hence generates more pollution.

So far, I have conducted the analysis on the basis of the pollution coefficients of the United States. It is true that the economic structures of Belgium and the United States are not the same, but it is unlikely that the emission coefficients will be drastically different. Next I shall use the pollution coefficients for the Netherlands given by Den Hartog and Houweling (1974). Unfortunately, the classification of pollutants for the United States and the Netherlands is not the same. Thus it will not be possible to compare the two sets of results. The Netherlands' coefficients include both air and water pollution. Although there is an overlap in the definitions of the five types of pollutants for the United States and the seven types in the case of the Netherlands, in a sense this is an advantage since policymakers can decide which coefficients to use and for what purposes.

The seven classifications are:

1. Public water pollution.
2. Private water pollution.
3. Sulphur pollution from gas oil.
4. Sulphur pollution from residual oil.
5. Solid waste.
6. Pollution from passenger cars.
7. Pollution from trucks and vans.

The input-output coefficient matrix can be extended to include not only production and consumption of ordinary goods but also the generation and elimination of pollutants. The extended matrix will look like

$$
\begin{array}{|c|c|}
\hline
A & Q \\
\hline
P & S \\
\hline
\end{array}
=
\left[
\begin{array}{ccc|ccc}
a_{11} \ldots a_{1m} & & q_{1,m+1} \ldots q_{1n} \\
\vdots & & \vdots \\
a_{m1} \ldots a_{mm} & & q_{m,m-1} \ldots q_{mn} \\
\hline
p_{m+1,1} \ldots p_{m+1,m} & & S_{m+1,m+1} \ldots S_{m+1,n} \\
\vdots & & \vdots \\
p_{n1} \ldots p_{nm} & & S_{n,m+1} \ldots S_{nn}
\end{array}
\right]
$$

where a_{ij} = input of good i per unit output of good j (produced by sector j), structural coefficients.

q_{ig} = input of good i per unit eliminated pollutant g (eliminated by sector g).

p_{gi} = output of pollutant g per unit of output of good i (produced by sector i).

s_{gk} = output of pollutant g per unit of eliminated pollutant k (eliminated by sector k).

$g,k = m + 1 \ldots n.$

$i,j = 1,2 \ldots m.$

In the foregoing scheme, A is the usual matrix of interindustry coefficients, P is the matrix of direct pollution output coefficients, Q is the input structure coefficient, and S is the pollution output coefficients matrix for the antipollution activities sectors producing pollution-abating goods. In the matrixes Q and S, the coefficients denote inputs and outputs per unit of eliminated pollutant.

For Belgium, we take the same antipollution sectors as those in the Netherlands study, along with the matrixes Q and S given by Den Hartog and Houweling. The abatement sectors are:

Abatement sectors	Unit of measurement of pollutant
1. Public waste water treatment	1,000 of population equivalents BOD_5^{20}
2. Private waste water treatment and sanitation	1,000 of population equivalents BOD_5^{20}
3. Desulphurization of gas oil	100 tons of gas oil
4. Desulphurization of residual oil	100 tons of residual oil
5. Solid waste management	1,000 tons of solid waste
6. Adaptation of passenger cars	100 passenger cars
7. Adaptation of trucks and vans	100 trucks or vans (commercial vehicles)

When we consider full abatement (Den Hartog and Houweling 1974), the direct and indirect pollutions generated by units delivery to final demand are given by the elements of the matrix t, where

$$t = (P_dS)\begin{bmatrix} I - A & -B \\ -C & I - D \end{bmatrix}$$

and where $B = QM^{-1}$, $C = MP_d$, $D = MS$, and P_d is the pollution coefficient matrix.

Q = the input structure matrix of pollution abatement goods.

S = the pollution coefficient matrix of pollutant abatement goods (Table 4–10).

M = the pollution elimination cost matrix (Table 4–11).

Table 4-10   Matrix S: Direct 1973 Pollution Coefficients of Abatement Sectors

	(1)	(2)	(3)	(4)	(5)	(6)	(7)
1	0.0	0.0	0.0	0.0	0.41989	0.0	0.0
2	0.0	0.0	0.0	0.0	0.0	0.0	0.0
3	0.0	0.0	0.0	0.0	0.0	0.0	0.0
4	0.0	0.0	0.81898	0.81898	0.0	0.0	0.0
5	0.14950	0.73698	0.0	0.0	0.0	0.0	0.0
6	0.0	0.0	0.00025	0.00025	0.0	0.0	0.0
7	0.00104	0.00497	0.00006	0.00006	0.01082	0.0	0.0

Abatement Sectors

Source: M. Chatterji, "Interindustry Linkage and Pollution in Belgium," *Environmental Management* 2, no. 4 (1978).

Table 4-11 Matrix *M*: Abatement Cost per Unit of Pollutant Eliminated (in million 1965 BF)

	(1)	(2)	(3)	(4)	(5)	(6)	(7)
1	0.048157	0	0	0	0	0	0
2	0	0.04884	0	0	0	0	0
3	0	0	0.01035	0	0	0	0
4	0	0	0	0.01904	0	0	0
5	0	0	0	0	0.17387	0	0
6	0	0	0	0	0	0.29304	0
7	0	0	0	0	0	0	0.39073

Abatement Sectors

Source: M. Chatterji, "Interindustry Linkage and Pollution in Belgium," *Environmental Management* 2, no. 4 (1978).

The direct and indirect pollution coefficients after full abatement are given in Table 4–12. The coefficients in Table 4–12 represent potential gross coefficients since the net pollution will be zero with full abatement.

Responsibility for Cleaning Pollution: Use of Balanced Input-Output Model

One of the problems arising in environmental management and planning is the allocation of responsibility for cleaning up the environment.[a] This problem arises at the international, national, and regional levels. The developing countries argue against any established standard of goods based on environmental considerations. According to them, the developed countries of the world have indiscriminately destroyed the balance in nature and, consequently, should assume the major responsibility for abiding by any regulations that need to be imposed. They point out that, in the name of environment, the growth rates of the economies of the developing countries might be reduced significantly if these countries were required to abide by worldwide standards on pollutant emissions.

When we come to the question of pollution on the regional level, it can be argued—say, in the case of water pollution—that an upstream region pollutes the river and thus intensifies the pollution problem of the region located downstream. Similarly, in the case of air pollution, the polluted air of one industrialized region can move to another area. The question, then, is: What should be the basis of sharing the responsibility for cleaning and managing the environment?

The problem is not simple. Nonetheless, it is necessary to confront it. In this section we will employ a balanced regional input-output model to begin to identify responsibility for pollution generation and control, especially when the several regions are contained within a single nation. Although what is presented here can be considered only a first attempt to analyze this problem, it does provide some insights that may be useful, especially for developing regions in which resources may permit the construction of only a national input-output table for environmental research purposes.

Notation

Consider a set of U regions in the nation. Each region produces n goods, of which m goods are useful goods and the remaining $(n - m)$ goods are

---

[a]This section develops material found in M. Chatterji (1975a). It is presented here with the kind permission of the Regional Science Association.

Table 4–12 Transposed Matrix of Cumulated Cross-Pollution Coeffients with Complete Abatement

1	0.01138	0.06586	0.01786	0.10890	0.00838	0.00440	0.00247
2	0.00132	0.00473	0	-.00002	0.01810	0.00064	0.00027
3	0.03982	0.04934	0.00578	0.05092	0.00819	0.00396	0.00121
4	0.03044	0.16632	0.01345	0.07976	0.01507	0.00619	0.00244
5	0.04074	0.07432	0.00708	0.04126	0.00902	0.00816	0.00158
6	0.03843	0.07012	0.00624	0.08464	0.00795	0.00561	0.00184
7	0.04933	0.09913	0.01410	0.08276	0.01212	0.00661	0.00241
8	0.00650	0.00882	0.00356	0.03770	0.00310	0.01511	0.00157
9	0.03093	0.06336	0.01763	0.06497	0.00227	0.01964	0.00144
10	0.01887	0.03874	0.00868	0.41668	0.00747	0.00649	0.00088
11	0.00499	0.00745	0.00672	0.30533	0.00273	0.00523	0.00182
12	0.01530	0.03151	0.00712	0.07945	0.00834	0.00422	0.00084
13	0.09253	0.03563	0.01287	0.07231	0.03727	0.00807	0.00204
14	0.03960	0.02390	0.00698	0.03903	0.01966	0.1421	0.00158
15	0.02891	0.05646	0.01306	0.10651	0.01405	0.00676	0.00179
16	0.02877	0.04989	0.01082	0.09306	0.01357	0.00658	0.00151
17	0.08491	0.17527	0.00944	0.08192	0.01909	0.00739	0.00139
18	0.06931	0.14360	0.00615	0.05222	0.01472	0.00577	0.00107
19	0.00617	0.01293	0.00369	0.03720	0.02189	0.00297	0.00093
20	0.01276	0.02587	0.01202	0.13897	0.01710	0.00638	0.00127
21	0.00853	0.01750	0.00949	0.12873	0.01747	0.00501	0.00105
22	0.00992	0.01116	0.01942	0.05200	0.01227	0.00766	0.00134
23	0.03307	0.06888	0.01816	0.06447	0.01336	0.00470	0.00090
24	0.04220	0.08740	0.02217	0.07070	0.01719	0.00585	0.00118
25	0.00943	0.01290	0.00748	0.05001	0.01066	0.00811	0.00153
26	0.01042	0.01082	0.00748	0.03908	0.01115	0.00946	0.00182
27	0.00763	0.00987	0.00726	0.03536	0.00789	0.00652	0.00110
28	0.01237	0.00813	0.00620	0.03199	0.01045	0.00818	0.00190
29	0.01454	0.01160	0.00782	0.05024	0.01288	0.00916	0.00203

	(1)	(2)	(3)	(4)	(5)	(6)	(7)
30	0.02881	0.01285	0.01090	0.03090	0.02073	0.01692	0.00394
31	0.01225	0.00442	0.00476	0.02535	0.00929	0.00808	0.00184
32	0.01994	0.01241	0.02607	0.03999	0.01659	0.00911	0.00148
33	0.00976	0.01295	0.01681	0.03920	0.01917	0.00912	0.00212
34	0.01201	0.00948	0.00906	0.27878	0.00748	0.00793	0.00175
35	0.00367	0.00645	0.00702	0.03541	0.00291	0.00809	0.00670
36	0.00471	0.00842	0.00735	0.06054	0.00244	0.00822	0.00684
37	0.00887	0.01317	0.00768	0.08148	0.00367	0.00779	0.00466
38	0.00322	0.00344	0.00389	0.02292	0.00187	0.00373	0.00367
39	0.00662	0.00889	0.00631	0.05298	0.00382	0.00612	0.00425
40	0.00351	0.00472	0.00607	0.00878	0.00191	0.00947	0.00363
41	0.00246	0.00498	0.00579	0.00865	0.00135	0.00746	0.00689
42	0.01082	0.00494	0.00795	0.00629	0.00205	0.00907	0.00049
43	0.01635	0.01047	0.01098	0.01394	0.01235	0.00064	
44	0.01252	0.00884	0.00828	0.02596	0.00265	0.00912	0.00049
45	0.01666	0.03485	0.01019	0.02733	0.00573	0.01197	0.00428
46	0.00298	0.00149	0.01252	0.00438	0.01526	0.00651	0.00158
47	0.00418	0.00632	0.00206	0.01491	0.00220	0.01049	0.00381
48	0.02999	0.06673	0.01672	0.04572	0.01195	0.00376	0.00076
49	0.01630	0.01688	0.00886	0.02131	0.00362	0.00947	0.00052
50	0.01345	0.00833	0.00963	0.02254	0.00411	0.01055	0.00087
51	0.00132	0.00473	—0.00000	—0.00002	0.01810	0.00054	0.00037
52	0.00361	0.00534	0.00198	0.01355	0.00181	0.01055	0.00383
53	0.01062	—0.00047	—0.00031	—0.00531	0.15003	—0.00022	0.00128
54	0.05397	0.00303	—0.00049	—0.01203	0.74062	—0.00047	0.00631
55	—0.00083	—0.00160	—0.00048	0.082550	—0.00050	—0.00002	0.00001
56	—0.00083	—0.00160	—0.00048	0.82550	—0.00050	—0.00002	0.00001
57	0.42125	—0.00107	—0.00064	—0.00495	0.02991	—0.00050	0.01098
58	—0.00147	—0.00197	—0.00066	—0.01848	—0.00085	—0.00066	—0.00014
59	—0.00147	—0.00197	—0.00066	—0.01848	—0.00085	—0.00066	—00014

pollutants generated by the production of the m useful goods. Each of the useful goods is classified as either local, regional, or national.

According to the well-known classification of balanced regional input-output, some commodities such as aircraft and motor vehicles are national, since their production and consumption balance only within the nation as a whole. They can be transported over great distances because they have a low weight-to-value ratio. Other goods, like cement, are designated as regional; their supply-and-demand balance within the region as well as the nation since their transportability is restricted by weight and other factors. Still other goods, like soft drinks and shoe repair services, are local; their supply and demand balance in the local area as well as regionally and nationally. Although the analysis can be performed using all three classes of commodities, for simplicity it will be restricted to only two classes here. (The reader can extend the model that follows to three classes following the standard procedures in the literature.)

$$
\begin{array}{cc}
\textit{Useful Goods} & \textit{Pollutants} \\
\end{array}
$$

Goods $1, 2, \ldots h,\ h+1, \ldots m,\quad m+1, m+2, \ldots, n$
balanced in the region
balanced in the nation

There are U regions, $A, \ldots J, K, L, \ldots U$. The national outputs of regional and national useful goals and of pollutants are denoted by

$$
X_R = \begin{bmatrix} X_1 \\ \cdot \\ \cdot \\ \cdot \\ \cdot \\ X_h \end{bmatrix} \rightarrow \text{Regional} \qquad X_N = \begin{bmatrix} X_{h+1} \\ \cdot \\ \cdot \\ \cdot \\ \cdot \\ X_m \end{bmatrix} \rightarrow \text{National}
$$

$$
X_T = \begin{bmatrix} X_{M+1} \\ \cdot \\ \cdot \\ \cdot \\ X_n \end{bmatrix} \rightarrow \text{Pollutants.}
$$

The total output vector is given by

$$X = \begin{bmatrix} X_R \\ X_N \\ X_T \end{bmatrix}$$

In a similar fashion, the national final demand vectors are denoted by

$$Y_R = \begin{bmatrix} Y_1 \\ \cdot \\ \cdot \\ \cdot \\ \cdot \\ Y_h \end{bmatrix} \rightarrow \text{Regional} \qquad Y_N = \begin{bmatrix} Y_{h+1} \\ \cdot \\ \cdot \\ \cdot \\ \cdot \\ Y_m \end{bmatrix} \rightarrow \text{National}$$

$$Y_T = \begin{bmatrix} Y_{m+1} \\ \cdot \\ \cdot \\ \cdot \\ \cdot \\ Y_n \end{bmatrix} \leftarrow \text{Pollutants,}$$

where Y_T denotes the acceptable levels of pollution generated by the productive processes.

The total final demand vector is denoted by

$$Y = \begin{bmatrix} Y_R \\ Y_N \\ Y_T \end{bmatrix}$$

For the jth region $(j = A, \ldots, J, K, L, \ldots U)$, the corresponding notations for the outputs are $_jX_{R'}{}_jX_{N'}{}_jX_T$ and $_jX$; and the symbols for the final demand are $_jY_{R'}{}_jY_{N'}{}_jY_T$ and $_jY$.

Following the usual definition of input-output analysis, we set

$$a_{RR} = \begin{bmatrix} a_{11} & a_{12} & \cdot & \cdot & \cdot & a_{1n} \\ \cdot & & \cdot & & & \cdot \\ \cdot & & & \cdot & & \cdot \\ \cdot & & & & \cdot & \cdot \\ a_{h1} & a_{h2} & \cdot & \cdot & \cdot & a_{hh} \end{bmatrix} \qquad a_{RN} = \begin{bmatrix} a_{1,h+1} & \cdot & \cdot & \cdot & a_{1m} \\ \cdot & \cdot & & & \cdot \\ \cdot & & \cdot & & \cdot \\ \cdot & & & \cdot & \cdot \\ a_{h,h+1} & \cdot & \cdot & \cdot & a_{hm} \end{bmatrix}$$
$(h \times h)$ \hspace{4cm} $[h \times (m - h)]$

In the a_{RR} partition, the matrix pertains to the interrelations of industries producing regional goods. Here the coefficients—say, $a_{rr'}$ $(r, r' = 1, \ldots, h)$—denote the input of regional good r per unit output of regional good r' (produced by sector r'). In the a_{RN} partition, the input-output coefficients— say, a_{rn} $(r = 1, 2, \ldots h; \ n = h + 1, \ldots m)$—denote the input of the rth (regional) industry per unit output of the nth (national) industry. We also have

$$
\begin{array}{c}
a_{NR} = \\
[(n-h) \times h]
\end{array}
\begin{bmatrix}
a_{h+1,1} & \cdots & \cdots & \cdots & a_{h+1,h} \\
\cdot & & & & \cdot \\
\cdot & & & & \cdot \\
\cdot & & & & \cdot \\
\cdot & & & & \cdot \\
\cdot & & & & \cdot \\
a_{m1} & \cdots & \cdots & \cdots & a_{mh}
\end{bmatrix} .
$$

$$
\begin{array}{c}
a_{NN} = \\
[(m-h) \times \\
(m-h)]
\end{array}
\begin{bmatrix}
a_{h+1,h+1} & \cdots & \cdots & a_{h+1,m} \\
\cdot & & & \cdot \\
\cdot & & & \cdot \\
\cdot & & & \cdot \\
a_{m,h+1} & \cdots & \cdots & a_{mm}
\end{bmatrix} .
$$

In the a_{NR} partition, the input-output coefficients—say, a_{nr} $(n = h + 1, \ldots m; \ r = 1 \ldots h)$—denote the input of the nth (national) industry per unit output of the rth (regional) industry. In the partition a_{NN}, the input-output coefficients—say, $a_{nn'}$ $(n, n' = h + 1, \ldots m)$—denote the input required from the nth industry (national) for the unit production of the n'th (national) industry.

Let

$$
\begin{array}{c}
a_{RT} = \\
[h \times (n-m)]
\end{array}
\begin{bmatrix}
a_{1,m+1} & \cdots & \cdots & \cdots & a_{1n} \\
a_{2,m+1} & \cdots & \cdots & \cdots & a_{2n} \\
\cdot & & & & \cdot \\
\cdot & & & & \cdot \\
\cdot & & & & \cdot \\
\cdot & & & & \cdot \\
\cdot & & & & \cdot \\
a_{h,m+1} & \cdots & \cdots & \cdots & a_{hn}
\end{bmatrix} .
$$

In a_{RT}, the input-output coefficients—say, $a_{rt}(r = 1, \ldots h, \ t = m + 1 \ldots$
n)—denote input required from the rth regional industry per unit of pollution-abatement activity t. Let

$$
\begin{array}{c}
a_{NT} = \\
[(m - h) \times (n - m)]
\end{array}
\begin{bmatrix}
a_{h+1,m+1} & \cdots\cdots\cdots & a_{h+1,n} \\
 & & \\
 & & \\
 & & \\
 & & \\
 & & \\
 & & \\
a_{m,m+1} & \cdots\cdots\cdots & a_{mn}
\end{bmatrix}
$$

In a_{NT}, the input-output coefficients—say, $a_{nt}(n = h + 1, \ldots m, \ t = m + 1, \ldots n)$—denote the input requirements from the nth (national) industry per unit output of the tth pollution-abatement industry. Let

$$
\begin{array}{c}
a_{TR} = \\
[(n - m) \times h]
\end{array}
\begin{bmatrix}
a_{m+1,1} & a_{m+1,2} & \cdots\cdots & a_{m+1,h} \\
 & & & \\
 & & & \\
 & & & \\
 & & & \\
a_{nl} & a_{n2} & \cdots\cdots & a_{nh}
\end{bmatrix}
$$

In a_{TR}, the input-output coefficients—say, a_{tr} ($t = m + 1, \ldots n, \ r = 1 \ldots h$)—denote the output of pollutant t per unit output of regional good r. Furthermore,

$$
\begin{array}{c}
a_{TN} = \\
[(n - m) \times (m - h)]
\end{array}
\begin{bmatrix}
a_{m+1,h+1} & \cdots\cdots\cdots\cdots & a_{m+1,m} \\
 & & \\
 & & \\
 & & \\
 & & \\
 & & \\
a_{n,h+1} & \cdots\cdots\cdots\cdots & a_{nm}
\end{bmatrix}
$$

In a_{TN}, the input-output coefficients—say, $a_{tn}(t = m + 1, \ldots n, \; h = h + 1, \ldots m)$—denote the output of pollutant t per unit level of output of the national industry n. Finally,

$$
\begin{array}{c}
a_{TT} = \\
[(n - m) \times (n - m)]
\end{array}
\begin{bmatrix}
a_{m+1,m+1} & \cdots\cdots\cdots & a_{m+1,n} \\
\vdots & & \vdots \\
\vdots & & \vdots \\
\vdots & & \vdots \\
\vdots & & \vdots \\
a_{n,m+1} & \cdots\cdots\cdots & a_{nn}
\end{bmatrix}
$$

In a_{TT}, the input-output coefficients—say, a_{tt} $(t = m + 1, \ldots n, \; t = m + 1, \ldots n)$—denote the output of pollutant t per unit of activity of the pollution-abatement industry t.

The Balanced Model

The complete input-output matrix is given by

$$
G = \begin{bmatrix}
a_{RR} & a_{RN} & a_{RT} \\
a_{NR} & a_{NN} & a_{NT} \\
a_{TR} & a_{TN} & a_{TT}
\end{bmatrix}
=
\begin{bmatrix}
R^A \\
N^A \\
T^A
\end{bmatrix}
$$

The inverse matrix is

$$
(I - G)^{-1} = M = \begin{bmatrix}
R^{AR} & R^{AN} & R^{AT} \\
N^{AR} & N^{AN} & N^{AT} \\
T^{AR} & T^{AN} & T^{AT}
\end{bmatrix}
$$

For the jth region ($j = A \ldots J, K, L \ldots U$), the usual input-output equation is given by

$$
\begin{bmatrix}
_jX_R \\
_jX_N \\
_jX_T
\end{bmatrix}
=
\begin{bmatrix}
a_{RR} & a_{RN} & a_{RT} \\
a_{NR} & a_{NN} & a_{NT} \\
-a_{TR} & -a_{TN} & (-a_{TT}-I)
\end{bmatrix}
\begin{bmatrix}
_jX_R \\
_jX_N \\
_jX_T
\end{bmatrix}
+
\begin{bmatrix}
_jY_R \\
_jY_N \\
_jY_T
\end{bmatrix}
$$

The foregoing well-known equation stipulates that the production of regional, national, and pollutant goods equals the exogenous section demand goods plus the final demand.

From the foregoing relations, obtain the following equations:

$$(I - a_{RR})_j X_R - a_{RNj}X_N - a_{RTj}X_T = {}_jY_R. \qquad (4.17)$$

$$-a_{NRj}X_R + (I - a_{NN})_j X_N - a_{NTj}X_T = {}_jY_N. \qquad (4.18)$$

$$+a_{TRj}X_R + a_{TNj}X_N + (a_{TT} - I)_j X_T = {}_jY_T. \qquad (4.19)$$

Next assume that

$$_jX_N = {}_jLX_N = {}_nL_N A Y; \qquad (4.20)$$

That is, the region j, the output of national goods is some fixed percentage $_jL$ of the national goods produced in the nation. $_N A$ denotes the portion of the inverse matrix M that gives the direct and indirect requirements of national goods for the production of the items in the final demand—that is, in Y.

The matrix $_jL$ is given by

$$_jL = \begin{bmatrix} {}_jr_{h+1} & 0 & \cdot & \cdot & \cdot & \cdot & \cdot & 0 \\ 0 & {}_jP_{h+2} & \cdot & \cdot & \cdot & \cdot & \cdot & 0 \\ \cdot & \cdot & \cdot & & & & & \cdot \\ \cdot & \cdot & & \cdot & & & & \cdot \\ \cdot & \cdot & & & \cdot & & & \cdot \\ \cdot & \cdot & & & & \cdot & & \cdot \\ 0 & \cdot & \cdot & \cdot & \cdot & \cdot & \cdot & {}_jr_m \end{bmatrix},$$

where $_jr_m$ denotes the proportion of national good m produced in the jth region relative to the total output of national good m for the nation. Substituting equation 4.20 into equations 4.17–4.19 yields

$$(I - a_{RR})_j X_R - a_{RNj}L_n A Y - a_{RTj}X_T = {}_jY_R. \qquad (4.21)$$

$$+ a_{NRj}X_R + (I - a_{NN})_j 1_N A Y - a_{NTj}X_T = {}_jY_N. \qquad (4.22)$$

$$a_{TRj}X_R + a_{TNj}L_N A Y + (a_{TT} - I)_j X_T = {}_jY_T. \qquad (4.23)$$

From equation 4.23 it follows that

$$_jX_T = (I - a_{TT})^{-1}a_{TRj}X_R + (I - a_{TT}A)^{-1}A_{Tnj}L_N A Y$$
$$- (I - a_{TT})^{-1}{}_jY_T. \qquad (4.24)$$

Substituting equation 4.24 into 4.21 then yields

$$\{(I - a_{RR}) - a_{RT}(I - a_{TT})^{-1}a_{TR}\}_jX_R -$$
$$\{a_{RN} + a_{RT}(I - a_{TT})^{-1}a_{TN}\}_jL_NAY +$$
$$a_{RT}(I - a_{TT})^{-1}_jY_T = {}_jY_R, \qquad (4.25)$$

or

$$_jX_R = C^{RR}_jY_R + C^{RR}D^{RN}_jL_NAY$$
$$- C^{RR}a_{RT}(I - a_{TT})^{-1}_jY_T \qquad (4.26)$$

where $C^{RR} = \{(I - a_{RR}) - a_{RT}(I - a_{TT})^{-1}a_{TR}\}^{-1}$.
$\qquad D^{RN} = a_{RN} + a_{RT}(I - a_{TT})^{-1}a_{TN}$.

Equation 4.26 is important because it links the output of the regional goods in region j with (1) national final demand, (2) the final demand of the region for regional goods, and (3) the tolerable (acceptable) level of pollution final demand. If there is some change in any of these three exogenous factors, then the change in the output of the regional goods in the region j can be calculated through equation 4.26. Substituting equation 4.26 in 4.24 yields the required output $_jX_T$ of pollution-abating industries in the jth region in terms of the same three exogenous factors. That is,

$$_jX_T = (I - a_{TT})^{-1}a_{TR}C^{RR}D^{RN} + (I - a_{TT})^{-1}a_{TNj}L_NAY$$
$$+(I - a_{TT})^{-1}a_{TR} \ C^{RR}a_{RT}(I - a_{TT})^{-1}_jY_T$$
$$+(I - a_{TT})a_{TR}C^{RR}_jY_R. \qquad (4.27)$$

It can now be seen that equations 4.26 and 4.27 can be used for policy decisions. For example, suppose a power plant (which produces the regional good electricity) must be constructed in region j. Then the responsibility for the pollution associated with its operations can be assigned relative to the two exogenous factors, national final demand (because of the demands of all regions) and final demand in region j for the regional goods, after adjustment for the acceptable level of pollution , $_jY_T$, in region j. In short, after this adjustment, the responsibility for the pollution emitted by the particular power plant can be allocated by region for policy analysis and formulation. Similarly, the responsibility for the pollution from journey-to-work transportation and other activities in any region can be related to the demands of that region and of all others. Thus equations 4.26 and 4.27 help us to fix responsibility for pollution. This analysis can be extended to pricing and value added by production. For a discussion of this procedure, see Chatterji 1975b and 1975c.

Industrial Complex Analysis and Programming Techniques

There are several crucial assumptions involved in the application of this model—namely, fixed coefficient, linear production function, full capacity utilization, and so on. The data difficulty is also serious, and it required considerable time and resources to construct an input-output table. To avoid these difficulties and take into account such items as transport cost, labor cost, and other processing cost differentials; scale economies; localization; and urbanization economies, we use the methods of industrial complex analysis. An industrial complex may be defined as a set of activities occurring at a given location and belonging to a group (subsystem) of activities that are subject to important production, marketing, or other relations (Chatterji 1963; Hirsch 1959; Hoch 1959). For example, we may have a joint production of two or more commodities from a single class of raw materials, such as food, fertilizer, and industrial products derived from livestock. Consider, for example, a region that has some cheap labor and good access to sources of oil. The problem may then be to study the ways in which the use of these two sources can be limited in order to identify desirable industrial development in this region. A large number of products can be produced from oil, and there are many ways of producing each. Again, each of these products has some market constraints, such as price, demand, or transport costs; they are also subject to economies of scale, localization economies, and urbanization economies. The situation thus does not permit the use of an input-output framework. The problem is to select a complex that is most efficient in the sense that it yields minimum cost or maximum profit. Industrial complex analysis is essentially an input-output system without the latter's restrictive assumptions. The idea of industrial complex analysis can be extended to an interregional setting, which then can be termed *interregional–industrial complex analysis.* For details of industrial complex analysis, see Isard (1960).

The initial calculation in industrial complex analysis starts with a comparative cost analysis. For any given industry this typically proceeds on the basis of an established or anticipated pattern of markets and a given geographic distribution of raw materials and other productive factors. The objective of the study is to determine in what region or regions the industry could achieve the lowest cost of producing and delivering its product to market. It is obvious that this simple concept of comparative cost will not work in many instances. Many factors, such as past industrial growth, political pressure, and the like, play an important part in the location decision. In many low-income countries these factors may be an important, if not the most important, factor in industrial location decisions. Thus these factors have to be considered in the framework of comparative cost study. For the application of a comparative cost approach, numerous indexes and coefficients are often used. These include location quotient, coefficient of localization, localization curves, ratios, and so on. These indexes indicate, in a crude way, the efficiency of one region over another from the point of view of location (Florence 1968).

Although input-output analysis has many advantages, it is not an optimization technique. Given some goals with respect to the sectors of a regional economy, it only states a suggested output so that these goals can be achieved, taking interindustry linkage into consideration. This does not take into account resource restrictions or the price to be paid for the achievement of the goal. In this respect, interregional linear programming techniques become quite useful.

Linear Programming Technique

Linear programming technique helps us choose the level of a given activity in a region at which the income generated by pursuing the activity at this level is maximum, subject to resource restrictions. Consider, for example, a region with two activities and four resources. The amount of input required per unit level of each activity is as follows.

		Act 1	Act 2	Resource Limitation
1.	Water	a_{11}	a_{12}	P_1
2.	Land	a_{21}	a_{22}	P_2
3.	Labor	a_{31}	a_{32}	P_3
4.	Capital	a_{41}	a_{42}	P_4

Let X_1 stand for the level of activity number 1 and X_2 for the level of activity number 2. Let C_1 and C_2 be the amount of income generated by unit level of activities 1 and 2, respectively, so that total income is

$$Y_1 = C_1 X + C_2 X_2. \tag{4.28}$$

The problem is to find the value of X_1 and X_2 such that Y is maximum subject to the restrictions:

$$a_{11}X_1 + a_{12}X_2 \leq P_1,$$

$$a_{21}X_1 + a_{22}X_2 \leq P_2,$$

$$a_{31}X_1 + a_{32}X_2 \leq P_3,$$

$$a_{41}X_1 + a_{42}X_2 \leq P_4. \qquad (4.29)$$

When we have two activities, this linear programming problem can be solved graphically. However, when the number of activities is greater than two, then obviously the problem cannot be solved by graphical methods. Instead, we have to use the simplex method (Dorfman, Samuelson, and Solow 1958). The linear programming model can be extended to the interregional case (Stevens 1959). The symbolic representation is just a straightforward extension of the single-region case except that we must take into account the question of transport cost between two regions. This is an extremely powerful tool, and it is extensively used in regional planning problems.

The interregional linear programming model can be used effectively to satisfy different goals for two regions, one urban and the other rural. Let us denote the activities level in the urban area by $x_1^U, \ldots x_n^U$ and the rural areas by $x_1^R, \ldots x_n^R$ in their original unit. If the prices are denoted by p, then the gross regional product is given by:

$$G^U = \sum_{i=1}^{n} x_i^U p_i^U , \qquad (4.30)$$

and

$$G^R = \sum_{i=1}^{n} x^R p_i^R . \qquad (4.31)$$

The national product is given by

$$G = G^U + G^R. \qquad (4.32)$$

The production function of different activities in the two regions can be quite different. They may use different types of inputs and different combinations of labor and capital. Again, one or more activities in one region may depend on the other region. As is commonly the case, this interdependence in the case or rural and urban areas can be quite complicated. This interregional interindustry linkage can be captured by the input-output type of coefficient, as shown in Table 4-2.

The level of production for each activity in each region is also restricted by economic, technological, and supply factors. For example, the production of many activities in the urban areas depends on the importation of agricultural inputs from the rural areas. For such an activity, the restriction may look like

$$a_{i1}^U x_1^U + a_{i2}^U x_2^U \ldots + a_{in}^U \underset{R \to U}{x_n^U} \leq E_i,$$

where E_i^{R-U} denotes the export of its resource from the rural areas to the urban areas.

A set of restrictions can be written as follows: for the urban area,

$$a_{11}^U x_1^U + a_{12}^U x_2^U \ldots + a_{1n}^U x_n^U \leq R_1^U \qquad (4.33)$$
$$\vdots$$
$$a_{S1}^U x_1^U + a_{S2}^U x_2^U \ldots + a_{Sn}^U x_n^U \leq R_S^U$$

A similar set of restraint equations exists for the rural region. Let us use the following matrix notation to express such equations.

$$X = \begin{bmatrix} x_1^U \\ x_2^U \\ x_n^U \\ \vdots \\ \vdots \\ \vdots \\ x_1^R \\ \vdots \\ x_n^R \end{bmatrix} \quad (2n \times 1) \qquad\qquad R = \begin{bmatrix} R_1^U \\ R_2^U \\ \cdot \\ \cdot \\ R_n^U \\ R_1^R \\ R^R \\ \cdot \\ R_n^R \end{bmatrix} \quad (2n \times 1)$$

and the input-output type coefficient

$$a_{ij} = \begin{bmatrix} a_{11}^U \ldots a_{1n}^U & & \\ \cdot & \cdot & \\ \cdot & \cdot & \cdots \\ a_{n1}^U \ldots a_{nn}^U & \cdot & a_{11}^R \ldots a_{1n}^R \\ \cdots & \cdot & \cdot \\ & \cdot & \cdot \\ & \cdot & a_{n1}^R \ldots a_{nn}^R \end{bmatrix} \quad (2n \times 2n)$$

It is noteworthy in the foregoing matrix that we do not consider the coefficient y of the type a_{ij}^{RU}, which signifies the input required from rural to urban areas from the ith sector in rural areas to the jth sector in urban areas.

This requirement is taken into consideration in the import of that commodity from the rural areas to the urban areas. The price vector is denoted by

$$p = (p_1^U, p_2^U \ldots p_m^U, p_1^R, p_2^R \ldots p_n^R).$$

The objective is to maximize G in equation 4.32 subject to the equation set 4.4. In the matrix mentioned, we are to choose the different activity levels $x_1^U, \ldots x_n^U, \ldots x_1^R, \ldots x_n^R$ in such a way that max $Z = px$, subject to

$$ax \leq R \qquad (4.34)$$

and

$$x \geq 0 \text{ (nonnegative condition).}$$

The linear programming model can be an effective tool in urban and regional planning in the developing countries. For example, it is usually observed that there is a great discrepancy in the income level of a region in developing countries. If we want to stipulate that the per capita income level in the rural area should be at least greater than one-third of that of the urban areas, then this condition can be expressed as

$$\sum W_e^R a_{ei} x_i^R \geq \tfrac{1}{2} \sum W_e^U a_{ei} x_i^U,$$

where W_e^R and W_e^U denote the wage rate in the rural and urban areas, respectively. It should be mentioned here that the goal of reducing the income differential between the regions will entail reduction in the GNP.

If a decision is made that equity and social justice are more important than economic efficiency, then different restrictive conditions—say, making one region artificially dependent on a smaller region—can be imposed. The linear program can also be used to affect decisions on the micro level—say, within a region with respect to land and pollution, agricultural development, balanced industrial growth, and so on. The data requirement for the linear programming technique is quite modest. What we need are the price levels of different activities, the I-O coefficients, and the constraint quantities. The usefulness of the model is to specify the objective function and constraint set appropriately. The solution procedure by the computer is routine.

Of course, the programming need not be linear. There are many situations in which the objective function and/or the constraints are nonlinear. The linear formulation does not consider clearly the economics of scale. There are other situations in which the effects are not additive. Although linear programming can be used as an approximation for a nonlinear case, recent advances in solution techniques with the computer (straightforward nonlinear programming) can be prepared where structural nonlinearity is believed to exist or empirical data suggests such a relationship. Nonlineality usually develops when the coefficients in the programming model are probabilities. Quadratic programming is a special case of nonlinear programming. The general case of nonlinear programming can be defined as

$$\text{Maximize } G(x_1 \ldots x_n), \qquad (4.35)$$

subject to $C_i(x_1, x_2 \ldots x_n) \leq 0 \qquad i = 1, 2, \ldots m,$
where the g and c are real-valued, nonlinear, but well-behaved functions of n variables.

In the linear programming model we are assuming that the variables x_j can take any value, including fractions. In some situations, however, the variable is constrained to take only integral values. One such case is the location of a facility like a plant or hospital. In this case the variable x_j can only take the value 0 or 1. If all the variables are restricted to take integer values, the problem is known as a pure-integer programming problem. Otherwise, it may be a mixed-integer programming problem. In mathematical notation, an integer programming problem can be stated as follows:

$$\text{Optimize } \sum_{j=1}^{n} C_j x_j,$$

subject to

$$\sum_{j=1}^{n} a_{ij}x_j \leq b_i \qquad i = 1, \ldots m,$$

$$X_i \geq 0,$$

$$X_j \text{ integer values } j = 1, \ldots p(\leq n).$$

$$\qquad (4.36)$$

For example, the transportation problem, given as

$$\text{Minimize } \sum_{i=1}^{m} \sum_{j=1}^{n} C_{ij}X_{ij} = \text{Total transport cost,}$$

subject to

$$\sum_{j=1}^{n} X_{ij} \leq S_i \text{ supply constraint,} \qquad (4.37)$$

has a value of either 0 or 1. There are mainly two computer algorithms to solve integer programming, namely (1) cutting-plane algorithm and (2) backtrack, or Branch and Brand, algorithm.

In a real-life situation the coefficients C_i in the objective functions and a_{ij} in the constraints set are not deterministic but usually have a probability distribution. For example, in this transportation problem the transport cost C_{ij} may be subject to chance, since we may not be sure of the price of oil. Again, the demand and supply quantities are obviously subject to change because of the changing nature of the consumer behavior and the functioning of production plants, respectively. Although the mathematics of the stochastic programming model can be quite complicated, the idea is clear that in the usual linear programming model, in place of the variable X_j, the coefficient C_j, and the coefficients a_{ij}, we use their expected value.

So far we are assuming that we have only one objective—say, the production of electricity. Besides the production of electricity, however, we may have the additional objective of reducing the amount of environmental pollution. In a national planning problem there may be two objectives— namely, to maximize the national income and to decrease interregional differences in income. For their purpose, we can use multiple-objective decision making. In another type of programming, known as *goal programming,* the decision maker specifies a desired level for one or more variables in the form of rank priorities.

So far we are speaking in terms of a static solution, but in a real situation there is a complicated dynamic interdependence that forces us to formulate the problem in terms of dynamic programming. The dynamic programming problem tries to allocate scarce resources among competing sectors, each over an interval of time from the initial period to a terminal time, by choosing the time path for certain variables, called control variables, from a given class of variables called control sets, so that a function, depending on the time path, is maximized (Intriligator 1971).

Pollution Abatement and Regional Welfare:
A Control Theory Approach

One of the significant aspects of environmental pollution is that it is not uniformly dispersed over space.[a] Also, higher pollution levels are usually concentrated in areas of lower income. It is often found that an area suffers pollution in order to produce inputs directly and indirectly needed for final demand in other areas. It can be argued that the regions consuming the

---

[a]This section develops material in M. Chatterji and F. Moulaert, "Pollution Abatement and Regional Welfare: A Control Theory Approach," *Tijdschrift voor Ekonomie en Management* 21, no. 2 (1976).

product should pay for partial cleaning of pollution generated in other areas. Sometimes this adjustment is made through the price mechanism, but the question of equity still remains to be resolved since it is seldom evident what this amount of adjustment should be. In an earlier paper (Chatterji 1975a), a balanced regional input-output framework was suggested to measure the magnitude of this adjustment.

If this income transfer from the consuming areas to pollution-suffering areas cannot be carried out as a result of nonexistence of any suitable mechanism, an alternative is to relocate industries so that the pollution is more evenly dispersed. The industries that are movable are usually those that serve national markets (known as national sectors). Coupled with this may be the diversion of capital from producing sectors to pollution-abating sectors. Both relocation and abatement, however, will have an adverse economic impact on the region. Besides, the relocation should be technologically feasible; the resulting unemployment should be tolerable; and it should consider the feedback effect through unemployment, migration, and the resulting chain reactions. A framework for such a dynamic relocation model has been indicated (Chatterji 1975b), and an extended static linear pro-gramming model that takes diffusion processes into consideration has been presented elsewhere (Chatterji 1975c).

The objective here is to generalize further. The optimal control theory helps us to investigate the nature of the policy variables at each point of time so that some objective functions can be optimized over the planning horizon, subject to the restriction that the state variables follow the usual equations of primary form, secondary form, or any other form, i.e. a demand for national and regional goods, and the level of tolerance of pollution in each region, such that the welfare of all the regions of the planning period (t_0, t_1) is maximized subject to the technological path of the production variables, population growth and migration, and other restrictions. Formally, the problem can be stated as follows (Chatterji and Moulaert 1976).

With this expanded definition of sectors and hierarchical systems of goods presented earlier in this chapter, the input-output coefficient matrix can be defined as follows:

$$A = \begin{bmatrix} a_{RR} & a_{RN} & a_{RT} \\ a_{NR} & a_{NN} & a_{NT} \\ a_{TR} & a_{TN} & a_{TT} \end{bmatrix} = \begin{bmatrix} R^A \\ N^A \\ T^A \end{bmatrix}$$

In the matrix A, a_{RR}, a_{RN}, and so on denote submatrixes of input-output coefficients between regional goods, regional and national goods, and so on. In particular, the elements in the submatrix a_{TT} denote the generation of pollution of different kinds by the unit level of production of corresponding pollution-abating industry.

Analogous to A, we define the capital coefficients matrix

$$B = \begin{bmatrix} b_{RR} & b_{RN} & b_{RT} \\ b_{NR} & b_{NN} & b_{NT} \\ b_{TR} & b_{TN} & b_{TT} \end{bmatrix}$$

In the foregoing matrix, the submatrixes b_{RR}, b_{RN}, and so on have meanings similar to those of the corresponding submatrixes in A, except that they denote capital inputs. For the sake of simplicity, it is assumed that the production and capital coefficients are invariant over time—for example, independent of t. Note that b_{TR}, b_{TN}, and b_{TT} can be interpreted as permanent damage to society or nature.

Specification of the Regional Structure

With this dichotomy of regional and national goods, we now specify the dynamic input-output structure of each regional economy.

$$X_{jN} = a_{jNR}X_{jR} + a_{jNT}X_T + a_{jNN}X_{jN}$$
$$+ b_{jNR}\mathring{X}_{jT} + b_{jNT}\mathring{X}_{jT} + b_{jNN}\mathring{X}_{jN} + Y_{jN} \quad (4.38)$$

Equation 4.38 simply states that in any region ($j \in I$, where I is the set of regions), the total output of the national goods at any point in time equals the sum of intermediate goods needed to produce the regional, national, and abatement goods during that period; the national goods needed to produce capital goods, and the final demand.

$$Y_{jN} = L_i Y_N. \sum_{j=1}^{U} L_j = 1 \quad (4.39)$$

for all $j \in I$.

This simple relation states that for the national goods, regional final demand is a fixed portion of national demand. It is possible to replace this equation with a more realistic formulation that takes into consideration changing interregional positions over time, existing in infrastructure, population, and and so on. The general thesis of this chapter, however, will remain the same, although its mathematics will be complicated. We would therefore like to keep equation 4.39 as it stands. Structural relations for regional and pollution-abatement goods can be written similar to equation 4.38, and the three relations are conveniently given as

$$X_j = B_j \mathring{X}_j + A_j X_j + Y_j \qquad\qquad j \in I, \qquad (4.40)$$

or

$$\mathring{X}_j = B_j^{-1}[I - A_j]X_j - B_j^{-1}Y_j \qquad j \in I, \qquad (4.41)$$

assuming B_j^{-1} exists.

For computational convenience, and to obtain a more clear-cut economic interpretation, we assume that X_{jR}, X_{jN}, and X_{jT} are scalars—that is, that there exists only one commodity of each kind. Under this assumption,

$$B_j^{-1} = {}_j\Delta^{-1}\begin{bmatrix} b_{NN}b_{TT} - b_{TN}b_{NT} & -(b_{RN}b_{TT} - b_{TN} & b_{RT}),b_{RN}b_{NT} - b_{NN}b_{RT} \\ -(b_{NR}b_{TT} - b_{NT}b_{TR}),b_{RR}b_{TT} - b_{RT}b_{TR} & , & -(b_{RR}b_{NT} - b_{NR}b_{RT}) \\ b_{NR}b_{TN} - b_{NN}b_{TR} & -(b_{RR}b_{TR} - b_{TR}b_{RN}),b_{RR}b_{NN} - b_{NR}b_{RN} \end{bmatrix}$$

where ${}_j\Delta$ is the determinant of matrix B_j. In this particular scalar case, and in the general case when X_{jR}, X_{jN}, and X_{jT} are vectors, we shall denote the inverse matrix in simpler notation:

$$B_j^{-1} \equiv \begin{bmatrix} b_{j1} & b_{j2} & b_{j3} \\ b_{j4} & b_{j5} & b_{j6} \\ b_{j7} & b_{j8} & b_{j9} \end{bmatrix} \qquad \text{and} \qquad (4.42)$$

$$B_j^{-1}[I - A_j] \equiv \begin{bmatrix} k_{j1} & k_{j2} & k_{j3} \\ k_{j4} & k_{j5} & k_{j6} \\ k_{j7} & k_{j8} & k_{j9} \end{bmatrix} \qquad \text{for all } j \, \varepsilon \, I \quad (4.43)$$

The interpretation of the coefficients of both matrixes is straightforward. For example, in the region j,

$$-b_{j5} = L_j \frac{\partial \mathring{X}_{jN}}{\partial Y_N}$$

is the marginal impact of a unit change in final demand for the national goods on its rate of change of production (multiplier effect).

$$k_{j5} = \frac{\partial \mathring{X}_{jN}}{\partial X_{jN}}$$

measures the acceleration effect.

It indicates to what extent the rate of change of production of a national good in region j will rise or fall because of the initial impulse of a rise (or fall) in its production.

From equations 4.41, 4.42, and 4.43, it results that

$$\mathring{X}_{jR} = k_{j1}X_{jR} + k_{j2}X_{jN} + k_{j3}X_{jT} - b_{j1}Y_{jR} - b_{j2}Y_{jN} - b_{j3}Y_{jT} \qquad (4.44)$$

$$\mathring{X}_{jN} = k_{j4}X_{jR} + k_{j5}X_{jN} + k_{j6}X_{jT} - b_{j4}Y_{jR} - b_{j5}Y_{jN} - b_{j6}Y_{jT} \qquad (4.45)$$

$$\mathring{X}_{jT} = k_{j7}X_{jR} + k_{j8}X_{jN} + k_{j9}X_{jT} - b_{j7}Y_{jR} - b_{j8}Y_{jN} - b_{j9}Y_{jT} \qquad (4.46)$$

If we define $\mathring{x}_R \equiv$
$$\begin{bmatrix} \mathring{X}_{1R} \\ \cdot \\ \cdot \\ \cdot \\ \mathring{X}_{jR} \\ \cdot \\ \cdot \\ \cdot \\ \mathring{X}_{UR} \end{bmatrix}$$
, and $\mathring{x}_N, \mathring{x}_T, y_R, y_N, y_T,$

in a similar way as $\mathring{x}_R$, we get

$$\mathring{x}_R = \hat{K}_1 x_R + \hat{K}_2 x_N + \hat{K}_3 x_T - \hat{B}_1 y_R - \hat{B}_2 y_N - \hat{B}_3 y_T \qquad (4.47)$$

$$\mathring{x}_N = \hat{K}_4 x_R + \hat{K}_5 x_N + \hat{K}_6 x_T - \hat{B}_4 y_R - \hat{B}_5 y_N - \hat{B}_6 y_T \qquad (4.48)$$

$$\mathring{x}_T = \hat{K}_7 x_R + \hat{K}_8 x_N + \hat{K}_9 x_T - \hat{B}_7 y_R - \hat{B}_8 y_N - \hat{B}_9 y_T \qquad (4.49)$$

Respectively, the redefined vectors x_R, x_N, and x_T belong to the Uh, $U(m-h)$, $U(n-m)$ dimensional Euclidean space. The matrixes $K_i B_i$ ($i = 1, \ldots 9$) in Equations 4.47, 4.48, and 4.49 can be written in a still more compact way as

$$\mathring{x} = Kx - \bar{B}y \qquad (4.50)$$

for $x \equiv \begin{bmatrix} x_R \\ x_N \\ x_T \end{bmatrix}$, $y \equiv \begin{bmatrix} y_R \\ y_N \\ y_T \end{bmatrix}$, $k \equiv \begin{bmatrix} \hat{K}_1 & \hat{K}_2 & \hat{K}_3 \\ \hat{K}_4 & \hat{K}_5 & \hat{K}_6 \\ \hat{K}_7 & \hat{K}_8 & \hat{K}_9 \end{bmatrix}$

$$\text{and } \bar{B} \equiv \begin{bmatrix} \hat{B}_1 & \hat{B}_2 & \hat{B}_3 \\ \hat{B}_4 & \hat{B}_5 & \hat{B}_6 \\ \hat{B}_7 & \hat{B}_8 & \hat{B}_9 \end{bmatrix} \quad . \text{ Both } k \text{ and } \bar{B} \text{ are of order } Un.$$

Let us next consider the demographic structure of the region. As mentioned before, any plan for relocation of national industries and/or abatement of pollution will lead to unemployment and migration. As such, demographic factors are crucial. It is true that the resulting impact will be different, depending on the age-sex structure of the population. For example, the relocation of apparel industry from New York City will be harmful to women workers. Although it is not difficult to consider this in our model, it will complicate our notational system. Therefore, we restrict ourselves to the simple formulation, namely,

$$\mathring{P} = B - D + M \tag{4.51a}$$

where $\mathring{P}$ = rate of change in population.

B = birth rate.

D = death rate.

M = net migration rate.

They are all vectors each having U elements (corresponding to the number of of regions).

In a regional economy, besides the production of useful goods, externalities are generated. These will be denoted by the word *pollution*. However, our framework covers not only air, water, and noise pollution, but also such things as crime, landscape destruction, and so on.

Pollution is generated in the intermediate as well as in the final demand sectors. Considering the pollution from the first source only, we have

$$a_{jTR}X_{jR} + a_{jTT}X_{jT} + a_{jTN}X_N$$

$$+ b_{jTR}\mathring{X}_{jR} + b_{jTT}\mathring{X}_{jT} + b_{jTN}X_{jN} - X_{jT} = - Y_{jT}, j \, \varepsilon \, I \tag{4.51b}$$

Equation 4.51 states that given there is no built-in pollution-control equipment in the products; and, assuming full abatement, the pollution-abatement sector's output equals the pollution generated by regional and national goods plus the tolerance level Y_{jT} (note that $Y_{jT} \leq 0$). Considering the pollution generated in the final demand sector, the increase in pollution from two sources is:

$$\mathring{R} = -y_r + \hat{p}_1 \hat{L} Y_N + \hat{p}_2 y_R, \tag{4.52}$$

where $\hat{p}_1$ and $\hat{p}_2$ are diagonal matrixes of pollution coefficients P_{1j}, P_{2j}, of the final sector for each region j. L is a diagonal matrix with elements L_j, allocation coefficients of the product of national goods among regions (see equation 4.39). Besides local final demand sectors, we include nonlocal consumption, state and federal government purchases, defense purchases, and so on.

Relocation of national industries and restrictive antipollution laws will generate unemployment. The unemployment in a region j can be obtained from the difference of the number of people seeking jobs (first term of relation 4.53), less the number of jobs created by the regional and national industries, plus the loss of employment due to the investment in pollution control and/or legal restrictions with respect to environmental standards.

$$u_j = (1 - k) s_j P_j - \Theta (X_{jR} + X_{jN} - \alpha_0 X_{jT}). \tag{4.53}$$

It is often said that environmental standards set by federal and state agencies either closed down many plants or adversely affected the production level (say, in the case of paper industry). The first term in the (second) bracket is the total output of the regional good in the jth area. The second is the total output of the national good in the jth area. The third denotes the net amount of loss in the output that will result from the channeling of investment for the production of pollution-abating industry. It is assumed that this loss is a fixed portion (α_0) of the total output of pollution abating industry.

Notice that Θ is a constant term that converts the output figure into an employment figure (Θ is an average labor intensity for the economy as a whole); s_i, a labor force participation rate; and k, a structural unemployment ratio.

Substituting equations 4.45, 4.46 and 4.51a in 4.53, we get

$$\begin{aligned}
\mathring{u}_j = &(1-k) s_j (B_j - D_j + M_j) - \Theta(k_{j1} + k_{j4} - \alpha_0 k_{j7}) X_{jR} \\
&- \Theta(k_{j2} + k_{j5} - \alpha_0 k_{j8}) X_{jN} - \Theta(k_{j3} + k_{j6} - \alpha_0 k_{j9}) X_{jT} \\
&+ \Theta(b_{j1} + b_{j4} - \alpha_0 b_{j7}) Y_{jR} + \Theta(b_{j2} + b_{j5} - \alpha_0 b_{j8}) Y_{jN} \\
&+ \Theta(b_{j3} + b_{j6} - \alpha_0 b_{j9}) Y_{jT}
\end{aligned} \tag{4.54}$$

Classification of Variables

As indicated in the introduction, we shall now formulate the problem in a control theory framework. To this end, let us classify the variables as follows.

State Variables. Let S be the set of state variables. The evolution of the state (of nature) of each region $j \in I$ is described by the values of its state variables. They can be either stock (at any point of time during the planning period) or flow (for any interval of time during the planning period) variables. In our system for each region the state variables are:

- Flows: X_{jR}, X_{jN}, $X_{jT} (j \in I)$ denoting production of regional goods, national goods, and antipollution activities, respectively.
- Stocks: P_j, R_j, and u_j, respectively, referring to total population, total pollution, and unemployment in region $j \in I$.

S contains $U(n + 3)$ elements.

Control or Policy Variables. Let C be the set of control variables. It contains Y_{jR}, $Y_{jT} (j \in I)$, and Y_s, respectively, referring to final demand of regional goods, pollution norms, and final demand for national goods. C contains $U(h + n - m) + 1$ elements.

Identification Variables. These variables contribute to the identification of the feasible region defined by relations between state and control variables. They are mathematically specified by means of stimulus-response and definitional relations (see equations 4.60–4.62).
In our system these variables are;

$m = (M_{ij})$, the matrix of immigration balances of region $j (j \in I)$.
$M_j =$ the total immigration balance of region j (with respect to all $i \in I$).
$Y_{jN} =$ final demand for national production in region j (that is, intraregional demand plus exports minus imports).

Predetermined Variables. The variables B_j (birth figures in period t, $t + dt$), D_j (mortality), and d_{ij} (economic distance between region i and region j) are predetermined to the model. In this deterministic model, their mathematical character corresponds to that of the parameters.

The initial state of the multiregional economy at time t is described as follows:

● Flow values:
Production of regional goods in period $(t_0, t_0 - dt)$:

$$x_R(t_0) = x_{R0}.$$

Production of national goods in period $(t_0, t_0 - dt)$:

$$x_N(t_0) = x_{No}$$

Production of pollution abatement in period $(t_0, t_0 - dt)$:

$$x_T(t_0) = x_{T0}.$$

● Stock values:
Total population at time t_0:

$$P(t_0) = P_0.$$

Total pollution at time t_0:

$$R(t_0) = R_0.$$

Rate of unemployment at t_0:

$$u(t_0) = u_0.$$

(The whole set of initial conditions is denoted by IC.)

Maximization of Welfare

The question that naturally arises is how to choose the optimal set C of control variables at each point in time so as to maximize the national welfare. For simplicity it is assumed that the national welfare is obtained by summing the regional welfare. Regional welfare depends on the level of pollution R_j; unemployment u_j; final demands Y_N, Y_{jR}; and the pollution tolerance level Y_{jT}. Thus the increase in national welfare per unit of time is given by

$$W(t) \equiv \sum_{j=1}^{U} W_j(R_j, u_j, Y_{jR}, Y_{jT}, Y_N) \, dt \qquad (4.55)$$

In addition we assume that

$$\frac{\partial W_j}{\partial u_j} < 0, \frac{\partial W_j}{\partial Y_{jR}} > 0,$$

$$\frac{\partial W_j}{\partial Y_{jT}} < 0, \frac{\partial W_j}{\partial Y_N} > 0, \frac{\partial W_j}{\partial R_j} < 0, \qquad (4.56)$$

Over the whole planning period (t_0, t_1) policymakers will try to get the highest outcome for

$$W_T \equiv \int_{t_0}^{t_1} \left[\sum_{j=1}^{U} W_j(R_j, u_j, Y_{jR}, Y_N) \right] dt^7 \qquad (4.57)$$

by manipulating C, subject to equations 4.47–4.48, 4.49, 4.52, and 4.54.

In a centralized economy, the control C can be exercised directly, whereas in a free economy it can be done through taxes, interest and discount rates, and other fiscal and monetary policy instruments.

The Hamiltonian Criterion (H)

The optimization indicated in the previous section can be handled by Pontryagin's maximum principle (see Pontryagin 1962). To avoid complications in symbols, however, we assume that we have one regional good, one national good, and one pollution-abating good; that is, X_{jR}, X_{jN}, and X_{jT} are scalars and not vectors. The same is true for Y_{jR}, Y_{jN}, and Y_{jT} ($j \in I$). This will facilitate interpretation, but it is not a limiting assumption.

To visualize the problem and the technique of optimal control, the following chart will be useful.

Time derivatives of vectors of state variables $(\mathring{S})$	Equation number	Dimension of the vector $(6U)$	Corresponding vector of costate variables $(\tau(t))$
$\mathring{x}_R$	(10)	U	$\chi_R(t)$
$\mathring{x}_N$	(11)	U	$\chi_N(t)$
$\mathring{x}_T$	(12)	U	$\chi_T(t)$
$\mathring{P}$	(14)	U	$\pi(t)$
$\mathring{R}$	(16)	U	$\psi(t)$
$\mathring{u}$	(18)	U	$\eta(t)$

Performing an optimal policy will correspond to maximizing the Hamiltonian (H) for each period $(t, t + dt)$ over the set of control variables C. For simplicity, the discounted value of the welfare has not been taken into account. However, its inclusion is straightforward. For example, if r is the discount rate, we need to multiply the expression within the integral by e^{-rt}.

It should be noticed that, from a social justice point of view, social welfare is to be weighted equally over time; that is, r is to vanish.

$$\max_{C \in \Omega} H \equiv \sum_{j=1}^{U} W_j(R_j, u_j, Y_{jR}, Y_{jT}, Y_N)$$

$$+ \chi'_R(\hat{K}_1 x_R + \hat{K}_2 x_N + \hat{K}_3 x_T - \hat{B}_1 y_R - \hat{B}_2 y_N - \hat{B}_3 y_T)$$

$$+ \chi'_N(\hat{K}_4 x_R + \hat{K}_5 x_N + \hat{K}_6 x_T - \hat{B}_4 y_R - \hat{B}_5 y_N - \hat{B}_6 y_T)$$

$$+ \chi'_T(\hat{K}_7 x_R + \hat{K}_8 x_N + \hat{K}_9 x_T - \hat{B}_7 y_R - \hat{B}_8 y_N - \hat{B}_9 y_T)$$

$$+ \pi'(B - D + M)$$

$$+ \psi'(- y_T + \hat{p}_1 \hat{L} Y_N + \hat{p}_2 y_R)$$

$$+ \eta' f \tag{4.58}$$

Ω denotes the feasible region and replaces the extensive expression for $\mathring{U}$ in equation 4.54.

The Hamiltonian can also be written in scalar notation:

$$H \equiv \sum_{j=1}^{U} W_j(R_j, u_j, Y_{jR}, Y_{jT}, Y_N)$$

$$+ \sum_j \chi_{jR}(k_{j1} X_{jR} + k_{j2} X_{jN} + k_{j3} X_{jT} - b_{j1} Y_{jR} - b_{j2} L_j Y_N - b_{j3} Y_{jT})$$

$$+ \sum_j \chi_{jN}(k_{j4} X_{jR} + k_{j5} X_{jN} + k_{j6} X_{jT} - b_{j4} Y_{jR} - b_{j5} L_j Y_N - b_{j6} Y_{jT})$$

$$+ \sum_j \chi_{jT}(k_{j7} X_{jR} + k_{j8} X_{jN} + k_{j9} X_{jT} - b_{j7} Y_{jR} - b_{j8} L_j Y_N - b_{j9} Y_{jT})$$

$$+ \sum_j \pi_j(B_j - D_j + M_j)$$

$$+ \sum_j \psi_j(- Y_{jT} + p_{1j} L_j Y_N + p_{2j} Y_{jR})$$

$$+ \sum_j \eta_j [(1 - k)s_j(B_j - D_j + M_j) - \Theta(k_{j1} + k_{j4} - \alpha_0 k_{j7})X_{jR}$$

$$- \Theta(k_{j2} + k_{j5} - \alpha_0 k_{j8}) X_{jN} - \Theta(k_{j3} + k_{j6} - \alpha_0 k_{j9}) X_{jT}$$

$$+ \Theta(b_{j1} + b_{j4} - \alpha_0 b_{j7}) Y_{jR} + \Theta(b_{j2} + b_{j5} - \alpha_0 b_{j8})L_j Y_N$$

$$+ \Theta(b_{j3} + b_{j6} - \alpha_0 b_{j9}) Y_{jT}] \qquad\qquad (4.59)$$

The Region of Feasible Controls

Apart from the dynamic relations, the state and control variables are also linked through the identification variables. Definition relation 4.60 allocates total demand for national goods to each region (this relation was already referred to by equation 4.39); definitional relation 4.61 aggregates immigration balances from each region to region j; and the stimulus-response relations (4.62) determine the rates of migration from the other regions to region j.

$$Y_{jn} \equiv L_j Y_N, \sum_j L_j = 1, \qquad j \in I \qquad (4.60)$$

$$M_j \equiv \sum_{i \neq j} M_{ij}, \qquad j \in I \qquad (4.61)$$

$$M_{ij} = \beta_0 + \beta_1 u_i + \beta_2 u_j + \beta_3 X_{iN} + \beta_4 X_{jN} + \beta_5 P_i$$

$$+ \beta_6 P_j + \beta_7 d_{ij}. \qquad i,j \in I \qquad (4.62)$$

The parameters $\beta_0, \beta_1, \beta_2, \ldots \beta_7$ are assumed to have been estimated by, say, regression analysis outside the system. From common sense one can argue that

$$\beta_1 > 0, \beta_5 > 0.$$
$$\beta_2 < 0, \beta_6 < 0.$$
$$\beta_3 < 0, \beta_7 < 0,$$
$$\beta_4 > 0.$$

Necessary and Sufficient Conditions for the Existence
of a Solution for the Control Problem

By Pontryagin's maximum principle, the necessary conditions for $C(t)$ to be an optimal control vector and for $S(t)$, $\tau(t)$ to be the corresponding optimal and costate trajectory include (Bryson and Ho 1969; Intriligator 1971) the existence of an internal solution (we stick to the classical case only) for the problem

$$\max H$$

$$\{C(t)\} \in \Omega,$$

where Ω is the feasible region defined by relations 4.61 and 4.62. The unique solution of this problem will satisfy

$$\frac{\partial H}{\partial C} = 0 \text{ and} \tag{4.63}$$

$$v' \frac{\partial^2 H}{\partial C^2} v < 0, \text{ for every } (2U+1) \text{ dimensional vector } v \neq 0 \tag{4.64}$$

$$\overset{\circ}{S} = \frac{\partial H}{\partial \tau}, \; x_0 = x(t_0) \tag{4.65}$$

$$\overset{\circ}{\tau} = -\frac{\partial H}{\partial S} \tag{4.66}$$

$C(t)$, $S(t)$, and $\tau(t)$ are the vectors of control, state, and costate variables, respectively. Conditions 4.63 through 4.67 will be sufficient if

$$v' \frac{\partial^2 H}{\partial S^2} v < 0, \text{ for every } 6\,U \text{ dimensional vector } v \neq 0 \tag{4.67}$$

In terms of the expression for H in relation 4.59, in order for condition 4.64 to hold, it suffices that

$$\frac{\partial^2 W_j}{\partial Y^2_{jR}} < 0, \frac{\partial^2 W_j}{\partial Y^2_{jT}} < 0 \text{ and } \frac{\partial^2 W_j}{\partial Y^2_{N}} < 0, \quad j \in I \tag{4.68}$$

4.67 will be met if

$$\frac{\partial^2 W_j}{\partial u^2_j} < 0, \frac{\partial^2 W_j}{\partial R^2_j} < 0 \tag{4.69}$$

Explicit Form of the Optimality Conditions

We first elaborate the equations of motion of the costate variables as defined by equation 4.66. Notice that their economic meaning can be derived from

$$\tau = \frac{\partial H}{\partial \overset{\circ}{S}},$$

if we know that $H\,dt$ is the contribution of economic activities to welfare per unit of time (Moulaert 1975).

We know that $S'(t) \equiv [x'_R(t), x'_T(t), x'_N(t), R'(t), u'(t),$

$$p'(t)]$$

In view of equation 4.59, 4.66 will thus turn into:

$$\overset{\circ}{X}_{jR} = -\frac{\partial H}{\partial X_{jR}} = -[X_{jR}k_{j1} + X_{jN}k_{j4} + X_{jT}k_{j7}$$
$$-\Theta(k_{j1} + k_{j4} - \alpha_0 k_{j7})\eta_j], j \in I \qquad (4.70)$$

$$\overset{\circ}{X}_{jN} = -\frac{\partial H}{\partial X_{jN}} = -[X_{jR}k_{j2} + X_{jN}k_{j5} + X_{jT}k_{j8} + (U-1)\beta_4\eta_j$$

$$+ \beta_3 \sum_{i\neq j}^{U} \pi_j + (1-k)(U-1)\beta_4 s_j \eta_j$$

$$+ (1-k)\beta_3 \sum_{i\neq j}^{U} s_i \eta_i - \Theta(k_{j2} + k_{j5} - \alpha_0 k_{j8})\eta_j],$$

$$j \in I \qquad (4.71)$$

$$\overset{\circ}{X}_{jT} = -\frac{\partial H}{\partial X_{jT}}$$

$$= -[k_{j3}X_{jR} + k_{j6}X_{jN} + k_{j9}X_{jT} - \Theta(k_{j3} + k_{j6} - \alpha_0 k_{j9})\eta_j],$$
$$j \in I \qquad (4.72)$$

$$\dot{\pi}_j = -\frac{\partial H}{\partial P_j}$$

$$= -[(U-1)\beta_6\pi_j + \beta_5 \sum_{i\neq j}^{U} \pi_i$$

$$+ (1-k)(U-1)\beta_6 s_j \eta_j + (1-k)\beta_5 \sum_{i\neq j}^{U} s_i \eta_i], \; j \in I \quad (4.73)$$

$$\dot{\psi}_j = -\frac{\partial H}{\partial R_j} = -\frac{\partial W_j}{\partial R_j}, \qquad\qquad j \in I \quad (4.74)$$

$$\dot{\eta}_j = -\frac{\partial H}{\partial u_j}$$

$$= -\left[\frac{\partial W_j}{\partial u_j} + (U-1)\beta_2\pi_j + \beta_1 \sum_{i\neq j}^{U} \pi_i \right.$$

$$+ \left. (1-k)(U-1)\beta_2 s_j \eta_j + (1-k)\beta_1 \sum_{i\neq j}^{U} s_i \eta_i \right], \; j \in I$$
$$(4.75)$$

Let us now proceed to the explicit form of the first-order conditions for maximizing H (see Eq. 4.63). We repeat that the transposed vector of control variables

$$C'(t) \equiv [Y'_R, Y'_T, Y_N] \equiv [(Y_{jR}(t))', (Y_{jT}(t))', Y_N].$$

Consequently:

$$\frac{\partial H}{\partial Y_{jR}} = \frac{\partial W_j}{\partial Y_{jR}} - b_{j1}X_{jR} - b_{j4}X_{jN} - b_{j7}X_{jT}$$

$$+ p_{1j} \cdot \psi_j + \Theta(b_{j1} + b_{j4} - \alpha_0 b_{j7})\eta_j = 0, \qquad j \in I \quad (4.76)$$

$$\frac{\partial H}{\partial Y_{jT}} = \frac{\partial W_j}{\partial Y_{jT}} - b_{j3}X_{jR} - b_{j6}X_{jN} - b_{j9}X_{jT} - \psi_j$$

$$+ \Theta(b_{j3} + b_{j6} - \alpha_0 b_{j9})\eta_j = 0, \qquad j \in I \qquad\qquad (4.77)$$

$$\frac{\partial H}{\partial Y_N} = \sum_{j=1}^{U} \frac{\partial W_j}{\partial Y_N} - \sum_{j=1}^{U} b_{j2}L_jX_{jR} - \sum_{j=1}^{U} b_{j5}L_jX_{jN}$$

$$- \sum_{j=1}^{U} b_{j8}L_jX_{jT} + \sum_{j=1}^{U} p_{1j}L_j\psi_j$$

$$+ \Theta \sum_{j=1}^{U} (b_{j2} + b_{j5} - \alpha_0 b_{j8})L_j\eta_j = 0, \qquad j \in I \qquad (4.78)$$

The way to solve the equations for the optimal values for $C(t)$, $S(t)$, and (t) is as follows:

1. Solve for $C(t)$ from equations 4.76, 4.77, and 4.78.
2. Introduce the solution for $C(t)$ into the equations of motion of state and costate variables such that we obtain a system of differential equations

$$\begin{bmatrix} \mathring{S}(t) \\ \mathring{\tau}(t) \end{bmatrix} = g(S, \tau) \qquad\qquad (4.79)$$

subject to $S(t_0) = S_0$.

There are some problems to solve in this system. First of all, $g(t)$ is probably not linear in S. Second, we are missing initial conditions for $\tau(t)$. These could be introduced by adding a final function of the state variables to the welfare function $W(t)$.

Economic Interpretation

The interpretation of relations 4.70–4.75 and 4.76–4.78 is not that straightforward. $\tau(t)$ is a vector of valuation coefficients giving a value to differential economic activities—that is, economic activities that did not occur in the previous period. These differentials are expressed as $\mathring{S}$; marginal price (see relation 4.58) can be interpreted as

$$\tau(t) = \frac{\partial H}{\partial \mathring{S}}$$

It follows that the valuation of the increase of the stock variable, population, over period $(t_0 \, t_1)$ equals

$$\int_{t_0}^{t_1} \mathring{P}'(t)\pi(t)\, dt \qquad\qquad \text{for } P(t_0) = P_0$$

which implies a kind of vintage approach to population. For flow variables (say, x_R) this kind of expression does not make sense and should be replaced by an expression such as $x'_R(t)X_R$ where regional production in period $(t, t + dt)$ for the whole nation is valued at prices $\mathring{X}_R(t)$ of new production x_R. The value of total production over the whole period will equal

$$\int_{t_0}^{t_1} x'_R(t)\chi(t)\, dt, \qquad\qquad x_R(t_0) = x_R \qquad (4.80)$$

Let us now interpret some of the optimality conditions obtained in the previous section. Equation 4.75 tells that the marginal social disutility of changes in unemployment falls at the rate that unemployment generates social disutility through the economic activities it pertains: subjective disutility $\partial W_j/\partial u_j$, and objective disutility or cost. See Moulaert (1975), which consists of:

1. The marginal cost of the emigration from regions $i \in I$ $(i \neq j)$ due to a one unit rise in the unemployment rate in regions i (third term of equation 4.75), corrected for the benefit of emigration from region j (second term of 4.75). The cost and benefit are both expressed in utility or disutility of one additional inhabitant (a one-unit change of P_j, P_i).
2. The gain in terms of a fall in unemployment in region j due to emigration from j, because of a unit change in the unemployment rate of region j (expressed in terms of disutility of one unit increase in unemployment in region j) (fourth term of 4.75).
3. The cost of an increase in unemployment in region j, as corresponding to similar effects as under 2, for regions i, valued at marginal disutility of unemployment in regions i.

The interpretation of first-order conditions like 4.76 and 4.77 is similar to the equalization of marginal utility to marginal cost in a static economic optimization problem. For example, in equation 4.76, marginal utility of final output of the regional good in region j equals the sum of the value of the marginal multiplier effects for the production of the regional good, the national good, and the antipollution goods, respectively; the marginal disutility of pollution generated by a unit increase of final demand for the regional good; and the marginal cost of labor inputs corresponding to the multiplier effect (valued at the marginal price of the rate of change in unemployment). Equation 4.78 for national goods can be interpreted similarly. However, instead of a unique pollution effect and unique multiplier effects, we have to take the sum of all the effects as they occur in each region. Clearly, the relative position of the effects of changes in final demand for the national good in each region depends on the mathematical specification of its welfare function W_j, the value of the parameters of this function, and the portion (L_j) of the national goods produced in that region.

Implementation of the Model

The empirical testing of the model is not easy, but it is not impossible. For a two-region model (say, for California and the rest of the United States) the data requirement is not that serious. For this purpose the concept of regional and national good can be taken as analogous to basic and service industries. The data may be available. The capital coefficients can be taken from some other recent estimates. The information relating to pollution sectors can be taken from official sources. The population and migration information can be obtained from Rogers (1968). Experiments can be made with some particular form of welfare functions. For a limited number of regions it does not pose any serious computational problem.

Instead of taking a linear welfare function, a quadratic criterion function can be used, such that the conditions 4.55, 4.56, 4.68, and 4.69 are met. The quadratic control function has the advantage of formalizing the law of decreasing marginal utility (if the matrixes of the quadratic forms are negative definite).

Formally, the problem would become

$$\max_{\{C\}} W_T = \int_{t_2}^{t_1} [z'S + h'C + \tfrac{1}{2}(S'DS + C'EC)]\, dt \qquad (4.81)$$

$$\text{sub } \mathring{S} = FS + GC,$$

where $S(t)$ is the $6U$-dimensional vector of state variables; $C(t)$ the $(2U + 1)$ dimensional vector of control variables; z and h coefficient vectors of dimension $6U$ and $(2U + 1)$, respectively; and D and E are negative (semi-) definite matrixes of appropriate order. The matrixes of coefficients F and G in the equations of motion are of dimensions $(6U \times 6U)$ and $[6U \times (2U + 1)]$, respectively. For the solution of this problem we refer to Bryson and Ho (1969).

We think that the model suggested here, though complicated, has some good features. It contains both abatement and relocation as two means of pollution control. As an input-output type of model, it can take the productive as well as the ecological system through an infinite number of chain reactions. It also integrates the demographic and employment variables. More important, it employs control theory, which makes the situation more realistic. The policy variables suggested can be controlled directly and indirectly in both a free and a socialist economy. However, a multiregional framework rather than a more realistic interregional framework has been used. Diffusion of pollution between regions has not been taken into account, but its inclusion is straightforward. The constancy of the I-O coefficients and the only primary input have been assumed. Empirical testing is not difficult, and it is hoped that it can be done in the future.

The task of regional economic development in developing countries requires the integration of input-output and programming techniques, since we are faced with the task of deciding the levels of different activities with economic, social, political, and resource constraint. Many of these constraints cannot be expressed in terms of quantifiable variates, so this necessarily has to be a simulation job with an alternative design of development.

References

Blumenfeld, Hans. 1955. "The Economic Base of the Metropolis." *Journal of the American Association of Planners* 21 (Autumn):114–32.

Bryson, A. E., Jr., and Ho, Yu-Chi. 1969. *Applied Optimal Control.* Waltham, Mass.: Blaidsell Publishing Company.

Chatterji, Manas. 1963. "Studies in the Structure of the Calcutta Economy." Doctoral dissertation, University of Pennsylvania, Philadelphia.

_____. 1975a. "A Balanced Regional Input-Output Model for Identifying Responsibility for Pollution Created by Industries Which Serve National Markets." *International Regional Science Review* 1, no. 1.

_____. 1975b. "A Dynamic Balanced Regional Input-Output Model of Pollution Control." *Environment and Planning A* 7, no. 1.

_____. 1975c. "Responsibility for Cleaning Pollution: An Interregional Linear Programming Model." *Kybernetes* 5.

Chatterji, M. and F. Moulaert. (1976) "Pollution Abatement and Regional Welfare: A Control Theory Approach," *Tijdschrift voor Ekonomie en Management* 21, no. 2.

Czamanski, Stanislaw. 1963. "A Model of Urban Growth." Doctoral dissertation, University of Pennsylvania, Philadelphia.

Den Hartog H., and Houweling, A. 1974 "Pollution, Pollution Abatement and the Economic Structure: Empirical Results of Input-Output Computations for the Netherlands." Paper presented to the Sixth International Conference on Input-Output Techniques, Vienna, April.

Dorfman, Robert; Samuelson, Paul; and Solow, Robert. 1958. *Linear Programming and Economic Analysis.* New York: McGraw-Hill.

Florence, Sargent P. 1968. *Investment Location and Size of Plant.* Cambridge: Cambridge University Press.

Hirsch, Werner, Z. 1959. "An Application of Area Input-Output Analysis." *Papers of the Regional Science Association* 5: 79–94.

Hoch, Irving. 1959. "A Comparison of Alternate Interindustry Forecasts for the Chicago Region," *Papers of the Regional Science Association* 5: 217–236.

Intriligator, Michael. 1971. *Mathematical Optimization and Economic Theory.* London: Prentice-Hall.

Isard, Walter. 1960. *Methods of Regional Analysis.* Cambridge, Mass.: MIT Press.

_____. 1969. *General Theory: Social, Political, Economic, and Regional.* Cambridge, Mass.: MIT Press.

_____ and Thomas Schooler. (1964). "An Economic Analysis of Local and Regional Impacts on Reduction of Military Expenditures." Peace Research Society (International Papers), Vol. 1.

Leoutief, Wasily W., and Ford, D. 1972. "Air Pollution and Economic Structure: Empirical Results of Input-Output Computations." In A. Brody and A. P. Carter, eds., *Input-Output Techniques.* Amsterdam: North-Holland, Pp. 9–30.

Moulaert, F. 1975. "Dual Stability of the Cyclical Output and Valuation Gaps in a Dynamic Linear Economy with a Quadratic Welfare Function. *Regional Science Research Paper* no. 1. Leuven: Centrum voor Economische Studien.

National Institute of Statistics, Government of Belgium, 1970. "De Input-Output Tabellen Van 1965." In *Statistisch Tijdschrift,* Brussels, pp. 7–28.

Pontryagin, Lev S., et al. 1962. *The Mathematical Theory of Optimal Process.* New York: Wiley.

Rogers, A. 1968. *Matrix Methods for Population Growth.* Berkeley: University of California Press.

Stevens, Benjamin. 1959. "Interregional Linear Programming" Ph.D. dissertation, University of Pennsylvania, Philadelphia.

Tejano, A. R., and Brauer, W. 1974. "Analysis of the 1965 Input-Output Table of Belgium." Leuven: Centrum voor Economische Studien.

Bibliography

Adams, G.; Brooking, C. G.; and Glickman, N. J. 1975. "Description et simulation d'un modèle économétrique regionale: un modèle pour l'état du Mississippi." Discussion Paper no. 266, Economics Department, University of Pennsylvania, Philadelphia.

Allen, R. G. D. 1972. *Mathematical Economics.* London: Macmillan.

Barten, A., and D'Alcantara, G. 1974. "The Linking of Models of the E.E.C. Countries." Louvain: CORE. Multilith.

Brown, M.; Di Palma, M.; and Ferrara, B. 1972. "A Regional-National Econometric Model of Italy." *Papers of the Regional Science Association* 29: 25–44.

Chatterji, Manas. 1965. "Local Impact of Disarmament, Foreign Aid Programs, and Development of Poor World Regions: A Critique of Leontief and Other Growth Models." *Papers of the Peace Science Association (International)* 4:39–66.

_____. 1981. "Health Care Cost Containment in New York State: An Econometric Study." Mimeograph.

Cumberland, J. H. 1966. "A Regional Inter-Industry Model for Analysis of Development Objectives." *Papers of the Regional Science Association* 17: 65–94.

Daly, Herman E. 1968, "On Economics as a Life Science." *Journal of Political Economy* 76 (May–June): 392–405.

De Corel, L.; Thys, F.; and Van Rompuy, Paul. 1973. "Een Econometrisch Model voor het Plan 1976–1980." RENA. Brussels: Planbureau.

Dramais, A. 1974, 1975. "Desmos III." *Cahiers Economiques de Bruxelles* 64: 473–514; 65: 53–108; 66: 201–259.

Glejser, H.; Van Daele, G.; and Lamprecht, M. 1973. "First Experiments with an Econometric Regional Model of the Belgian Economy." *Regional and Urban Economics* 3: 301–304.

Glickman, N. J. 1974. "Son of 'the Specification of Regional Econometric Models.' " *Papers of the Regional Science Association* 32: 155–177.

Isard, Walter. 1953. "Some Empirical Results and Problems of Regional Input-Output Analysis." In W. W. Leontief et al., eds., *Studies in the Structure of the American Economy.* New York: Oxford University Press.

Kneese, A. V. 1971. "Environmental Pollution: Economics and Policy." *American Economic Review (Papers and Proceedings)* 61.

Koo, Anthony. 1974. "Environmental Repercussions and Trade Theory." *Review of Economics and Statistics* 56: 235–244.

Leontief, Wasily W. 1970. "Environmental Repercussions and the Economic Structure." *Review of Economics and Statistics* 52 (August): 262–271.

Mangasarian, O. L. 1966. "Sufficient Conditions for the Optimal Control of Nonlinear Structured Systems." *SIAM Journal of Control*, 4, no. 1.

National Institute of Statistics, Government of Belgium. 1970. *Statistisch Jaarbock*. Brussels, pp. 3–11.

Nijkamp, P., and Paelinck, J. 1973. "Some Models for the Economic Evaluation of the Environment." *Regional Science and Urban Economics* 3, no. 1.

Organization for Economic Cooperation and Development. 1971. *Economic Implications of Pollution Control.* OECD, pp. 28–29.

Van Wynsberghe, D. 1975. "Le Projet de modèle I.R.I.S., modèle interregional et intersectoriel de la Belgique." Brussels: Economic Council for Brabant. Multilith.

5 PROVIDING INFRASTRUCTURE FOR REGIONAL DEVELOPMENT

Requirements for Urban-Regional Growth in the Developing Countries

Although the urban population in the Third World in terms of numbers and growth rate has assumed a staggering proportion, the essential fact remains that all these countries are basically agricultural. For optimum urban growth and industrialization, a strong agricultural sector is essential. To adopt such a strategy, we must identify the linkage of agricultural development and urban growth with the help of some sort of econometric model, as mentioned in Chapter 3. The objective in this chapter will be to show how development or decline in the agricultural sector influences economic activity in urban areas through increased demand for urban-oriented activities or decline in employment opportunities in the rural areas.

One such linkage is the result of the incessant flow of population from rural to urban areas in most developing countries. The elusive pull factor of cities and the continuous push factor of rural areas, due to population growth and lack of employment opportunities, have created urban villages everywhere— in all cities, from Calcutta to Rio and São Paulo to Lagos and Nairobi. It seems that there is no other alternative except population control, but the question remains how to accomplish this. Although birth control information should be propagated by every means possible, the basic key is education.

In the diffusion of information about birth control and population policies, we can use the diffusion models of regional science to structure an optimum network of communication. Side by side with agricultural and urban-regional planning, we need to develop strategies for educational planning. In many countries, because of the excessive importance placed on the development of traditional areas of education, a surplus pool of urban elites has been created without any job opportunities. Meanwhile, the vast agricultural sector has remained stagnant and illiterate. The focus thus should be changed from the creation of urban elitism to mass education in the agricultural sector. This cannot be imposed from above. Grass-roots movements on the Gandhian model need to be introduced within the framework of existing social, religious, and other institutions. The task is not easy, but a beginning must be made.

Fundamental to modernization are changes in the role of women in the society. Advanced education and communication have given urban women new challenges and opportunities. These changes are already visible in many countries. In many professions women now outnumber men, even in absolute numbers. The situation for these women is even more promising than in the developed countries. The vast majority of women in the villages, however, have not yet benefited from this. More important, the new role for urban women will lead to a demand for child care and health services. Substantial changes in the structure of the urban family will create new problems in addition to those already existing in the area of housing, transportation, and social services.

The problem of creating a healthy population in the developing countries depends primarily on the provision of adequate food nutrition. Not to speak of the quality of the food, a vast majority of the people are not getting the minimum nutritional standard, and millions are starving. So economic development and health planning are intricately related. Still, there is a crying need for environmental and preventive health care. Although medical science and technology have become highly sophisticated in these countries, regional variation (between urban and rural areas) is staggering. Many doctors in urban areas in such countries are unemployed, but millions in the villages go uncared for. The population policy, health education, and social service requirements can be determined via an interregional input-output table. This is a gigantic task.

Such an input-output analysis can give us only the global values of the policy variables for determining the level of different services in a specific urban area. We also need a micro study. For example, consider the situation in the Calcutta Industrial Region. This area not only suffers from economic deprivations and unemployment but also lacks basic urban services such as water supply, transportation, drainage, health care, and education. To analyze these problems in terms of municipal income and expenditures, it will be worthwhile to construct an econometric model of the following type.

Municipal Income and Expenditure: An Analytical Study

We can identify a number of dependent and independent variables and run a regression analysis with appropriate independent variables (see Table 5–1 for the list of variables). One of the crucial variables is the population of the community. If the value of the population at a future date is known, then the required expenditure on a specific service can be estimated (for a base period quality in, say, 1960.).

The first dependent variable considered is the expenditure on public health and conveniences. This includes conservancy, health and sanitary outlays, market maintenance, and public works. Equation 1 in Table 5–2 gives the relationship of this variable to population in each town. It will be seen from that relation that the regression coefficient is significantly different from zero and that the correlation is high. When we introduce an additional variable— namely, the area of each town—the regression coefficient of the population variable is slightly changed, but we get a negative coefficient for the area. This means that, the higher the area of a town, the lower the expenditure level.

This apparent contradiction can be explained by saying that the system of income and expenditure in the CMD is not an equilibrium state and that the higher area means a lower density and less expenditure. When we consider the age of the municipality and want to find out whether it has any effect on the expenditure, we see from equation 3 in Table 5–2 that it did not improve the situation much. The regression coefficient for the new variable is found to be statistically insignificant. If we have some idea about the total expenditure and want to know how much of it has to be spent on public health and conveniences, equation 4 can be used.

Let us next divide this expenditure into its constituent parts. Consider the expenditure on conservancy. This relationship with population is given by equation 5, which has a significant regression coefficient and a high correlation. When we introduce the area and age of the municipality, the resulting equation 6 shows that the last variable is insignificant; the area variable has a negative sign. This may mean that the amount of money available for conservancy is more or less decided and that a larger area implies inferior

Table 5-1   List of Variables

	A. Expenditure Variables	*Symbols*
1.	General administration expenditure (1960–61)	E^A
2.	General administration and collection charges (1950–51) (percentage of total ordinary expenditure of major head)	$E^{AC}_{p.51}$
3.	Total expenditure (general administration and collection charges) (1960–61)	E^{AC}
4.	General administration and collection charges (1960–61) (percentage of total ordinary expenditure on major head)	$E^{AC}_{p.61}$
5.	Expenditure on collection of taxes (1960–61)	E^{CX}
6.	Lighting expenditure (1960–61)	E^L
7.	Lighting (1950–51) (percentage of total ordinary expenditure on major head)	$E^L_{p.51}$
8.	Lighting (1960–61) (percentage of total ordinary expenditure on major head)	$E^L_{p.61}$
9.	Drainage establishment (1960–61)	E^D
10.	Drainage (1950–51) (percentage of total ordinary expenditure)	$E^D_{p.51}$
11.	Drainage (1960–61) (percentage of total ordinary expenditure on major head)	$E^D_{p.61}$
12.	Conservancy (1960–61)	E^C
13.	Conservancy (1950–51) (percentage of total ordinary expenditure on major head)	$E^C_{p.51}$
14.	Conservancy (1960–61) (percentage of total ordinary expenditure on major head)	$E^C_{p.61}$
15.	Health, sanitary, etc. (1960–61)	E^H
16.	Sanitation medical relief (1950–51) (percentage of total ordinary expenditure on major head)	$E^H_{p.51}$
17.	Sanitation medical relief (1960–61) (percentage of total ordinary expenditure on major head)	$E^H_{p.61}$
18.	Total public health and convenience, etc. (1960–61)	E^{HC}
19.	Roads (1950–51) (percentage of total ordinary expenditures on major head)	E^R
20.	Roads (1960–61) (percentage of total ordinary expenditure on major head)	$E^R_{p.61}$

21.	Education (1950–51) (percentage of total ordinary expenditure on major head)	E^E
22.	Education (1960–61) (percentage of total ordinary expenditure on major head)	$E^E_{p.61}$
23.	Water supply (1950–51) (percentage of total ordinary expenditure on major head)	$E^W_{p.51}$
24.	Water supply (1960–61) (percentage of total ordinary expenditure on major head)	$E^W_{p.61}$
25.	Public instruction—contributions (1960–61)	E^{EC}
26.	Total expenditures (1960–61)	E
27.	Total (ordinary) expenditure (1950–51)	E_{51}
28.	Per capita ordinary expenditure (1960–61)	E_p
29.	Expenditure on Public Works (1960–61)	E^{PW}
30.	Extraordinary and debt (1960–61)	E^D

B. Income Variables

1.	Water supply—income (1960–61)	I^W
2.	Lighting—income (1960–61)	I^L
3.	Conservancy—income (1960–61)	I^C
4.	Government grants—subventions (1960–61)	I^{GS}
5.	Government grants—M.V. tax (1960–61)	I^{MV}
6.	Grants and contributions—total (1960–61)	I^G
7.	Per capita government grants (1960–61)	I^G_P
8.	Total ordinary income (1960–61)	I
9.	Extraordinary debt (1960–61)	I^D
10.	Total receipts (including opening balance) (1960–61)	I^R
11.	Per capita ordinary income (1960–61)	I_p
12.	Number of rate-payers (1963)	N
13.	Rates and taxes—houses and land (1960–61)	I_H
14	Rates and taxes—miscellaneous (1960–61)	I_m
15.	Rates and taxes—total (1960–61)	I_r
16.	Per capita taxation (1960–61)	T/P

(Continued next page)

Table 5–1   (continued)

B. Income Variables

17.	Percentage of rate-payers (1963)	N_p
18.	Outstanding balance as % of col. 6 (total demand) (1960–61)	B_p
19.	Rates levied on annual value—holding (1963) (per Rs. 100)	r_H
20.	Rates levied on annual value—conservancy (1963) (per Rs. 100)	r_C
21.	Rates levied on annual value—lighting (1962) (per Rs. 100)	r_L
22.	Closing balance (1960–61)	B

C. Demographic and Other Variables

1.	Area square miles	A
2.	Population (1951)	P^{51}
3.	Population (1961)	P
4.	Percentage growth in population (1941–51)	G^{41-51}
5.	Percentage growth in population (1951–61)	G^{51-61}
6.	Density of population (1951)	D^{51}
7.	Density of population (1961)	D^{61}
8.	Total votes against Congress party (1952) (percentage)	V_{52}
9.	Total votes against Congress party (1957) (percentage)	V_{57}
10.	Occupied houses (1951)	H
11.	Age of the municipality in 1961	A^G

A. Expenditure Variables

Variable Number	Mean	Standard Deviation
1	21 619.968 7	15 801.293 0
2	11.716 1	2.653 3
3	63 565.558 6	57 416.972 7
4	13.273 5	4.471 6
5	39 960.793 0	44 722.054 7
6	24 704.351 6	15 647.121 1
7	4.340 9	3.309 3
8	6.277 6	2.179 2

9	30 886.468 7	44 334.531 2
10	5.601 2	3.905 6
11	7.077 3	7.765 4
12	127 540.969 7	92 059.750 0
13	33.377 5	13.042 1
14	29.918 1	11.341 4
15	32 719.437 5	31 215.625 0
16	8.219 7	7.046 9
17	8.133 8	8.099 4
18	299 766.242 4	227 302.232 1
19	11.086 7	9.121 1
20	8.931 4	6.815 5
21	7.045 3	8.367 9
22	7.618 2	8.475 4
23	7.730 6	8.767 6
24	8.810 9	6.966 8
25	41 770.058 6	89 333.125 0
26	452 729.909 1	343 239.175 1
27	352 965.2	
28	7.316 8	3.876 1
29	60 842.320 3	82 736.062 5
30	70 797.562 5	

B. Income Variables

Variable Number	Mean	Standard Deviation
1	52 096.175 8	89 552.000 0
2	32 814.851 6	25 709.378 9
3	90 067.250 0	76 346.687 5
4	81 379.500 0	
5	13 329.734 4	53 982.972 7
6	96 059.375 0	
7	1.668 8	2.786 1
8	477 703.545 5	366 541.795 8
9	50 434.644 5	51 047.472 7
10	884 026.4	
11	7.717 6	4.375 6
12	7 572.144 5	8 296.863 3
13	139 020.393 9	121 035.892 5
14	33 768.910 2	31 755.890 6
15	351 574.697 0	290 806.276 9

(continued next page)

Table 5–1   (continued)

16	5.351 2	2.448 3
17	11.955 8	7.154 4
18	38.174 0	17.507 0
19	7.911 8	1.627 0
20	6.632 4	1.614 6
21	2.163 5	0.759 5
22	72 198.750 0	80 990.312 5

C. Demographic and Other Variables

Variable Number	Mean	Standard Deviation
1	3.922 6	2.444 7
2	44 601.675 8	30 711.445 3
3	64 372.203 1	42 813.039 1
4	39.411 8	30.006 2
5	50.573 4	41.608 9
6	15 192.410 2	13 167.488 3
7	20 286.203 1	14 963.933 6
8	55.647 0	13.080 0
9	59.735 3	7.081 0
10	10 313.968 7	8 312.101 6
11	73.647 0	42.704 0

service. The relationship between conservancy expenditure and total expenditure is given by equation 7.

In the case of health and sanitary services, the population emerges as the only significant explanatory variable; area and age variables do not seem to have any significant effect in equations 8–10. As before, the relation between total expenditure and health and sanitary expenditures is given by equation 11.

In the case of the drainage establishment expenditure, the same conclusion follows. The population is an important variable, but the correlation is not that high (equation 12). If we include an area variable, the correlation increases a little, and it becomes a significant variable, though remaining negative (equation 13). Inclusion of age variables does not change the situation (equation 14). The relationship between the public works expenditure and the total expenditure is given in equation 15. Data for the water

Table 5-2 List of Equations
(Figures in parentheses denote the standard error of the regression coefficient.)

(a) *Total Public Health Convenience Expenditure, 1960–61*
(Water Supply + Drainage + Conservancy + Health Sanitary + Market pounds + Public Works)

$$E^{HC} = 1\ 253.952\ 7 + \underset{(0.503\ 2)}{4.535\ 9P}$$
$$R = 0.850\ 8 \qquad \ldots(1)$$

$$E^{HC} = 64\ 354.798\ 5 + \underset{(0.497\ 7)}{5.290\ 5P} - \underset{(8\ 688.947\ 8)}{28\ 202.89\ 0A}$$
$$R = 0.892\ 0 \qquad \ldots(2)$$

$$E^{HC} = 120\ 724.616\ 2 + \underset{(0.491\ 8)}{5.267\ 5P} + \underset{(8\ 675.933\ 0)}{26\ 513.350\ 0A}$$
$$\underset{(684.296\ 9)}{-\ 906.465\ 8}\ A^{G}$$
$$R = 0.898\ 5 \qquad \ldots(3)$$

$$E^{HC} = 22\ 712.300\ 0 + \underset{(0.045\ 5)}{0.612\ 0E}$$
$$R = 0.924\ 1 \qquad \ldots(4)$$

(b) *Conservancy Expenditure, 1960–61*

$$E^{C} = 4\ 948.719\ 6 + \underset{(0.206\ 9)}{1.862\ 8P}$$
$$R = (0.850\ 6) \qquad \ldots(5)$$

(Continued next page)

Table 5-2 (continued)

$$E^C = 30\ 816.946\ 3 + 2.120\ 2P- \qquad \ldots (6)$$
$$(0.218\ 8)$$
$$-9\ 556.321\ 8A \quad 67.619\ 8A^G$$
$$(3\ 859.908\ 5) \quad (304.442\ 6)$$
$$R = 0.879\ 8$$

$$E^C = 20\ 676.510\ 7 + 0.236\ 0E \qquad \ldots (7)$$
$$(0.024\ 3)$$
$$R = 0.867\ 7$$

(c) *Health and Sanitary Expenditure, 1960–61*

$$E^H = 1\ 160.481\ 4 + 0.481\ 5P \qquad \ldots (8)$$
$$(0.101\ 7)$$
$$R = 0.647\ 7$$

$$E^H = 7\ 004.437\ 8 + 0.551\ 4P \qquad \ldots (9)$$
$$(0.113\ 7)$$
$$R = 0.671\ 8$$

$$E^H = 8\ 287.358\ 8 + 0.550\ 9P$$
$$(0.115\ 7)$$
$$-2\ 573.501\ 4A \quad -20.630\ 26A^G \quad - \quad 2\ 611.953\ 8A \qquad \ldots (10)$$
$$(2\ 040.562\ 6) \quad (160.945\ 3) \quad (1\ 985.029\ 00)$$

$$E^H = 5\ 895.514\ 0 + 0.059\ 5E \qquad \ldots (11)$$
$$(0.012\ 7)$$
$$R = 0.644\ 8$$

(d) *Expenditure in Drainage Establishment, 1960–61*

$$E^D = -4\ 777.556\ 8 + 0.553\ 5P$$

$$E^D = 13\,878.636\,7 + \underset{(0.160\,4)}{}$$
$$R = 0.526\,9 \qquad \ldots (12)$$

$$E^D = + \underset{(0.162\,5)}{0.776\,6P} \quad - \quad \underset{(2\,836.674\,7)}{8\,338.378\,0A}$$
$$R = 0.662\,7 \qquad ..13$$

$$E^D = 11\,668.491\,3 + \underset{(0.165\,3)}{0.777\,5P} \quad - \quad \underset{(2\,915.659\,6)}{8\,404.621\,7A}$$
$$+ \quad \underset{(229.966\,8)}{35.540\,7A^G}$$
$$R = 0.663\,0 \qquad \ldots (14)$$

(e) *Total Expenditure on Public Works, 1960–61*

$$E^R = -9\,590.949\,5 + \underset{(0.033\,2)}{0.158\,6E}$$
$$R = 0.651\,0 \qquad \ldots (15)$$

(f) *Expenditure in General Administration, 1960–61*

$$E^A = 2\,739.915\,5 + \underset{(0.033\,7)}{0.041\,9E}$$
$$R = 0.896\,3 \qquad \ldots (16)$$

(g) *General Administration and Collection Charges, 1960–61*

$$E^{AC} = -4\,980.801\,0 + \underset{(0.012\,7)}{0.153\,6E}$$
$$R = (0.908\,4) \qquad \ldots (17)$$

$$E^C = -661\,6.390\,5 + \underset{(0.014\,3)}{0.014\,7E}$$
$$R = 0.796\,2 \qquad \ldots (18)$$

(Continued next page)

Table 5-2 (continued)

$$E^A = 7\,598.155\,5 + 0.218\,5E^{AC}$$
$$(0.030\,4)$$
$$R = (0.790\,6) \qquad \dots(19)$$

$$E^A = 12\,895.719\,2 + 0.215\,9E^C$$
$$(0.050\,7)$$
$$R = 0.607\,6 \qquad \dots(20)$$

$$E^{AC} = 14\,009.165\,0 + 1.238\,6E^C$$
$$(0.061\,6)$$
$$R = 0.963\,8 \qquad \dots(21)$$

$$E^A = 2\,579.181\,4 + 0.290\,6P$$
$$(0.042\,9)$$
$$R = 0.772\,4 \qquad \dots(22)$$

$$E^C = 2\,657.139\,9 + 0.579\,5P$$
$$(0.159\,2)$$
$$R = 0.547\,3 \qquad \dots(23)$$

$$E^{AC} = 3\,146.965\,4 + 0.932\,9P$$
$$(0.178\,0)$$
$$R = 0.685\,5 \qquad \dots(24)$$

$$E^A = 6\,622.546\,5 + 0.338\,9P \qquad - \qquad 1806.180\,4H^{51}$$
$$(0.045\,6) \qquad\qquad (795.703\,5)$$
$$R = 0.809\,8$$

$$E^A = 16\,039.005\,0 + 0.337\,0P \qquad - \qquad 1\,665.420\,1H^{51}$$
$$(0.045\,3) \qquad\qquad (798.361\,3)$$
$$- 76.056\,4A \qquad \dots(25)$$

(Continued next page)

$$E^A = 7\,948.834\,2 + \quad\quad 1.302\,1H^{51} \qquad \cdots(26)$$
$$(62.969\,2) \qquad\qquad (0.255\,8)$$
$$R = (0.819\,92) \qquad\qquad R = 0.674\,8 \qquad \cdots(27)$$

(h) *Lighting Expenditure, 1960–61*

$$E^L = 6\,944.009\,9 + 0.039\,6E \qquad \cdots(28)$$
$$(0.004\,3)$$
$$R = 0.858\,4$$

$$E^L = 4\,290.144\,3 + 0.331\,0P \qquad \cdots(29)$$
$$(0.036\,0)$$
$$R = (0.842\,0)$$

$$E^L = 10\,294.224\,8 + 1.382\,0H^{51} \qquad \cdots(30)$$
$$(0.236\,0)$$
$$R = (0.724\,7)$$

$$E^L = 4\,312.752\,1 + 0.292\,4P + 0.126\,2H^{51} \qquad \cdots(31)$$
$$(0.066\,8) \qquad (0.342\,7)$$
$$R = 0.842\,8$$

(i) *Income*

$$I^L = 8\,068.827\,4 + 0.052\,5I \qquad \cdots(32)$$
$$(0.008\,6)$$

$$I^C = 16\,649.822\,5 + 0.156\,6I \qquad \cdots(33)$$
$$(0.025\,0)$$

Table 5-2 (continued)

$$I^L = 7\ 269.596\ 9 + 0.073\ 7r \qquad \qquad \cdots(34)$$
$$(0.009\ 1)$$

$$I^C = 18\ 130.198\ 9 + 0.028\ 6r \qquad \qquad \cdots(35)$$
$$(0.029\ 4)$$

$$I = 118\ 127.882\ 0 + 8\ 867.281\ 0r_C - 131\ 036.845\ 8r_L$$
$$(25\ 353.229\ 4) \qquad (53\ 463.650\ 6)$$
$$+ 18\ 453.490\ 8r_H + 6.607\ 24P \qquad \qquad \cdots(36)$$
$$(24\ 604.849\ 4) \qquad (0.983\ 3)$$
$$R = 0.814\ 4$$

$$I = 115\ 177.104\ 0 + 2.607\ 7I_H \qquad \qquad \cdots(37)$$
$$(0.276\ 6)$$
$$R = 0.861\ 1$$

$$I = 132\ 128.865\ 0 + 10.420\ 1I_L \qquad \qquad \cdots((38)$$
$$(1.701\ 7)$$
$$R = 0.739\ 9$$

$$I = 153\ 662.409\ 0 + 3.542\ 3I_C \qquad \qquad \cdots(39)$$
$$(0.569\ 8)$$
$$R = 0.744\ 9$$

$$I = 197\ 111.544\ 1 + 8.209\ 8I_m \qquad \qquad \cdots(40)$$
$$(1.420\ 2)$$
$$R = 0.720\ 3$$

$$I = 58\ 601.995\ 9 + 1.991\ 2I_H - 0.375\ 28I_L$$
$$(\ 0.349\ ) \qquad (2.322\ 01)$$
$$+ 1.691\ 5I_C$$

$$I = 33\,805.078\,2 - \quad \begin{array}{c}(0.700\ 9)\end{array}$$
$$R = 0.900\ 8 \qquad \dots (41)$$

$$I = \quad 2.007\ 9I_H \quad - \quad 2.013\ 77I_L$$
$$\begin{array}{cc}(0.282\ 6) & (1.911\ 7)\end{array}$$
$$+ \quad 0.979\ 8I_C \quad + \quad 4.152\ 17I_m$$
$$\begin{array}{cc}(0.593\ 4) & (1.026\ 3)\end{array}$$
$$R = 0.938\ 6 \qquad \dots (42)$$

$$I = 313\,133.923\ 2 + 1.672\ 3I^G$$
$$(0.398\ 5)$$
$$R = 0.602\ 0 \qquad \dots (43)$$

$$I = 71\,990.453\ 97 + 77\,219.704\ 5\,(T/P)$$
$$(21\,317.482\ 1)$$
$$+ \quad 18.224\ 8N$$
$$(6.271\ 6)$$
$$R = 0.628\ 3 \qquad \dots (44)$$

Source: M. Chatterji, "An Econometric Model of Municipal Finances of Calcutta Metropolitan District," *Indian Journal of Public Administration* (January–March 1970).

supply expenditure were incomplete. Hence we could not determine any relationship between this and related variables.

We next turn our attention to the expenditure in general administration. It is seen from equation 16 that about 5 percent of the total expenditure is spent on this item of expenditure. If collection charges are included, then it is 15 percent (equation 17). The collection charges as such are about 10 percent (equation 18). The relationship between expenditure in (1) collection charges, (2) administration, and (3) collection charges plus administration are given by equations 19–21. In all cases the regression coefficients are significant and the correlation coefficients are high. If the population of any town is known, and if we are interested in estimating the three different heads of expenditure, then equations 22–24 can be used. If we introduce the number of houses as an additional variable besides population, then from equation 25 it is seen that the variable has a negative sign. This is not quite significant. The same is true when we include the area variable (equation 26). However, from equation 27 it is clear that the relationship between administration expenditure and the number of houses is a positive one. It is noteworthy in this connection that the number of houses refers to the year 1951. When we relate the expenditure on lighting to the total expenditure, we see from equation 28 that it represents only 4 percent of it. The relationships between population and housing variables are given in equations 29–31. It is seen from these equations that, although the sign of housing variables is positive, it is not significant, whereas the correlation coefficients are reasonably high. If we know the total income of a municipality, then the income from taxes on lighting and conservancy taxes are given by equations 32 and 33, respectively. If we have estimates of total tax income and we want to find lighting and conservancy income, we can use equations 34 and 35. In all these cases the regression coefficients are significant and the correlation coefficient is high.

On the other hand, if we have information on income received under different items such as house tax and conservancy tax, and we wish to estimate the total income, we can use equations 36–40 for this purpose. They can also be used simultaneously through equations 41 or 42. If we have different tax rates and want to find out their relationship with the total income, equation 36 can be used. Equation 43 gives the relationship of government grants to total income where the relationship of per capita taxation and the number of taxpayers with the total income is given by equation 44.

At the end a few remarks seem to be in order. All of the foregoing equations have been estimated on the basis of cross-section data for the first thirty-three towns (see Figure 1–1), so the relationships should be taken as an average. If we square the correlation coefficients, we shall get a coefficient of determination that will give the percentage of total variance explained by the independent variables. Admittedly, this is low in many cases. The possible existence of spurious correlations should also be kept in mind.

I do not intend to imply in this study that this is the only possible approach. A great many methods are open to us. The objective was to emphasize the need for a more sophisticated technical approach in analyzing municipal finances and link it with the growth in regional income. We hope more powerful comprehensive models will be forthcoming in the future and will facilitate improved urban and municipal research in India.

It is noteworthy that when we mention the econometric models in the foregoing analysis and also in the materials presented in Chapter 3, we are talking in terms of a single-equation least-square estimation procedure. A more refined model using an equation systems approach estimated by such methods as the maximum-likelihood method needs to be developed. It should be emphasized that the solution found in developed countries cannot be used indiscriminately to attack such problems as housing or transportation. For example, it is neither possible nor desirable, in my judgment, to clear the slums and build high-rise apartments, since in almost all cases this leads to permanent eviction of the poor and increased landholding by the rich with the use of illegally acquired money. Renovation and provision of minimum municipal services are the keys of housing policies. Urbanization should act as the principal force for eradicating social problems such as the caste problem in India, social discrimination, and the existence of urban elites. However, experience shows that increased affluence in the urban sector has created the polarization and domination of interest groups in both rural and urban areas.

Energy-Econometric Modeling

One factor that will hinder the growth of infrastructure is the high price and scarcity of mineral resources, particularly energy. The developing countries are the worst sufferers as a result of the rising cost of energy. Energy is the lifeblood of economic development. When energy prices go up, so do fertilizer prices. As a consequence, food grain production is also affected. Thus it should be worthwhile to construct an energy-econometric model through which to evaluate the impact of higher energy prices on economic activities in different points in space. The framework for such a model is as follows (for details, see Chatterji 1981).

Figure 5–1 gives the different types of developing regions in the world. The names of the individual countries within each region can be found in Leontief et al. (1977). For each country, the total population at any time is taken as a sum of urban and rural populations. The rural population in a given period is determined by the sum of (1) the population in the previous period plus natural growth, and (2) migration from the rural to the urban areas. The migration equation can be estimated as a function of urban-rural wage differentials and attraction of urban employment. Labor force can be obtained by multiplying population by the labor force participation rate (see Figure 5–2).

Total food production is a function of number of workers, animal energy input, fertilizer, water, pesticides, and irrigated land. Cash crop production levels are determined by export of cash crops. The demand for energy can be estimated on the basis of total population, fertilizer need, and available biomass and other nontraditional energy sources.

Figure 5–3 gives a Klein-Goldberger (1954) type of econometric model for the organized manufacturing sector containing (1) activity submodel (see Chatterji 1982) (ASM): employment, and (2) activity submodel (ASM):

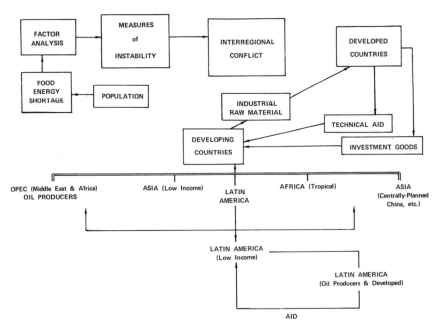

Figure 5–1. Definition of the Developing Countries

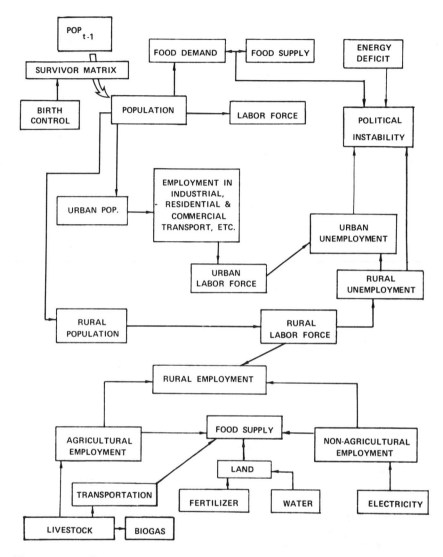

Figure 5–2.   Demographic-Agricultural Submodel. Source: M. Chatterji, "Energy Modeling with Particular Reference to Spatial Systems," *Regional Science and Urban Economics* 10. Reprinted with the courtesy of the North-Holland Publishing Company.

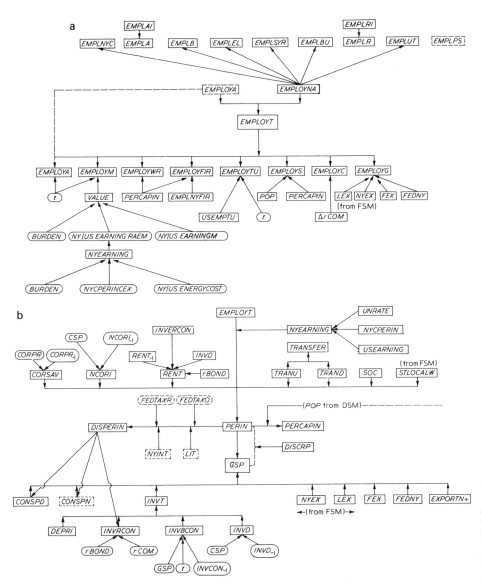

Figure 5–3. (a) Activity Submodel (ASM): Employment; (b), Activity Submodel (ASM): Income and Product Account. Source: M. Chatterji, "Energy Modeling with Particular Reference to Spatial Systems," *Regional Science and Urban Economics* 10. Reprinted with the courtesy of the North-Holland Publishing Company.

income and product account. A framework of an integrated energy, demographic, and econometric model is shown in Figure 5-4. This figure helps us to find out the impact of the exogenous level of energy availability and price effects, not only on the organized manufacturing sector, but also on food production, fertilizers, rural to urban migration, and so on. An arrow in this figure refers to a regression-type relation.

Once an interregional input-output table is available and the resource constraints with respect to health, social services, and resources are known, they can be combined with an integrated input-output linear programming model.

Energy in Urban-Regional Development

One of the basic problems in the field of energy management and policy is to forecast the demand at a future date in terms of (1) policy variables, prices, taxes, and so on, and (2) data variables such as population, incomes, and so on. This is usually achieved by the development of what is called an *energy model*, which connects energy with various other variables—such as price, income, and temperature—that affect the demand for energy. If we need a more disaggregated model, the energy consumption is divided into several categories of demand—residential, industrial, transportation, and commercial.

Similarly, the models can be extended by taking into consideration several types of fuel, such as coal, petroleum, natural gas, and so on. The relationships are usually established on the basis of (1) past information about economic, social, and behavioral variables, and (2) past, present, and future technological information.

Numerous energy models, both national and regional, are currently available in many countries. Some of the sophisticated models constructed in the United States are indicated in Table 5-3. These models required considerable resources in their development. Therefore, the ability of these models to predict the values of the endogenous variables on the basis of the stipulated value of the exogenous variables should be weighed against the cost.

Sometimes, to avoid the high cost of model building and some methodological problems, some simple formulations can be used to obtain results as good as those obtained from the sophisticated models. Time-series models of energy are usually estimated on the basis of past data. Clearly, however, the future scenario will be completely different from that of the recent past. Because the demand for energy then was quite insensitive to price, for that

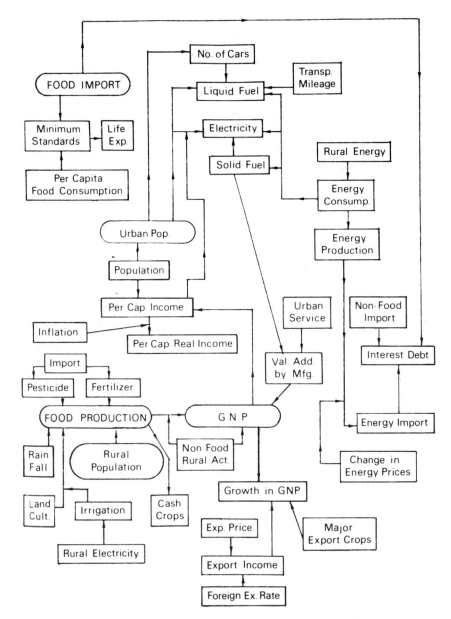

Figure 5-4. An Integrated Energy, Demographic, and Econometric Framework

Table 5–3   Some Mathematical Models for Energy Consumption in the United States

Source	Comments
Institute for Energy Analysis (IEA)	IEA projected low (101.4) and high (125.9) figures, of which 114 is the midpoint.
CONAES Demand-Conservation Panel	Study projected four principal cases to the year 2010. The 111-quad figure, a subsidiary version of case B, conforms most closely to our midrange economic and demographic projections (see Chapter 4) and assumes a real energy price rise of 2 percent yearly. The figure is interpolated from a 1975–2010 time path.
MOPPS	Figure is described as the base case projection.
EPRI-Demand 1977	Figure is described as baseline, falling between a conservation case (146) and a high case (196).
RFF-NIH Study	Baseline case; study featured wide variety of additional cases.

Source: Sam Schurr et al., *Energy in America's Future: The Choices before Us* (Baltimore, Md.: Johns Hopkins University Press, 1979), p. 180.

Notes:

IEA: Institute for Energy Analysis, Oak Ridge Associated Universities, *U.S. Energy and Economic Growth, 1975–2010* (Oak Ridge, Tenn.: IEA, September 1976).

CONAES: National Academy of Sciences, Committee on Nuclear and Alternative Energy Systems (CONAES), "Outlook for Energy Demand and Conservation," Report of the Panel on Demand and Conservation (in preparation). The acronym CONAES, denoting the parent committee, is used here as it has been elsewhere. For a summary discussion of the panel's findings, particularly with respect to low-energy futures, see "U.S. Energy Demand: Some Low Energy Figures," *Science*, April 14, 1978, pp. 142–152.

MOPPS: U.S. Department of Energy, "Market Oriented Program Planning Study (MOPPS)," Final Report, vol. 1, "Integrated Summary." (Reference applies to the December 1977 review draft version of this document.)

EPRI: Larry J. Williams, James W. Boyd, and Robert T. Crow, *Demand 77: EPRI Annual Energy Forecasts and Consumption Model*, EPRI EA-621-SR, vol. 1 (Palo Alto, Calif.: Electric Power Research Institute, March 1978). A summary account appears in Robert T. Crow, "Demand 77," *EPRI Journal* (December 1977): 20–23.

RFF-NIH: See Ronald G. Ridker and William D. Watson, Jr., "Energy," in *To Choose a Future: Resources and Environmental Problems of the U.S., A Long-Term Global Outlook*, Chapter 5, an RFF study sponsored by the National Institutes of Health (in preparation). A compressed account appears in Ronald G. Ridker, William D. Watson, Jr., and Adele Shapanka, "Economic, Energy, and Environmental Consequences of Alternative Energy Regimes, An Application of the RFF/SEAS Modeling System," in Charles J. Hitch, ed., *Modeling Energy and Economic Interactions: Five Approaches* (Washington, D.C.: Resources for the Future, 1977). However, this latter discussion, though a lucid description of the approach followed in the RFF-NIH project, introduces and tests the effect of somewhat different underlying assumptions so as to conform to identical assumptions governing other contributions to the Hitch volume.

period, the price cannot be used to predict the demand for energy. After the 1973 price increase, price did become a factor. It is worthwhile to compute the price elasticities, cross-elasticities, and so on after that period. What we are suggesting is that instead of using a long time series for the related variables, we should subdivide the time period into different parts. For each period we connect the relevant variables for that period and then integrate the results. The objective of this study is to present some results based on this principle on the international, national, state, and local levels.

International

We divided the countries of the world into two groups: (1) developed and (2) developing. The definition of development was the same as that given in *World Energy Consumption* (1976). The following variables were defined:

Developed Countries
C_{TOT} = total commercial energy consumption.
C_{SF} = solid fuels consumption.
C_{LF} = liquid fuels consumption.
C_{NG} = natural gas consumption.
C_{HNE} = hydronuclear electricity consumption.
C_{POP} = an index of population.

Developing Countries
C_{XTOT} = total commercial energy consumption.
C_{XCF} = solid fuels consumption.
C_{XLF} = liquid fuels consumption.
C_{XNG} = natural gas consumption.
C_{XHNE} = hydronuclear electricity consumption.
C_{XPOP} = an index of population.

A straight line of regression relation was established between the related variables, and the following results were obtained using time-series data between 1950 and 1974:

Developed Countries
$$C_{SF} = \underset{(24.76)}{1,057.27} + \underset{(.007)}{.007 C_{TOT}} \qquad R^2 = .04$$

$$C_{LF} = \begin{matrix} -721.79 \\ (15.11) \end{matrix} \begin{matrix} + .660C_{TOT} \\ (.004) \end{matrix} \qquad R^2 = .99$$

$$C_{NG} = \begin{matrix} -313.23 \\ (13.14) \end{matrix} \begin{matrix} + .298C_{TOT} \\ (.004) \end{matrix} \qquad R^2 = .99$$

$$C_{HNE} = \begin{matrix} -24.05 \\ (3.11) \end{matrix} \begin{matrix} + .034C_{TOT} \\ (.0009) \end{matrix} \qquad R^2 = .98$$

$$C_{SF} = \begin{matrix} 1{,}016.399 \\ (90.23) \end{matrix} \begin{matrix} + 94.822C_{POP} \\ (134.59) \end{matrix} \qquad R^2 = .02$$

$$C_{LF} = \begin{matrix} -6{,}136.69 \\ (404.07) \end{matrix} \begin{matrix} + 11{,}163.425C_{POP} \\ (602.72) \end{matrix} \qquad R^2 = .94$$

$$C_{NG} = \begin{matrix} -2{,}788.86 \\ (161.75) \end{matrix} \begin{matrix} + 5{,}087.003C_{POP} \\ (241.278) \end{matrix} \qquad R^2 = .95$$

$$C_{HNE} = \begin{matrix} -306.466 \\ (18.096) \end{matrix} \begin{matrix} + 578.608C_{POP} \\ (26.993) \end{matrix} \qquad R^2 = .95$$

$$C_{TOT} = \begin{matrix} -8{,}213.240 \\ (591.835) \end{matrix} \begin{matrix} + 16{,}922.815C_{POP} \\ (883.793) \end{matrix} \qquad R^2 = .94.$$

Developing Countries

$$C_{XCF} = \begin{matrix} 43.984 \\ (3.467) \end{matrix} \begin{matrix} + 1.32C_{XTOT} \\ (.008) \end{matrix} \qquad R^2 = .91$$

$$C_{XLF} = \begin{matrix} -14.877 \\ (2.274) \end{matrix} \begin{matrix} + .644C_{XTOT} \\ (.006) \end{matrix} \qquad R^2 = .99$$

$$C_{XNG} = \begin{matrix} -26.413 \\ (1.789) \end{matrix} \begin{matrix} + .184C_{XTOT} \\ (.004) \end{matrix} \qquad R^2 = .98$$

$$C_{XHNE} = \begin{matrix} -4.322 \\ (.224) \end{matrix} \begin{matrix} + .040C_{XTOT} \\ (.0005) \end{matrix} \qquad R^2 = .99$$

$$C_{XCF} = \begin{matrix} -51.555 \\ (5.230) \end{matrix} \begin{matrix} + 99.602C_{XPOP} \\ (3.560) \end{matrix} \qquad R^2 = .97$$

$$C_{XLF} = \begin{matrix} -448.470 \\ (24.995) \end{matrix} \begin{matrix} + 462.846C_{XPOP} \\ (17.016) \end{matrix} \qquad R^2 = .96$$

$$C_{XNG} = \begin{matrix} -148.374 \\ (10.281) \end{matrix} \begin{matrix} + 130.975C_{XPOP} \\ (6.999) \end{matrix} \qquad R^2 = .93$$

$$C_{XHNE} = \begin{matrix} -31.062 \\ (1.731) \end{matrix} \begin{matrix} + 28.584C_{XPOP} \\ (1.179) \end{matrix} \qquad R^2 = .96$$

$$C_{XTOT} = \begin{matrix} -678.006 \\ (32.088) \end{matrix} \begin{matrix} + 722.162C_{XPOP} \\ (21.845) \end{matrix} \qquad R^2 = .97$$

The results of the analysis are satisfactory. In the developing countries the coefficients of determination range from .91 to .99, and the standard errors are small. The same is generally true in the developed countries, with the exception of the two equations in which C_{SF} was the dependent variable and C_{TOT} and C_{POP} were the independent variables, respectively. This inconsistency may be explained if one examines the role of solid fuels in the developed countries over the past twenty-five years. With advanced technology and the growing concern for protecting the environment from polluting fuel sources, the growth rate for solid fuels has not kept pace with either total energy needs or population growth. Hence the results of these regression analyses show a very low R^2 (.04 and .02). Also, the standard error is higher than would generally be accepted. This inconsistency does not extend to the developing countries because here the issue of environmental control has not become significant; nor has technology advanced to the point where other sources of energy are more practical.

In summary, this analysis lends strong support to the significance of the correlations between total energy consumption and consumption of individual energy sources and between population and the consumption of these same energy sources. Also, as discussed earlier, such an analysis can be instrumental in pointing out inconsistencies that exist in the general scheme of energy consumption. The low correlation between consumption of solid fuels and total consumption in the developed countries brings out the importance of technology and environmental control in determining the amount of solid fuel consumption. An interesting extension of this study might be to correlate solid fuel consumption with the increase in technological development and environmental controls over the past twenty-five years.

In the next stage we considered only the demand for electricity and related it to such variables as population and income. Population growth often means a growth in the demand for goods and thus, ultimately, a growth in the production of those goods. Given the nature of this growth, and holding equal other relevant facts—such as the state of technology, capital investment, prices, and cultural tastes—it should be possible to estimate the demand and, ultimately, the production of certain goods. A good example of this is the production of electrical energy. Production and demand for this energy good are closely related since the difficulty of transporting it over long distances requires that it be produced and consumed within a given locality and produced largely on the immediate demand of consumers. Given the rate of population growth, therefore, we should be able to estimate production of electrical energy quite accurately, particularly if we differentiate between developed and developing nations, which have a substantially different mix of technology and capital investment.

Using figures for population and electrical energy production from 1950–1974 given by *World Energy Statistics,* several linear and log linear equations were developed to explore this relationship. These equations are summarized in Table 5–4.

A number of conclusions can be drawn from these equations. One is that knowledge of changes in population allow us to predict total electrical energy production with a high degree of accuracy. R^2 is very high for all the equations, and the standard errors of estimate are small in comparison with the coefficients. The best estimates of production will be obtained through the use of the log linear equations, as R^2 is 3 or 4 points higher than when the linear equation is used. This suggests that the rate of growth in electrical energy production is exponential: for every increase in population, the production will increase at an increasing rate.

It is interesting to note that the developed countries expand at an even faster rate than the developing nations. This may be the result of a more advanced technological level and a greater capacity for capital investment. It may also be due to a more complex demand in the developed nations. Consumers in these areas undoubtedly use a wider variety and a greater number of products that require electricity.

Breaking down electrical energy production into its public and industrial sectors suggests an interesting comparison. In both developed and developing countries, the industrial sector expands at a fairly constant rate, whereas the public sector expands at an exponential rate. The best prediction of industrial production is a linear equation that has a higher R^2 in both cases, although for developed nations the linear equation is only slightly better than the log linear equation. On the other hand, the best estimate for public sector production is the log linear equation, which has an R^2 almost five points higher in both equations.

The reason for this difference can probably be explained by the fact that public demand for electrical energy is more direct than industrial demand, which is derived. Industrial consumption is based ultimately on the demand for the finished goods of the industries, which in many cases may rise at a slower rate than the population. Public consumption is more direct. Each additional person will produce a proportional increase in demand. Increases in industrial consumption may also require greater increments of capital expenditures and technology, which would have a tendency to slow growth, particularly in developing nations. The regression analysis supports this explanation. In developed countries the linear model is only slightly better than the log linear model, meaning that industrial electrical energy consumption approaches exponential growth.

The breakdown into public and industrial sectors also reveals that the public sector is growing at an increasingly faster rate than the total production. It is the public sector that pulls up the total growth to an

Table 5-4 Regression Relationship between Population and Production of Electricity

	Developing Nations				Developed Nations		
	b_0	b_1	R^2		b_0	b_1	R^2
Linear regression							
Total	−570.70	532.025	.965	Total	−11,050.85	19,825.99	.953
	(30.72)[a]	(20.92)			(612.35)	(913.51)	
Industrial	−46.54	55.21	.983	Industrial	−918.61	1,813.96	.992
	(2.22)	(1.51)			(22.39)	(33.41)	
Public	−523.01	475.96	.953	Public	−10,147.68	18,035.08	.947
	(32.27)	(21.98)			(594.79)	(887.31)	
Log linear regression							
Total	1.54	4.20	.995	Total	4.42	6.40	.995
	(.0097)	(.0568)			(.0169)	(.0939)	
Industrial	1.06	2.73	.936	Industrial	3.22	4.40	.984
	(.0254)	(.1484)			(.0205)	(.1142)	
Public	1.39	4.55	.997	Public	4.41	6.76	.994
	(.0089)	(.0518)			(.0185)	(.1030)	

Note: Figures in thousand million kilowatt hours.
[a]Standard errors of the coefficients in parentheses.

exponential rate, whereas the slower industrial growth dampens the rate of total growth. Thus our analysis bears out our expectation that the growth in production of electrical energy would be closely related to the growth of population.

Next we considered natural gas consumption separately for developed and developing countries and computed the regression equations in Figures 5–5 through 5–10. Figures 5–5 and 5–6 refer to developed countries, and Figures 5–7 through 5–10 refer to developing countries. For the developed countries, total natural gas consumption is first matched with time (Figure 5–5) and then with population (Figure 5–6). For the developing countries both total consumption (Figure 5–7) and log (total consumption) (Figure 5–8) were matched with time. Then total consumption (Figure 5–9) and log (total consumption) (Figure 5–10) were matched with population.

Beginning with the developed country, the dependent variable studied was total gas consumption (C). Its relationships to the independent variables, time and population, were studied separately. A linear relationship was found in both cases with a high degree of statistical correlation (see Figure 5–5).

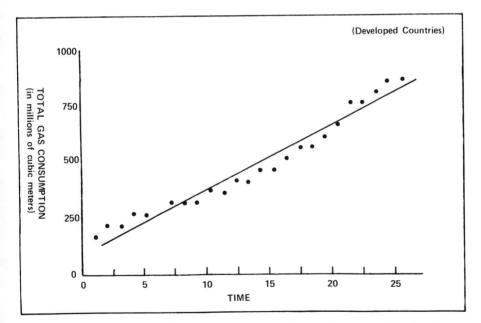

Figure 5–5.   Total Gas Consumption versus Time, Developed Countries

The regression equation for Fig. 5.5 is

$$C = 81.740 + 28.949T$$
$$(18.32)\quad\ (1.23)$$

$R^2 = .9600$

Average proportional deviation $= .1010$

D.W. $= .1133$ (Durbin-Watson test score for autocorrelation)

Standard deviation of regression $= 44.433$

When we regress total consumption on population, we get Figure 5–6.

$$C = 2{,}097{,}071 + 3{,}824.209P$$
$$(121.10)\qquad (180.65)$$

$R^2 = .9512$

Average proportional deviation $= 1.064$

 D.W. $= .1080$

Standard deviation of regression $= 49.080$

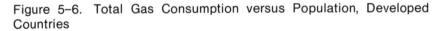

Figure 5–6. Total Gas Consumption versus Population, Developed Countries

As would be expected, the data for developed countries indicate a direct linear relationship between gas consumption and time and between gas consumption and population. This is even more logical since time and population are also directly related.

The relationships for the developing countries are shown in Figures 5–7 through 5–10. The same variables are used as for the developed countries. The relationships found are more complicated, however. The first regression run was between total gas consumption and time. The following equation is obtained for Fig. 5.7:

$$C = -11.62 + 3.27T$$
$$(3.66) \quad (0.24)$$

$R^2 = 0.8849$

Average proportional deviation $=$ N.A.

D.W. $=$ N.A.

Standard deviation of regression $= 8.875$

Obviously, from the correlational data and from the graph in Figure 5–7, the linear relationship is not quite the right explanation for the data. If, however, we plot a much better logarithmic function (in base 10), a much better fit is observed.

The relationship between log (total consumption) versus time for the developing countries is as follows (see Figure 5–8):

$$\log C = \quad 0.632 \quad + \quad 0.054T$$
$$(0.011) \quad (0.0007)$$

$R^2 = .9959$

Average proportional deviation $= 0.171$

D.W. $= 1.614$

Standard deviation of regression $= 0.026$

From the Figure 5–8 graph we can see that this equation provides a much better explanation of the data. This exponential fit is intuitively explained by the fact that as a developing country's population increases, the amount of

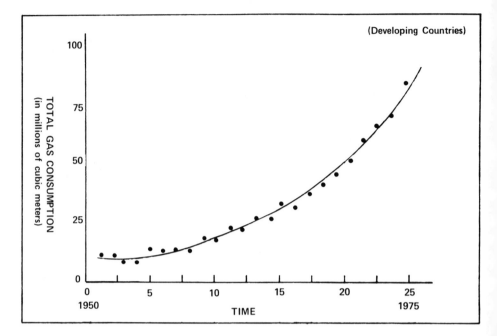

Figure 5-7.   Total Gas Consumption versus Time, Developing Countries

natural gas it consumes increases in a less than proportionate amount because:

1.   Not many people can afford gas at first.
2.   Technology lags behind population growth.
3.   It will take time for the local gas companies to realize the additional demand; and so on.

This relation will be directly observed in the next regression between total consumption versus total population.

$$C = -103.174 + 91.75P$$
$$(10.77) \qquad (7.26)$$

$R^2 = 0.8742$

Average proportional deviation $= 0.568$

D.W. $= 0.925$

Standard deviation of regression $= 9.276$

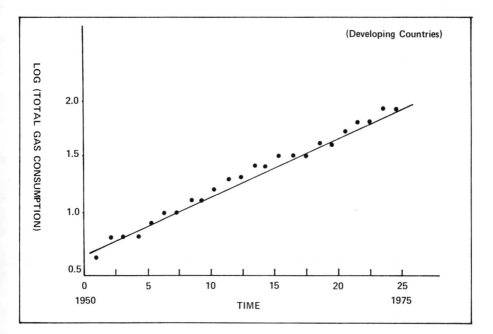

Figure 5–8. Log (Total Gas Consumption) versus Time, Developing Countries

Once again it is apparent that a linear relationship is not adequate to explain the data. When the regression is carried out on a logarithmic scale, the data indicate a much improved correlation. The R^2 improves from 87 percent to 96 percent. (The R^2 is the proportion of the total variation in consumption explained by fitting the regression.) This equation is given by

$$\text{Log } C = -0.848 + 1.491P$$
$$\phantom{\text{Log } C = }(0.095) \quad (0.064)$$

$R^2 = 0.9597$

Average proportional deviation $= 0.054$

D.W. $= 2.36$

Standard deviation of regression $= 0.0814$

From Figures 5–5 through 5–10, it is quite clear that simple formulations worked very well. However, if prices change drastically, the demand for energy will change; then it will be necessary for us to consider the price variables in the equations. Using the regression equation, we predicted the

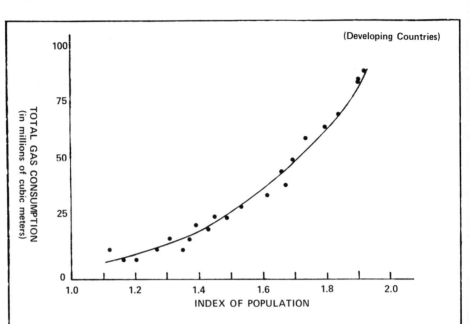

Figure 5–9. Total Gas Consumption versus Population, Developing
Countries

demand for 1978 and compared it with the actual demand. The differences
are not significant.

National

After concentrating on the international scene, we turn our attention to the
national (U.S.) energy demand. We collected data for each state for the
period 1960–1969 and hypothesized the following regression relations:

$$E_N = a + b_1 P + b_2 I, \qquad\qquad (5.1)$$

$$E_N = a + b_1 P + b_2 I^*, \qquad\qquad (5.2)$$

where E_N is energy consumption in BTUs, P is population, I is personal
income in actual dollars, and I^* is personal income in 1958 dollars. Table 5–
5 summarizes these results.

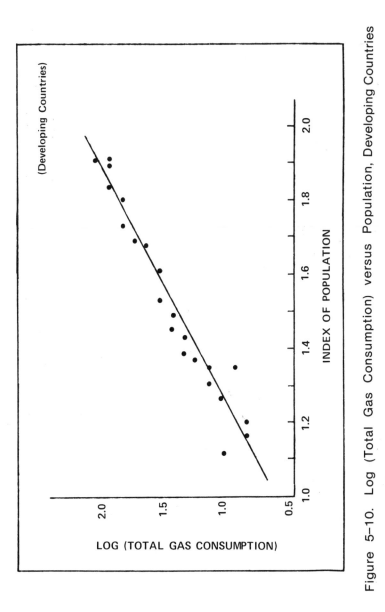

Figure 5–10. Log (Total Gas Consumption) versus Population, Developing Countries

Table 5-5 Results of Regression Analysis: Energy Consumption

$E_N = f(P,I) = a + b_1 (P) + b_2 (I),$

where E_N = total energy consumption (trillion BTUs)
   P = population (thousands)
   I = personal income in current dollars (100 million)
   I^* = personal income in 1958 dollars (100 million)
   $E_N = a + b_1 P + b_2 I^*$

	Y Intercept	Regression Coefficient b_1	Regression Coefficient b_2	R^2	R^2 (Equation 5.2)
United States	-15,716	.2215 (.0670)	4.1664 (.4189)	.997	.997
Maine	101	.0502 (.6109)	3.3161 (.8744)	.694	.563
Vermont	.4	.0978 (.2703)	2.4500 (1.9481)	.949	.956
Massachusetts	-3,745	.9059 (.3580)	.2524 (1.2685)	.941	.941
Connecticut	183	.0436 (.0561)	2.5101 (.4158)	.988	.977
New York	-2,610	.2512 (.1051)	2.5551 (.4318)	.974	.985
New Jersey	-476	.2152 (.0802)	1.9379 (.5902)	.983	.977
Ohio	-2,806	.4845 (.3656)	2.9786 (1.9721)	.972	.988
Indiana	-1,740	.6061 (.3565)	4.5628 (1.8384)	.995	.993
Illinois	-2,701	.4427 (.1289)	2.4785 (.6274)	.993	.994
Michigan	-3,967	.6984 (.2236)	1.2223 (1.3312)	.991	.992
Wisconsin	-1,424	.4839 (.1256)	3.7020 (.5919)	.995	.993

Minnesota	−622	.3116 (.4115)	3.4625 (1.7374)	.973	.980
Iowa	−5,053	1.9636(1.3417)	4.0678 (.7318)	.970	.963
Missouri	−210	.1334 (.3126)	4.7036 (1.5676)	.969	.937
South Dakota	−38	.0630 (.3408)	9.1945 (2.1277)	.864	.726
Nebraska	−51	.1157 (.1853)	5.9918 (.3880)	.972	.964
Kansas	131	.0660 (.2801)	7.0116 (.8323)	.970	.918
Maryland and DC	110	.0403 (.0758)	2.3184 (.5825)	.973	.962
Virginia	−219	.2116 (.0988)	1.9025 (.8048)	.975	.981
North Carolina	−1,358	.3864 (.2285)	3.8036 (1.7760)	.981	.984
South Carolina	146	.0356 (.1821)	4.4700 (1.5432)	.970	.942
Georgia	47	.0466 (.0558)	3.3076 (.4947)	.993	.992
Florida	−862	.2766 (.0599)	2.5143 (.6520)	.993	.994
Kentucky	−2,977	1.1094 (.3981)	4.8234 (1.7235)	.972	.963
Tennessee	513	.0047 (.3252)	5.2016 (2.337)	.891	.894
Alabama	487	.0750 (.1554)	8.7429 (1.0136)	.985	.971
Mississippi	129	.0762 (.2473)	13.4607 (1.5208)	.985	.966
Texas	1,964	.0575 (.2802)	8.7254 (2.3141)	.962	.966
Montana	−480	.8962 (.3144)	6.4421 (.8394)	.922	.832
Colorado	−14	.1647 (.1680)	3.9416 (1.5141)	.968	.965
Arizona	41	.0824 (.0435)	4.2624 (.5503)	.988	.982
Utah	86	.0877 (.2784)	5.8778 (2.7817)	.895	.927
California	−187	.1298 (.0371)	2.6164 (.3343)	.995	.996

Note: Standard errors are in parentheses.

Initially, I had expected the regression coefficients to be fairly consistent for states within a particular region of the nation. This was not the case. Instead, there seemed to be fairly large, unexplainable differences. These results may be due to the short time frame (ten years); the oversimplicity of the model; or a changing environment (birthrate decline, low energy costs, high inflation and growth).

In the second formulation we stipulated:

$$E_L = a + b_1 P + b_2 I, \qquad (5.3)$$

$$E_L = a + b_1 P + b_2 I^*, \qquad (5.4)$$

where E_L is total electric energy sales in kilowatt-hours, P is population, I is personal income (actual), and I^* is personal income in 1958 dollars. The regression equations are shown in Table 5–6. The data used in Table 5–6 refer to the time period 1960–1969.

The value of R^2 was above .8 for all states except two—Kentucky and Wyoming. The standard error of the regression coefficient (b_2) was satisfactory for all states except Vermont and Illinois. Both these states had a very low stable population growth, one well below the national average. This very flat rate may have distorted the regression analysis. Population showed a better correlation with total electric sales than with total energy sales in the models used. The standard errors for the population regression coefficients were also larger than is normally acceptable.

The value of R^2, the coefficient of determination, was above .8 for all the states except Maine, Rhode Island, and Oklahoma. The standard errors of the regression coefficients were satisfactory for most states. The correlation between energy consumption and personal income was good, except as just noted. On the other hand, although population showed some correlation with energy consumption, the standard errors were large and the signs of the regression coefficients inconsistent.

A comparison between the two equations (5.1 and 5.2) showed personal income (actual) correlated better with energy consumption (equation 5.1). This was an expected result since personal income (actual) is both a measure of the amount of money available to be spent and a measure of production. Attempts to use disposable personal income in place of personal income (actual) generally had poorer results. Again, this was expected since disposable income, though a better measure of the amount of money available to be spent, would be a lesser measure of production.

Attempts to use a logarithmic model $\log E_N = f(\log P, \log I)$ also failed to show any improvement in R^2. Therefore, the results of this model are not shown.

Personal income (actual) again had a better correlation than did personal income in 1958 dollars. The regression coefficient (b_2) showed some regional consistency, but large deviations were present. Overall, personal income correlated well with electric energy sales, and the model had a good fit.

Using equations 5.1–5.4, we predicted the demand in 1977 and compared it with the actual demand. The difference was not significant.

The results in Tables 5–5 and 5–6 clearly show that even when we do not consider the effect of price, energy demand can be predicted fairly well by using population and income. The prices, industrial structure composition of products, public policies, emergence of alternative sources of energy, and so on are important, but only when a particular threshold level has been achieved. Energy prices in the United States have traditionally been quite low. Energy consumption increased despite a small but steady increase in price. However, the threshold level probably was not reached until 1973. Thus for data after 1973 the price variable needs to be used.

We took some individual states, such as Florida, Illinois, New Jersey, Texas, Vermont, Delaware, California, and Michigan, and used such independent variables as population income, number of motor vehicles registered, number of tourists, miles driven, and so on, and obtained excellent regression results. To limit the size of the book, the results are not shown here.

New York State Counties

Then we considered the situation in New York State. A detailed study of New York State has been reported elsewhere (Chatterji 1977). Here we are giving only some results. They refer to the relationship of the consumption of electricity in New York State counties with some socioeconomic characteristics. The consumption of electricity was examined both at the aggregate level (total consumption) and at the level of its components—namely, residential and public authorities, and commercial and industrial ones. The study was conducted separately for all counties in New York State, first including and then excluding the five boroughs of New York City.

The basic method of analysis for each consuming sector was to calculate three sets of regression equations. The first set used one independent variable, the second set used two, and the third set used three or more independent variables. An attempt was made to avoid inclusion of inter-dependent variables in the same regression equation. Because of the nature of the data, however, it is possible that some of the equations are deficient in this respect.

The variables used in this study are as follows:

ELECT	Total consumption of electricity (kwh/yr), 1976
ELECR	Consumption of electricity in the residential and public authorities sector (kwh/yr), 1976
ELECIC	Consumption of electricity in the industrial and commercial sector (kwh/yr), 1976
Pop:	Population (1975)
Emp:	Total employment (units), 1975
Pay:	Total payroll (millions of dollars), 1975
Man I:	Manufacturing income (millions of dollars), 1975
PI:	Personal income (millions of dollars), 1974
Value:	Value added by manufacturing (millions of dollars), 1972
Tunits:	Total housing units, 1970
Sunits:	Single structure units, 1970
PAC:	Percentage of housing units with air conditioning, 1970
Md Fam I:	Median family income (dollars), 1969
Den:	Population density (persons per square mile), 1975
Value M:	Value added, primary metals (millions of dollars), 1972
Value C:	Value added in chemicals and allied products (millions of dollars), 1972
R Sales:	Total retail sales (thousands of dollars), 1972

The regression equations are shown in Tables 5–7 through 5–13. (Note that the dependent variables is not the total demand. Rather, it is the proportion of the demand in ith county to total New York State demand. The

Table 5-6 Results of Regression Analysis: Electric Sales

$E_L = f(P,I) = a + b_1 (P) + b_2 (I),$

where E_L = total electricity sales (10 million KW-hrs)
P = population (thousands)
I = personal income in current dollars (100 million)

	k^2	Y Intercept	b_1 (Standard Error)	b_2 (Standard Error)
United States	.9997	−100,821	.629 (.076)	14.0 (.475)
Maine	.998	−929	.915 (.185)	16.3 (.265)
New Hampshire	.991	−43	.073 (.227)	12.7 (1.95)
Massachusetts	.999	−3,058	.619 (.161)	8.53 (5.70)
Rhode Island	.998	−558	.678 (.196)	8.86 (.696)
Connecticut	.999	−657	.268 (.071)	9.94 (.525)
New York	.994	−7,472	.516 (.135)	7.89 (.557)
New Jersey	.999	−2,650	.480 (.074)	9.06(.545)
Pennsylvania	.995	−17,852	1.64 (.736)	13.2 (2.10)
Ohio	.970	−1,453	.528 (.832)	9.47(4.49)
Illinois	.805	−26,685	2.97 (2.48)	.481(12.1)
Michigan	.998	−1,847	.283 (.277)	13.13(1.63)
Wisconsin	.995	−2,374	.643 (.337)	12.8 (1.39)
Minnesota	.996	−4,852	1.48 (.482)	9.12(2.04)
Iowa	.988	−8,836	3.22 (2.41)	13.1 (1.31)
Missouri	.997	−6,041	1.43 (.321)	11.3 (1.61)
North Dakota	.900	−140	.162 (.521)	15.6 (2.33)

(Continued next page)

Table 5-6 (continued)

Nebraska	.951	−344	.286 (.596)	14.4 (1.25)
Kansas	.979	−408	.275 (.475)	13.3 (1.35)
Deleware	.986	−910	1.93 (.524)	14.1 (5.56)
Maryland and DC	.998	−630	.004 (.108)	13.9 (.832)
North Carolina	.999	−2,731	.589 (.225)	21.6 (1.75)
South Carolina	.998	−1,555	.743 (.305)	23.8 (2.58)
Florida	.998	−3,382	.708 (.139)	14.7 (1.51)
Tennessee	.986	−3,393	1.76 (.563)	13.85(4.04)
Alabama	.996	−3,126	.968 (.384)	32.9 (2.50)
Mississippi	.998	−493	.127 (.176)	29.3 (1.06)
Arkansas	.996	−652	.282 (.203)	26.5 (1.68)
Oklahoma	.984	−2,774	1.19 (.479)	15.0 (2.76)
Texas	.988	−11,222	1.14 (.217)	19.5 (1.74)
Idaho	.967	−2,628	4.15 (1.88)	29.9 (8.28)
Colorado	.992	165	.383 (.230)	11.3 (2.08)
New Mexico	.988	−720	.698 (.190)	17.7 (1.05)
Arizona	.988	32	.043 (.173)	19.7 (2.18)
Utah	.998	−445	.596 (.081)	10.0 (.819)
Nevada	.911	−50	.925 (.455)	7.51(7.15)
Oregon	.997	−2,220	1.54 (.407)	21.7 (3.42)
California	.994	−4,350	.270 (.166)	13.0 (1.49)
Alaska	.982	−100	.437 (.182)	5.63(1.43)
Hawaii				

Note: Standard errors are in parentheses.

Table 5-7   Single Explanatory Variable Equations

Dependent variable: ELECT/TELECT—Total
consumption of electricity in county i as a proportion of the total of all counties.

Explanatory Variables (County as a Proportion of the Total)	a	b_1	$t(b_1)$	R^2
1. Population	.0041	.8021	11.0793	.7065
2. Employment	.0040	1.0390	13.2583	.7751
3. Manufacturing income	.0040	.6237	12.8951	.7653
4. Payroll	.0046	1.1141	12.6500	.7583
5. Personal income	.0056	.4439	10.2661	.6739
6. Value added by manufacture	.0030	1.1342	14.1421	.7968
7. Total housing stock	.0047	.8106	9.7754	.6520
8. One unit structure	.0079	180.2082	8.7678	.6012
9. Value added by primary metals	.0102	.1668	5.0465	.3331
10. Value added by chemicals and allied products	.0079	.4804	8.7678	.6012
11. Retail sales	.0043	3.9682	10.9023	.6998

Table 5-8   Single Explanatory Variable Equations

Dependent variable: ELECR/TELECR—Residential and
public authority consumption of electricity in the county as a proportion of the totals of all counties.

Explanatory Variables	a	b_1	$t(b_1)$	R^2
1. Population	.0053	1.6671	14.8906	.8130
2. Payroll	.0079	2.0968	11.3238	.7154
3. Personal income	.0099	.8340	9.3919	.6336
4. Total housing stock	.0064	1.7107	13.1998	.7736
5. One unit structure	.0165	251.4807	4.8073	.3118

Table 5-9   Single Explanatory Variable Equation

Dependent variable: $\dfrac{\text{ELECIC}}{\text{TELECIC}}$ —total

commercial and industrial consumption of electricity in county i as a proportion of the total of all counties

	Explanatory Variables				
1.	Population	.0046	.7343	7.8239	.5455
2.	Employment	.0043	.9854	9.5685	.6423
3.	Payroll	.0048	1.0551	9.2482	.6265
4.	Manufacturing income	.0036	.6341	11.6997	.7286
5.	Personal income	.0061	.4039	7.3431	.5139
6.	Value added by manufacture	.0024	1.1757	13.7995	.7888
7.	Value added by primary metals	.0095	.2000	6.3441	.4411
8.	Value added by chemicals and allied products	.0071	.5311	10.3378	.6769
9.	Total retail sales	.0049	3.5979	7.5820	.5299

Table 5-10   Equations with Two Independent Variables

Dependent variable: $\dfrac{\text{ELECR}_i}{\text{TELECR}}$ —Residential and public authority consumption of electricity in a county as a proportion of the total of all counties

				R^2
1.	$\dfrac{\text{ELECR}}{\text{TELECR}} = .0053 +$	1.5081 Pop + (7.0314)	.1057 PI (.8697)	.8158
2.	$\dfrac{\text{ELECR}}{\text{TELECR}} = .0053 +$	1.6858 Pop − (11.5826)	7.2088 Sunit (− .2034)	.8132
3.	$\dfrac{\text{ELECR}}{\text{TELECR}} = .0077 +$	2.3802 Pay (8.6964)	− 69.3768 Sunit (−1.3953)	.7261
4.	$\dfrac{\text{ELECR}}{\text{TELECR}} = .0060 +$	.2718 PI + (2.4610)	1.3081 Tunits (6.3795)	.7980

Table 5–11   Equations with Two Independent Variables

Dependent variables: $\dfrac{\text{ELECIC}_i}{\text{TELECIC}}$ —Industrial and commercial consumption of

electricity in a county as a proportion of the total of all counties

			R^2
1. $\dfrac{\text{ELECIC}}{\text{TELECIC}}$ = .0035 +	.0854 Pop + (.6442)	.5808 ManI (5.8660)	.7308
2. $\dfrac{\text{ELECIC}}{\text{TELECIC}}$ = .0024 +	.0067 Pop + (.0581)	1.1683 Value (7.5882)	.7888
3. $\dfrac{\text{ELECIC}}{\text{TELECIC}}$ = .0048 +	.3631 Pop + (4.0708)	.3826 ValueC (6.6074)	.7574
4. $\dfrac{\text{ELECIC}}{\text{TELECIC}}$ = .0048 +	.5267 Emp + (4.2156)	.3283 ValueC (5.0051)	.7617
5. $\dfrac{\text{ELECIC}}{\text{TELECIC}}$ = .0052 +	.5368 Pay + (3.8162)	.3382 ValueC (4.9654)	.7498
6. $\dfrac{\text{ELECIC}}{\text{TELECIC}}$ = .0051 +	.3915 ValueC + (6.2816)	1.6169 RSales (3.3878)	.7373

equations were estimated as a cross-section for sixty-two counties for the year 1976. R^2 and t values are mostly satisfactory.

In this study we have used some simple formulations to forecast energy consumption on the international, national, state, and local levels. Most of these formulations gave good results, but this does not mean that more sophisticated econometric and management science techniques will not improve the situation. Both approaches are necessary. The decision to choose one method depends on the cost of research and the benefit of the findings.

Table 5-12   Equations with Two Independent Variables

Dependent variable. $\dfrac{\text{ELECT}}{\text{TELECT}}$ —Total consumption of electricity in a county as a proportion of the total of all counties

		R^2
1. $\dfrac{\text{ELECT}}{\text{TELECT}} = .0039 +$	.8483 Emp + (4.2673) .8340 RSales (1.0438)	.7799
2. $\dfrac{\text{ELECT}}{\text{TELECT}} = .0035 +$	.4599 ManI + (5.8035) .2832 Tunits (2.5384)	.7921
3. $\dfrac{\text{ELECT}}{\text{TELECT}} = .0044 +$	.2628 PI + (4.0478) .4212 Tunits (3.4942)	.7879
4. $\dfrac{\text{ELECT}}{\text{TELECT}} = .0047 +$	.5342 Tunits + (6.3082) .2782 ValueC (5.3241)	.7779
5. $\dfrac{\text{ELECT}}{\text{TELECT}} = .0026 +$	.3064 Pop + (3.0688) .7959 Value (5.9862)	.8290
6. $\dfrac{\text{ELECT}}{\text{TELECT}} = .0042 +$	.5570 Pop + (7.2898) 94.7312 Sunits (5.0900)	.8067

Table 5-13   Equations with Three or More Independent Variables

		R^2
1. $\dfrac{\text{ELECT}}{\text{TELECT}} = .0045 +$ .1526 PI (2.3933) + .3472 Tunits (3.2981) + .0461 ValueM (2.1176)		
+ .1691 ValueC (2.8062)		.8147
2. $\dfrac{\text{ELECIC}}{\text{TELECI}} = .0052 +$ .4500 Pay (3.3823) + .0743 ValueM + (3.0819) .2819 (4.3000)		.7904

Note: Dependent variable is expressed as a proportion of the sum of all counties.

References

Chatterji, Manas. 1977. "A Study of the Structure of Growth in Some U.S. Cities." *Northeast Regional Science Review* 7, no. 2:218–38.
_____. 1981. "Health Care Cost Containment in New York State: An Econometric Study." Mimeograph.
Klein, Lawrence, and Goldberger, A. S. 1954. *An Econometric Model of the United States.* Amsterdam: North-Holland.
Leontief, Wasily W. 1977. *The Future of the World Economy: A United Nations Study.* New York: Oxford University Press.
World Energy Consumption, 1976. Report to the United Nations.
World Energy Statistics, 1950–1975. Report to the United Nations.

Bibliography

Adams, F. G., and Griffin, J. M. 1972. "An Economic-Linear Programming Model of the U.S. Petroleum Refining Industry." *Journal of the American Statistical Association* 67: 339, 542–551.
Carter, A. P. 1974. "Energy, Environment, and Economic Growth." *The Bell Journal of Economics and Management Science* 5, no. 2:578–592.
Chatterji, Manas. (1982). "Regional and Interregional Energy-Econometric Model Building." in W. Buhr and P. Friedrich (eds.) *Regional Development under Regional Stagnation.* Nomos Verlag, Baden Baden.
Chatterji, M. 1979a. "Regional Stagnation and Energy Crisis." In *Proceedings, Advanced Studies Institute in Regional Science,* Siegen, Germany (in German).
_____. 1979b. "An Econometric Model of New York State," *Applied Mathematical Modeling,* 3, 6:441–454.
Chatterji, M., & Van Rompuy, Paul, eds. 1975. *Environment, Regional Science, and Interregional Modeling,* Germany: Springer Verlag.
_____. 1976. *Energy, Regional Science, and Public Policy,* Springer Verlag, Germany.
Glassey, C. Roger. 1978. "Price Sensitive Consumer Demands in Energy Modelling—A Quadratic Programming Approach to the Analysis of Some Federal Energy Agency Policy." *Management Science* 24, no. 9:878–886.
Goettle, R. J., et al. 1977. "An Integrated Multi-Regional Energy and Interindustry Model of the United States." Upton, N.Y.: Brookhaven National Laboratory. Mimeograph.
Griffin, James M. 1974. "The Effects of Higher Prices on Electricity Consumption." *Bell Journal of Economics and Management Science* 5, no. 2:515–540.
Griffin, James M., and Gregory, Paul R. 1976. "An Intercountry Translog Model of Energy Substitution Responses." *American Economics Review* 66, no. 5:845–857.

Halvorsen, Robert. 1977. "Energy Substitution in U.S. Manufacturing." *Review of Economics and Statistics* 59:381–388.

———. 1978. "Energy Policy and U.S. Economic Growth." *American Economics Review* 68, no. 2:118–123.

Hudson, Edward A., and Jorgenson, Dale W. 1974. "U.S. Energy Policy and Economic Growth, 1975–2000." *Bell Journal of Economics and Management Science* 5, no. 2:461–515.

Kennedy, M. 1976. "An Economic Model of the World Oil Market." *Bell Journal of Economics and Management Science* 5, no. 2:540–578.

Klaassen, L., and Paelinck, J. 1977. *Long Run Energy Policies in an Economic Setting, Foundation of Empirical Economic Research,* no. 12, Netherlands Economic Institute.

Kosobud, Richard F., and Stokes, Houston H. 1978. "Economic Analysis of OPEC Using a Markov Chain Model." *Journal of Energy and Development* 4, no. 2:378–400.

Kraft, John, Kraft, Arthur, and Reiser, Eugene. 1976. "A National Energy Demand Simulation Model." In A. Askin and John Kraft, (eds.), *Econometric Dimensions of Energy Demand and Supply,* Lexington, Mass.: Lexington Books, D.C. Heath and Company.

Macavoy, P. W. 1967. *Economic Strategy for Developing Nuclear Fast Breeder Reactors.* Cambridge, Mass.: MIT Press.

Manne, A. S. 1976. "A Mode for Energy Technology Assessment," *Bell Journal of Economics* 7, no. 2:379–406.

Mead, Walter J. 1979. "The Performance of Government in Energy Regulations." *American Economic Review,* 69, no. 2:352–356.

Miernyk, M. 1976. "Some Regional Impacts of the Rising Costs of Energy," *Papers of the Regional Science Association* 37:213–227.

Nijkamp, Peter. 1977. *Theory and Application of Environmental Economics.* Amsterdam: North-Holland.

Paelinck, J., and Wagenaar, S. *Multiregional Sectoral Developments and Energy Price Differentials.* Foundation of Empirical Economic Research, no. 12, Netherlands Economic Institute.

Pindyck, Robert S. (1979) "Interfuel Substitution and Industrial Demand for Energy: An International Comparison." *Review of Economics and Statistics* 61, no. 2:169–179.

Schinnar, A. P. 1976. "A Multidimensional Accounting Model for Demographic and Economic Planning Interaction." *Environment and Planning A* 8:455–475.

Searl, Milton, F., ed. (1973) *Energy Modeling: Art, Science, Practice.* Washington, D.C.: Resources for the Future, March.

Stone, R. 1971. *Demographic Accounting and Model Building.* Paris: OECD.

Taylor, L. D. 1974. "The Demand for Electricity: A Survey." *Bell Journal of Economics and Management Science* 6:74–110.

United Nations. 1972–1976. *World Energy Supplies.* U.N. Series U, no. 21.

Uri, Noel. 1975. "A Spatial Equilibrium Model for Electrical Energy." *Journal of Regional Science* 15, no. 3:323–333.

Wavermans, Leonard. (Review by D. Kendrick). 1973. "Natural Gas and National Policy: A Linear Programming Model of North American Natural Gas Flows." *Bell Journal of Economics and Management Science* 4, no. 2:690–692.

6 POLITICAL DIMENSIONS OF REGIONAL ECONOMIC DEVELOPMENT

Military Expenditure and Economic Development

The developing countries face great challenges today. Population growth is excessive, resources are scarce, technology is outdated, the labor force is untrained, and capital formation is weak because of low income. These countries pay for imported capital since they must pay for the high import cost of energy. On the other hand, they allocate large sums of money for military expenditures even though their own people are starving.

Most developing countries are either caught in the power struggle of the superpowers or involved in feuds with neighboring countries. For this reason they must maintain continuously large armies and arsenals of weapons, which they buy from the developed countries at the expense of economic development. These countries should scale down military expenditures drastically and release resources to feed their own people. Although this may sound like a naive or utopian statement, everyone agrees that this is the only solution. The irony of the situation is that contesting countries can have the same level of relative security with much less defense expenditure.

Economic growth in the developing countries is very much contingent on the political realities of international and interregional conflict. In this

193

chapter we shall discuss different tools of conflict analysis and solution
procedures that can be linked directly with economic models.

Military Expenditure on the Indian Subcontinent:
An Example

Over the last decade or so, there has been a great increase in the literature of
conflict resolution models. More and more realities of the world have been
taken into account, and restrictive assumptions have been relaxed. The
testing of these models is becoming easier with the development of new
concepts and methods to measure qualitative variables. However, the scope
of these models can be enlarged in at least two respects. First, the spatial
relations of the contending parties—that is, the geopolitical aspects of the
conflict—can be considered. For example, when we look at the map of the
Indian subcontinent, we find that the geographical boundaries of two other
major powers—China and the USSR—meet the boundaries of India and
Pakistan. In considering political relations between India and Pakistan, this
factor is of crucial importance. The second factor is the political relationship
that exists between the contending parties. The rate of economic growth,
population growth rates, internal peace, and stability are some of the many
factors that greatly influence a country's foreign relations. This is particularly
true for Indo-Pakistan relations.

The case of India and Pakistan offers an excellent field of study in which
we can apply modern game-theoretical approaches to analyze their mutual
relationship. Here we have two countries that are interdependent from
geographic, economic, political, and social viewpoints. They have much to
gain by cooperating and much to loose by quarreling. Through cooperation,
the great powers can act as a moderating influence.

The emergence of India and Pakistan as two nations on the Indian
subcontinent ushered in a new phenomenon in Asia. Before 1947 these two
were one country, whose people struggled together for freedom from the
British rule. When the British decided to leave, the Moslem minority,
apprehensive of the Hindu majority, demanded a separate state. After bloody
riots, the country was divided. This division resulted in a complete
breakdown in the social, economic, and political system.

India has now about 650 million people, of whom 10 percent are Moslem.
Of Pakistan's 115 million people, most are Moslems. The enmity between
Hindus and Moslems on the subcontinent has not ended with the division of
the country. These groups are now archenemies who spend millions of rupees
on defense preparations. They have already fought three significant wars,

with extensive loss of lives and resources. Recently, the situation has worsened again. Any sensible person will agree that the very existence of these two countries depends on their mutual cooperation and friendship rather than on war or hostility. This friendship can be achieved in many ways. It must exist on the governmental and personal level, as well as through the auspices of other countries. One significant step would be in the field of disarmament, and this study throws some light on this issue. The intention is not to offer an easy solution, since conflict between nations is too complicated a matter to be solved easily. Rather, we are presenting an exercise in conflict resolution that takes the realities into consideration as far as possible.

Following Richardson (1960), we assume that there are three factors related to the arms race: (1) mutual suspicion and mistrust, (2) cost of military expenditure, and (3) grievances. Let us consider these factors for India and Pakistan in the context of their relationship and of other internal and external variables.

It is interesting to note that as far as India is concerned, there are two fronts to guard: Pakistan and China. India is suspicious of both. Thus it can be assumed that the rate of change in its military expenditure will depend on the military expenditures of Pakistan and China in the previous period. The lag in time period is appropriate since responses are never instantaneous, and there is always a time lag in the intelligence reports. A one-year time lag is assumed. So we have the following relation:

$$\frac{dm_{1t}}{dt} = kM_{2(t-1)} + nM_{3(t-1)}, \tag{6.1}$$

where M_{1t} = military expenditure (in millions of rupees) of India for the time period t.

$M_{2(t-1)}$ = military expenditure (in millions of rupees) of Pakistan in the time period $(t-1)$.

$M_{3(t-1)}$ = military expenditure (in millions of rupees or an index number) of the People's Republic of China in the period $(t-1)$.

The L.H.S. of equation 6.1 denotes the rate of change of Indian military expenditure; and k and n are positive constants, which, following Richardson's terminology, can be called *defense coefficients*. It is difficult to obtain data for China's defense expenditures. In their absence, we can try to have some index numbers or else use some proxy variables. Equation 6.1 represents India's mistrust and suspicion of Pakistan and China. Although it is true that mistrust is a qualitative aspect of state of mind, we are assuming that military expenditure is a satisfactory yardstick for measuring it.

The second factor involved in the arms race is the cost of keeping up the defenses. It can be assumed that a significant portion of the resources devoted to military efforts is complete wasted. Some military expenditure, such as road building, may have some economic value. It is not the purpose of this analysis to identify military items as useful and useless, nor do we want to make any estimate of them at this stage. Second, since the investment resources of India are limited, military expenditure implies sacrificing economic development in terms of an increase in gross national product that would have been achieved if the resources were used for national economic development. The third factor is the amount of benefit that would accrue to India if these two countries become friendly and cooperate in the field of international trade. There are many commodities, such as jute, tea, textiles, and so on, that would appreciably increase the income of both countries if they cooperate. These three factors have been combined in the following equation:

$$O_{1t} = a_1 M_{1t} + b_1 Y_{1t} + c_1 T_{1t}, \qquad (6.2)$$

where O_{1t} = the cost of defense.

   Y_{1t} = gross national product of India at time period t (GNP).

   T_{1t} = the foreign exchange income of India at time period t.

   a_1 = Constant that shows what percentage of the military expenditure can be treated as waste.

   b_1 = the percentage of Indian GNP that could have increased if there were a friendly relationship between the two countries. In the extreme case, b_1 may be taken as the percentage of Indian GNP that could have increased if there were no military spending. Since such a utopian situation is nowhere in sight in the near future, we shall take b_1 as the percentage of GNP that could be increased if the defense expenditure is kept at a normal level. We shall not confine ourselves to discussing the definition of *normal* but shall assume that such a figure has been reached by consensus.

   c_1 = a constant that shows the percentage of foreign exchange income that could be added with mutual cooperation between these countries.

The fourth factor related to conflict is the grievances. For simplicity let us assume that India's grievances against Pakistan consist of two parts: (1) Pakistan's alleged collusion with China and (2) allegedly Pakistani-inspired rebellions in tribal areas. As before, we do not want to verify the truth or falsity of these allegations. We take them as given. These two sources of grievances are assumed to be measurable in money terms. Some portion of it—say, military help from China to Pakistan—is measurable. The following equation then represents the fourth factor:

$$Q_{1t} = d_1 A_{2t}^c + e_1 I_{2t}, \qquad (6.3)$$

where Q_{1t} = the grievance of India against Pakistan at time period t.

A_{25}^c = military help from China to Pakistan in the time period t (in millions of rupees).

I_{2t} = Help (assumed to be expressed in terms of money value) given by Pakistan to the tribal rebels (in millions of rupees).

d_1 and c_1 = respective weights given by the Indian government to match these threats.

These constants (d_1, c_1) can also show what amount of money must be spent by India to face these dual fronts. The grievance equation involves some qualitative aspects that are assumed to be expressed in quantitative terms. It is easy to identify other costs and grievances, but for the sake of simplicity we assume that all these items can be expressed through the variables we have considered.

Combining the three factors together, we have

$$\frac{dM_{1t}}{dt} = kM_{2(t-1)} + nM_{3(t-1)} - O_{1(t-1)} Q_{1(t-1)}, \qquad (6.4)$$

which states that the rate of change in Indian military expenditure equals the sum total of the three factors in the previous period. Substituting the values of $O_{1(t-1)}$ and $Q_{1(t-1)}$ from equations 6.2 and 6.3, respectively, into equation 6.4, we get

$$\frac{dM_{1t}}{dt} = kM_{2(t-1)} + nM_{3(t-1)} - a_1 M_{1(t-1)} - b_1 Y_{1(t-1)}$$
$$- c_1 T_{1(t-1)} + d_1 A_{2(t-1)}^c + e_1 I_{2(t-1)}. \qquad (6.5)$$

Let us next make the following simplifying assumptions:

$$A_{2t}^c = f_1 M_{3t}, \qquad (6.6)$$

where f_1 is a constant. This equation states that the Chinese help to Pakistan is proportional to Chinese military expenditure.

$$T_{1t} = g_1 Y_{1t}, \qquad (6.7)$$

where g_1 is a constant. This equation states India's foreign exchange income proportional to its GNP.

The third substitution is

$$I_{2t} = h_1 Y_{1t}, \tag{6.8}$$

where h_1 is a constant that states that the grievances are proportional to GNP. The greater the grievance, the greater the portion of GNP set aside to meet these grievances.

Substituting equations 6.6, 6.7, and 6.8 into equation 6.5, we get

$$\frac{dM_{1t}}{dt} = kM_{2(t-1)} + \left(\frac{n}{f_1} + d_1\right) A_{2(t-1)}^c - a_1 M_{1(t-1)}$$
$$- b_1 Y_{1(t-1)} - c_1 g_1 Y_{1(t-1)} + e_1 h_1 Y_{1(t-1)}, \tag{6.9}$$

or

$$\frac{dM_{1t}}{dt} = kM_{2(t-1)} + \left(\frac{n}{f_1} + d_1\right) A_{2(t-1)}^c$$
$$- a_1 M_{1(t-1)} - Y_{1(t-1)}(b_1 + c_1 g_1 - e_1 h_1). \tag{6.10}$$

Let us transform this differential equation into its simplified difference equation form, as follows:

$$M_{1(t-1)} - M_{1t} = kM_{2(t-1)} + \left(\frac{n}{f_1} + d_1\right) A_{2(t-1)}^c \tag{6.11}$$

$$- a_1 M_{1(t-1)} - (b_1 + c_1 g_1 - e_1 h_1) Y_{1(t-1)}, \tag{6.12}$$

or

$$M_{1(t+2)} - M_{1(t+1)} + a_1 M_{1t} = kM_{2t} + \left(\frac{n}{f_1} + d_1\right) A_{2t}^c$$
$$- (b_1 + c_1 g_1 - e_1 h_1) Y_{1t}. \tag{6.13}$$

Equation 6.12 is a linear second-order difference equation of the form

$$Y_{t-2} + A Y_{t+1} Y_t = F(t).$$

We shall work in terms of a difference equation for the sake of simplicity. The difference equation formulation is realistic since the military expenditure decisions are made in several discrete steps rather than through instantaneous changes.

Equation 6.13 can be solved (in difference equation form) by available techniques, and the parameters of the equation can be estimated. Once the parameters are known, the equation can be used to predict the military expenditure as a result of changes in the exogenous variables (see Chatterji 1968).

A Suggested Cooperation Procedure

As mentioned before, international or interregional cooperation rather than competition can lead to a higher or equal level of security with much less expenditure.[a] We have few studies that use the techniques of conflict resolution and social science to show how interstate cooperation can lead to benefits for both parties. For this purpose the feedback system of interregional input-output analysis and recently developed concepts of growth points can be utilized effectively. A case in point is the sharing of river water by two regions. The water of a river can be used for different purposes in different regions. Again, the benefits that accrue as a result of the efficient use in one area can be transmitted to the other part; and a chain reaction can be generated to speed up the process of development. This will also stop the force of separatist interest of any particular state. The way the benefit is increased through cooperation can be explained by the following example.

Consider two contiguous states in India, West Bengal (A) and Bihar (B) sharing a common river basin (say, the Damodar River Basin area). Suppose they are interested in joint development of the area. Two aspects of this development are (1) the generation of power, and (2) irrigation and flood prevention. Let us say that each one has 10 million rupees to invest. The regional planning authority in A may estimate p^a, the rate of growth of its income for a combination of its own investment and that of B. For example, in Figure 6–1, A may estimate for itself an annual increase of gross regional product of Rs 1.59 million (p^a) if it were to undertake a program of Rs 2.5 million in irrigation and Rs 7.5 million in power generation when B divides its investment equally between 1 and 2. Each contour line of Figure 6–1 denotes all combinations of A's and B's expenditure program that yield A the specified level p^a (average annual increase in A's gross regional product). The contour line may be called A's p possibility curve.

---

[a]This discussion is heavily based on Isard (1969, Chapter 7).

If we examine Figure 6–1, we see that as we move vertically along A's possibility surface, the value of p^a increases. This means that as B undertakes more investment in irrigation, A profits more since it can divert more investment in power generation; its agricultural income increases simultaneously, since B's investment in irrigation indirectly benefits A. Assume that B's investment in irrigation prevents floods for A and supplies steady water through canals. Again, for any given expenditure program of B—say, Rs 5 million—we observe that p^a steadily increases up to a certain point and steadily decreases beyond that point. This relationship signifies that up to a certain point a rupee invested in irrigation tends to have a greater impact on A's gross regional product than does a rupee invested in electricity generation. Similar arguments can be made for B.

When the two states are not cooperating, then the equilibrium situation may be depicted by Figure 6–2,

If the initial proposals of the regions are $p^a_2 = $ Rs 8 million and $p^b_2 = $ Rs 9 million, then A's response to B's initial proposal and B's response to A's initial proposal are designated A_1 and B_1, respectively. Once these new proposals have been announced, however, A will respond to B_1 with a new

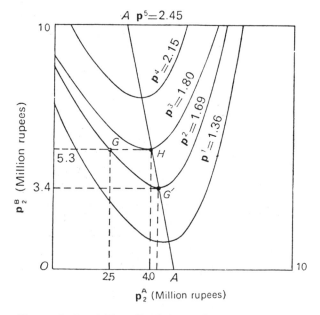

Figure 6–1. A Two-Participant Duopoly Game

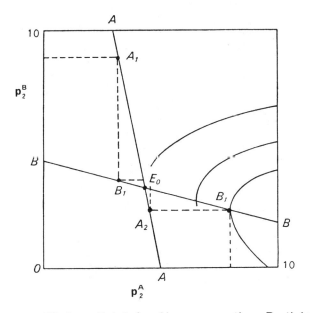

Figure 6-2. Equilibrium Point for Noncooperating Participants in Duopoly

proposal A_2, B will respond to A_1 with B_1, and so on. The process will continue until the equilibrium point E_0. It is evident that although states A and B have reached a stable equilibrium at E_0, both regions could do better. Both could increase their levels of p simultaneously if they get together and agree to shift their program proposals to some point in the shaded area of Figure 6-3. As a first step, each state comes to realize that the relevant range for bargaining over possible joint programs is given by points on arc MM. The point at which the compromise will be made depends on the cooperative arrangement. Suppose we assume the following:

1. In negotiating a joint decision, each region will have full power to veto any proposal.
2. No joint regional investment decision will be proposed that involves investment shifts exceeding any region's shift limit.
3. On any move a set of compatible proposals must be reached, which will then form the base for the next move.
4. No state will be asked to agree to a compromise proposal that does not yield it a p that is at least equal to that achieved by its and the other state's proposals.

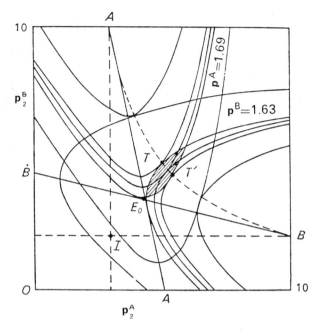

Figure 6-3. Equilibrium Process for Cooperating Participants in Duopoly

With these principles, a better solution E_n will emerge, as shown in Figure 6–4. Thus this example shows how cooperation among the two can lead them to better levels than independent action.

Often when there is some outstanding quarrel between two states, the progress of reconciliation is slow. The same is true in the case of conflicts among different groups. In this case, the central government can act as a third party and, through pressures and rewards, can keep the process moving. In this situation three-person game-theoretical approaches can be utilized profitably.

As in any other country in the world, conflict situations exist in India on international, national, regional, interregional, state, local, and group levels. On the positive side, there also exists an underlying unity of the Indian people through common heritage, goodwill, and determination to solve these conflicts in the framework of a democratic society.

With respect to conflicts and dissensions, these positive aspects should not be forgotten. In fact, they should be emphasized while steps are taken to resolve the conflicts. The efforts in this direction will ultimately result in the

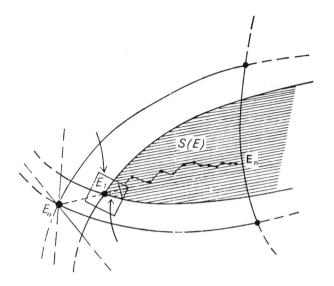

Figure 6–4.   Equilibrium Point for Cooperating Participants in Duopoly

all-around social and economic development of India and will set an example in the family of nations.

In this analysis, I have discussed in a small way the scope of application of conflict resolution research in regional planning in India, emphasizing the need for objective, scientific studies to explore the benefits of cooperation. This does not minimize the importance of using descriptive and historical research, since in essence the two methods are complementary. Nor is it implied that these models solve the problem. However, I do believe that they may offer some new insights and help us devise some objective steps that will help political leaders at all levels and the people at large to pursue the paths of peace true to their ancient tradition and the teachings of the father of the nation.

Internal Political Stability and Economic Development

One hypothesis that is generally made is that declining socioeconomic conditions, high level of population growth, inequality in the distribution of income, and so on lead to domestic conflict.

To see how these different factors affect conflict in a particular country, we can employ a factor analysis study. (For details, see Chatterji, 1978.) For each of a number of developing countries, three sets of variables can be identified:

A. Socioeconomic variables:
    1. Area of the country
    2. Population.
    3. Population density.
    4. Number of telephones.
    5. Primary school enrollment.
    6. Percentage literate.
    7. Physicians per inhabitant, and so on.
B. Political stability variables:
    1. Number of major constitutional changes.
    2. Effective executive (type).
    3. Effective executive (selection).
    4. Degree of parlimentary responsibility, and so on.
C. Conflict variables:
    1. Assassinations.
    2. General strikes.
    3. Riots, and so on.

On the basis of the cross-sectional data for the individual countries with respect to socioeconomic (A) and political (B) data, we can identify a number of factors by using factor analysis. Then, relating the conflict variables with the factor scores of those countries through regression analysis, we can predict domestic conflict at a future time if the values of the socioeconomic and political variables at that time are given.

It has been found that urbanization, spread of education, and liberalization of attitudes have always affected political opinion. However, it is difficult to define and measure political opinion. The definition and its measurements depend on the social, economic, and political system of the country in question. In most Western countries with a long history of democratic government, political opinion is a mode of expression of the way in which a person wants to be governed by the state. This preference is expressed through polls, meetings, and other forms of personal and collective communication systems. Despite the fact that the people of these countries are politically conscious and the democratic system is integrated with their way of life, it cannot be said that an individual's vote for a particular party is a true reflection of his wishes. This is so because the alternatives open to him are limited and because the individual always has to operate as a member of a group. The validity of polls in measuring political opinion is greatly weakened when we turn to the developing nations, which are either feudal or in the early stages of transition to a democratic society. In these countries the connotations of such terms as *freedom, equality,* and so on are different. Likewise, the ways of achieving these objectives vary as a result of the working of many historical forces. However, with the spread of education and industrialization to these countries, it is expected that a standard pattern of political behavior in the framework of a democratic society will ultimately develop, albeit not necessarily similar to that of the Western countries. In any case, for all practical purposes, the votes cast in an election can be taken as an index (though in some cases a poor one) of political preference for any particular party.

The voting pattern in all countries differs among various religious, ethnic, and social groups. It also varies over time and, although this is not so much discussed, over space. In fact, political opinion as measured by votes is interwoven with a country's social and economic system in a joint space-time dimension.

For example, in the towns of the CIR, the political opinion measured by votes changes depending on the density of population and the percentage of Bengali, non-Bengali, and refugee populations. Using 1952 and 1957 election results, we can obtain a regression relationship of the following types:

$$O_i^t = 44.0000 - .0391B_i + .2698R_i \qquad R^2 = .5632, \qquad (6.14)$$

$$O_i^t = 44.0000 - .0391B_i - .0260NB_i + .2698R_i \qquad R^2 = .7891, \qquad (6.15)$$

where B_i = number of Bengali-speaking nonrefugee people living in the ith town.

  NB_i = number of non-Bengali-speaking people living in the ith town.

  R_i = number of Bengali-speaking refugee people living in the ith town.

  d_i = distance of the ith town from Calcutta City.

  S_i = density of population in the ith town.

  O_i^t = percentage of votes cast against the ruling Congress party to the total votes cast in the ith town in the general election of 1957.

  O_i^{t-1} = percentage of votes cast against the ruling Congress party to the total votes cast in the ith town in the general election of 1952.

From equation 6.14 it is seen that the regression coefficient associated with variable NB_i is negative, indicating that towns with a larger number of non-Bengali population vote in favor of the Congress party. The fact that refugees generally vote against the Congress party is brought out by the positive sign of the variable R_i. From equation 6.15 it can be observed that as we go further out from Calcutta City, the Congress party becomes more and more popular.

The foregoing equations do not give a model of a regional pattern of political opinion in the Calcutta area, but they do point to the direction in which we can proceed. A large number of socioeconomic variables can be defined, and data for them can be collected in order to get a complete model. The analysis can be extended to all states in India, and an urban-rural classification will be quite meaningful. To test the effect of socioeconomic variables on the voting pattern, a number of metropolitan areas of similar type can be selected, and better estimates of the regression equations can be obtained. Once a stable relationship is attained, the effect of changes in socioeconomic variables (through urban and economic planning) on the voting pattern can be predicted. From the point of view of Congress party strategists, for example, it will be useful to know in what towns what types of programs are necessary to assure them a certain percentage of votes.

This is not to imply that the suggested models can completely characterize political opinion. Too many factors are involved, many of them are qualitative (caste, religion, language, and so on). Sudden events in international relations also influence these decisions. Nevertheless, when people vote for a party, they do have some motives. If some of these motives are identified and measured, then results can at least partially explain human decisions. Social science methodology is in a state of rapid change. What is now nonmeasurable and qualitative may become measurable in the future. It is possible to construct a set of variables for similar urban centers in India on the basis of existing data and information obtained from the survey. These variables may be the starting point for better future estimates. With the most recent values of these variables, what may be termed a regional model for political opinion can be constructed.

Political Ideology and Economic Development

Regional politics is very much influenced by the national and international political situation.[b] The political scene of a developing country is dominated

---

[b]This section relates to the material in M. Chatterji, "A Game Theoretical Approach of Coalition Politics in an Indian State," *International Interactions* 2, no. 4 (1978).

either by a military dictatorship or by the existence of a large number of political parties, out of which one or two have partial control over the electorate. In the latter case, it has led to politics of coalitions.

Consider, for example, the state of West Bengal in India. There are basically four political forces operating there.

CR = Congress party (controlled by Indira Gandhi).

ULF = (United Left Front) = coalition composed of leftist parties, such as:

1. Communist party of India—Marxist CP(M)
2. Forward Block—Marxist FB(M)
3. Revolutionary Socialist party (RSP)
4. Workers party of India (WP)
5. Socialist Unity Center (SUC)
6. Samuktya Socialist party (SSP)
7. Revolutionary Communist party RCP(M)

PULF = People's United Left Front = coalition composed of the following parties:

1. Communist party of India CP(I)
2. Bangla Congress C(B)
3. Praja Socialist (PS)
4. Bolshevik party (BP)
5. Gorkha League (GL)
6. Forward Block (F)
7. Lok Sevak Sangha (LS)

The lineup from ideological left to right would be like this:

CP(ML) CP(M) WP RCPI SUC RSP FB(M) SSP	CP(I) FB BP GL LS PS C(B) C(F)
ULF	PULF

In this line, CP(M/L) is an extreme Communist party, known as the Naxalites.

For the last twenty-five years these different parties have been involved in various coalitions among themselves. It will be interesting for us to formulate a model through which we can predict the resulting coalitions between different groups. Four of the groups are most important: (1) CPI(M), (2) ULF, (3) PULF, and (4) C(R-Indira).

In the whole conflict process, for each group, there are two possible strategies: to shift to the left or to shift to the right. However, these two options did not have the same connotation to each party. Consider, for example, the situation in the 1960s.

For C(R) moving toward the left, the strategy Q_1 meant, as follows:

1. Try to bring back old congressman who had defected.
2. Make active efforts for friendship with Russia and Bangladesh.
3. Take a strong position against the United States and China.
4. Support North Vietnam.
5. Keep the student movement alive but without violence.
6. Undertake programs of economic development.

The other alternative, Q_2, signified a move toward the right. It reflected an independent position, not caring for PULF or other parties. Q_2 should not be interpreted as low on socialism and high on capitalism, although it may lead to a friendly relationship with the United States.

For CP(M) the first strategy, P_1, denotes the position it held at that time:

1. Reject an alliance with the CP(M-L), while maintaining the same goals within the parliamentary democracy.
2. Infiltrate administrative structures.
3. Use the home portfolio to guide the police forces to its advantage.
4. Maintain neutrality toward the Chinese, with mild censure on specific issues like Bangladesh.
5. Take an uncompromising stance toward the CP(I).
6. Agitate among students and laborers to keep the situation in turmoil.

In short, from the point of view of the ULF partners, it signified (1) receiving help from the ULF to remain in power; (2) consolidating its hold; (3) encouraging the more radical elements of the ULF to defect to the CP(M); and (4) keeping up an uncompromising posture toward the United States and strongly supporting the National Liberation Front (NFL) of Vietnam, not to mention the USSR in its support for North Vietnam. The other position, P_2, called for (1) scaling down its extreme positions, (2) remaining calm over the home portfolio, (3) toning down its differences with the CP(I), (4) issuing a strong denunciation of China and mild ones of the USSR, and (5) giving up the demand for state autonomy/secession—in short, cooperating with the ULF and PULF against the C(R) with a moderate tone while striving for a radical program.

In the case of the ULF, the first strategy, R_1, will be to move toward the

CP(M); R_2 will be to move toward the PULF and the C(R). Similarly, for the PULF these strategies will be denoted by S_1 and S_2, respectively. It should be mentioned here that the calibration of the preference scale of ULF to move to the left toward the CP(M) (or for that matter to the right) is not of the same type as that for the PULF. For example, a given amount of shift by the ULF to the left to form a government with the CP(M) may not be equivalent to a move of the same amount to the right by the PULF to form a government with the C(R). This also depends on whether the C(R) shifts to Q_1 or Q_2. The foregoing situation can be shown as follows:

P_1	P_2	R_1	R_2	S_1	S_2	Q_1	Q_2
	CP(M)		ULF		PULF		C(R)

Let us denote a five-point preference scale as follows for each party.

1. Most preferable   Score $= +1$
2. Preferable   Score $= 0.5$
3. Neutral   Score $= 0$
4. Not preferable   Score $= -0.5$
5. Highly unfavorable   Score $= -1$

I am fully aware of the risk involved in dealing with a qualitative scale like this. However, this scale is often used in the literature as a consequence of the lack of availability of better approaches. It is also assumed that these preferences can be interpreted as the payoff and that the sum of these for any particular situation is zero. In essence, then, we are dealing with a four-person zero-sum game. For this game we have constructed the payoff Table 6–1. I have done so based on my belief and intuition. This is not to say that this table will be invariant for all situations.

From the payoff matrix it is seen that for the choice $P_1 Q_1 R_1 S_1$, the payoff to CP(M) is $+1$, indicating that this is the best situation for it. The ULF and PULF have moved toward it. It has not changed its own position. All this has happened despite the fact that the C(R) is interested in moving to the left, which is a bitter disappointment for the C(R). Consequently, its payoff is -1. The ULF is happy to have a united government against the C(R), but not very happy, since it is afraid that the CP(M) may destroy it. The PULF is not happy since it could not come out with the C(R), which has moved toward it. It has cooperated with strange bedfellows.

Similarly, take another choice, $P_1 Q_2 R_2 S_2$. Here the CP(M)) is unhappy, but not very unhappy since it knows the ULF will be reluctant to do business with the C(R), particularly if it moves to the right. The C(R) is very happy to

Table 6-1   Payoff Matrix for Congress

$C(R)$	$P_1R_1S_1$	$P_1R_1S_1$	$P_2R_1S_1$	$P_2R_2S_1$	$P_1R_2S_1$	$P_1R_2S_2$	$P_2R_1S_2$	$P_2R_2S_2$
Q_1	-1	0	$-.5$	0	0	$.5$	$-.5$	$.5$
Q_2	$-.1$	0	-1	0	$+.5$	$+1$	$-.5$	$.5$

see the PULF and ULF moving toward it despite the fact that it does not care for them. The ULF is unhappy, and the PULF is indifferent. All other cases can be explained likewise. Suppose now that the following coalition situation takes place. The question is: What will be the equilibrium coalition situation?

1. CP(M) versus others:

The game has a saddle point, and the resulting choice is $P_2Q_1R_2S_2$. It is interesting to note that this was the situation. Although the CP(M) expressed a desire to come to an understanding with the ULF and PULF, they have moved to the right toward the C(R), which in turn has moved to the left.

2. Congress versus others:

The payoff matrix for Congress is given by Table 6–1.

Again, there is a saddle point at $Q_2P_1R_1S_1$. Actually, this was the situation when Congress (R) was dominated by rightist leaders and the ULF and PULF vigorously moved to the left with the CP(M). If we consider the coalition between the CP(M) and the ULF versus the C(R) and the PULF, then the equilibrium situation will be $P_2R_1S_2Q_1$, which means the CP(M) has to move to the left and the PULF to the right. This is a reasonable position that can take place.

In the future it may also happen that there will be three contesting parties in the political scene: the C(R), the CP(M), and others. The third group forms coalitions with either of them, thus leading to a similar game theoretical situation. A three-person non-zero-sum game may arise with the central government as the fourth party, forcing it to a zero-sum game. Until that happens, the four-party situation would persist.

The interesting point is that the two groups, PULF and ULF, are placed in a situation like the prisoner's dilemma. If the PULF stands alone and does not cooperate with the ULF in supporting the CP(M) or the C(R), then it will be severed by punishment no matter who wins, and the ULF will be rewarded by power in the government, and vice versa. If they cooperate in supporting the winning party, however, both will be rewarded. The payoff matrix in the prisoner's dilemma case looks like this (C denotes cooperation; D denotes defection):

PRISONER'S DILEMMA
PULF

		C_2	D_2
ULF	C_1	R, R	S, T
	D_2	T, S	P, P

In the foregoing tables, C_1 and C_2 refer to the strategies of the ULF and PULF in cooperating among themselves in the election or on issues facing the state. The reward corresponding to the strategy is denoted by R. It is assumed that, as is generally the case in prisoner's dilemma situations, they are the same. The situation C_1D_2 denotes that the ULF stands alone in the election. The PULF makes a coalition with the C(R) and gets more than its parity norm share because of the strategic aspect of the game, whereas the ULF gets the punishment. The opposite situation is denoted by C_2D_1, wherein the PULF cooperates but the ULF defects to the CP(M). If they both defect—that is, if they do not cooperate in taking joint acions—they will get punishment P. The rewards in this matrix can be measured in terms of the number of seats in the ministry, the percentage of popular votes, and such things as public image, ideological considerations, and the like.

With this framework, if enough observations were available regarding the behavior of the PULF and ULF, it would be possible to estimate (following the Markov chain approach) the probability that they will cooperate in a particular case given their behavior on previous occasions. Since the time period is too short to generate such data, we cannot make such estimates. However, if we trace back the history of their behavior on issues rather than in electoral coalitions, this could be done. Alternatively, we could look at similar coalition politics in other states of India and make some estimates.

In this analysis I have tried to apply some game-theoretical concepts to political events in West Bengal State in the past decade. This type of approach, if properly carried out, can effectively explain the behavior of political parties in a coalition situation in India and other developing countries. It can also be applied in formulating a cooperative procedure to solve intergroup/interstate problems leading to efficient utilization of scarce resources for the benefit of all concerned.

The situation in the Indian subcontinent and West Bengal has changed drastically, as has the international situation, making the material in this chapter outdated. However, our objective was simply to indicate the approach that could be taken.

References

Chatterji, Manas. 1968. "A Model of Resolution of Conflict between India and Pakistan." *Papers of the Peace Research Society (International)* 12 (November): 87–102.

_____. 1978. "Conflict and Socio-Economic Structure: A Factor Analysis Study." *Northeast Peace Science Review* 1:7–21.

Isard, Walter. 1969. *General Theory: Social, Political, Economic, and Regional.* Cambridge, Mass.: MIT Press.

Richardson, L. F. (1960) *Arms and Security.* Pittsburgh: Boxwood Press.

Bibliography

Acayra, B. K. 1965. "India and China." *Indian and Foreign Review* 2, no. 11 (March 15):9–10, 19–20.

Alvares, Peter. 1968. "Kashmir and Power Balance in Asia." *Janata* 20, no. 43 (November 14):3–4, 6.

Alyar, S. P. 1967. "Union-State Relations in India: A Post-Election View." *United Asia* 19 (March–April):80–90.

"Assam—Federation within Federation?" 1967. *Parliamentary Studies* 11, no. 2–3 (February–March):12–14, 23.

Bandyopadhyaya, Jayantanuju. 1967. "Sino-Soviet Rift and India." *Shakti* 4, no. 2 (February):14–23.

Baranwal, G. S. 1965. "Role of Union Government in Financing the Development of Uttar Pradesh." *Prajna* 11, no. 1 (October):190–195.

Berelson, B., and Steinder, Gary. 1966. *Human Behavior: An Inventory of Scientific Findings.* New York: Harcourt, Brace and World.

Boulding, Kenneth. 1965. "The British Press and the War with Pakistan." *Vidura* 2, no. 4 (November):11–18.

_____. 1965. "The British Press on the India-Pakistan Conflict." *Foreign Affairs Report* 14, no. 12 (December):161–170.

_____. 1966."Towards a Theory of Peace." In Roger Fisher, ed., *International Conflict and Behavioral Science.* New York: Basic Books.

Catell, R. B. 1950. *An Introduction to Personality Study.* London and New York: Hutchinson's University Library.

Chelyshev, E. 1967. "Friendship Benefits Both Countries." *Amity* 4, no. 2–3 (April):5–9.

Chopra, R. N. 1965. "Adm. Org. for Regional Development—The Experience of

Punjab." *Indian Journal of Public Administration* 11, no. 4 (October–December):737–744.

Cooper, Brian C. 1967. "On East-West Understanding." *Aryan Path* 38 (September):415–418.

Dandavate, M. R. 1967. "Common Bonds of Nationalism." *Janata* 22, no. 37 (October–December):5–6.

Datta, Abhijit, and Bhattacharya, Mohit. 1967. "Functional Approach to Indian Federalism—Case Study of Urban Development." *Indian Journal of Public Administration* 13 (April–June):283–298.

Deshpande, A. M. 1967. "Federal-State Fiscal Relations in India." *United Asia* 19 (March–April):129–131.

Dutt, Vidya Prakash. 1966. "China and Indo-Pakistani Relations." *International Studies* 8, nos. 1–2 (July–October):126–133.

Dwivedy, Surendranath. 1967. "New Relationship between the Centre and States." *Janata* 22, no. 8 (March 12):2.

Gandhian Institutute of Studies.

A Case Work Study of Ganhiji's Method of Resolving Personal Conflicts.

A Comparative Study of Decentralization in Yugoslavia and India.

The Concept of Trusteeship.

A Directory of Gandhian Institutions and an Analysis of their Programmes.

An Economic History of a Cluster of Villages in U.P.

Emergence of Local Leadership.

Intermediate Technology and Its Implications for Rural Industrilization.

The Investment Pattern and the Emloyment Potential.

A Pilot Study of Gramdan Villages in Bihar.

Relations between the Modern and the Traditional Sectors of the Indian Economy.

A Sociological Study of the Dacoit Problem in the Chambral Valley.

The Structure of Power and Authority in Rural Communities.

Study of Basic Education.

A Study of Programmes Initiated by the Government for the Welfare of the Weaker Section of the Community.

A Study of Some of the Experiments in Rural Development—Sriniketan, Baroda and Etawah.

Gangal, S. C. 1966. "The Commonwealth and Indo-Pakistani Relations." *International Studies* 8, nos. 1–2 (July–October):131–149.

Ghatate, Narayan Madhav. 1966. "Disarmament in India's Foreign Policy, 1947–1965." Ph.D. dissertation, American University.

Guha, Samar. 1966. "When East Bengal Breaks Off." *Janata* 21, no. 2 (January):7–8, 12

Gulati, Hans Raj. 1967. "India and Pakistan—Their Mutual Antagonism." *Janata* 22, no. 35 (September):7–8.

Gupta, Sisir. 1966. "India's Policy towards Pakistan." *International Studies* 8, nos. 1–2 (July–October):29–48.

Hihman, Warren F. 1966. "Political Development and Foreign Policy: The Case of India." *Journal of Commonwealth Political Studies* 4, (November):216–230.

Isard, W., and Smith, T. 1965. "A Practical Application of Game Theoretical Approach to Arms Reduction." *Peace Research Society Papers,* vol. 4.

Jena, B. B. "Jurisdictional Contraditions in State Organisms in India (1965)." *Indian Journal of Political Science* 27, no. 4, section 3 (October–December):30–36.

Jha, C. S. "Non-alignment in a Changing World." 1967. *Indian and Foreign Review* 4, no. 23 (September 15):9–11, 17–19.

Kapur, Harish. 1966. "The Soviet Union and the Indo-Pakistan Relations." *International Studies* 8, nos. 1–2 (July–October):150–157.

Karanakaram, K. P. 1966. "China in India's International Relations." *China Report* 2, no. 6 (November–December):35–39.

Lakdawala, Dansukhial Tulsidas. 1967. *Union-State Financial Relations.* Bombay: Lalvani Publishing House.

Misra, K. P. 1965. "The Indo-Pakistan Conflict," *Africa Quarterly* 5, no. 3 (October–December):203–217.

Mohan, Surendra. 1967. "Regionalism—Unresolved Dilemma." *Janata* 22, no. 37 (October):3, 15.

Nath, V. 1966. "Region for Planning." *Indian Journal of Public Administration* 12, no. 1 (January–March):1–17.

National Academy of Administration. 1964. "Bibliography on Union State Relations (General)." *Journal* 9, no. 1 (January):55–61.

Prabhakar, Purushottam. 1967. "Indo-Japanese Cooperation: Need for New Openings." *Foreign Affairs Reports* 16, no. 10 (October):6–10.

Proceedings of the seminar "On the Relations between the Centre and States in India." 1967. *Indian Advocate* 7, no. 1–2, (January–June):3–116. (Speeches by K. Subha Rao, M. C. Setalvad, M. Hidayatullah, K. S. Hegde, J. L. Kapur. Papers by C. B. Agarwala, Uma Meht, S. R. Narayana Ayyar, V. G. Ramachandran, B. R. L. Iyengar.)

Ramachandran, G. 1966. "Union State Relations in Finance and Planning." *Indian Journal of Public Administration* 12, no. 3 (July–September):378–388.

Ramakant, 1967. "India-Pakistan Relations: Some Aspects." *Political Science Review* 6 (April–June):236–246.

Raman, A. "Centre-State Financial Relations—The Impact of Changed Political Conditions." *Economic Studies* 8 (July):25–50.

Rao, P. Chandrasekhara. 1965. "Indo-Pakistan Agreement on the Rann of Kutch: Form and Contents." *Indian Journal of International Law* 5, no. 2 (April):176–185.

Rapaport, Anatal. 1957. "Lewis Fry Richardson's Mathematical Theory of War." *Journal of Conflict Resolution* 2 (November).

Rath, P. K. 1965. "Governmental Set-up in the States of the Indian Union—Some Aspects of Its Working." *Indian Journal of Political Science* 27, no. 4, section 3 (October–December):18–22.

Ray, Amal. 1966. *Inter-governmental Relations in India: A Study of Indian Federalism.* Bombay and New York: Asia Publishing House. p. 184.

Ray, Asmini K. 1966. "Pakistan as a Factor in Indo-Soviet Relations." *Economic and Political Weekly* 2, no. 12 (November 5):503–506.

Ray, Jayant Kumar. 1966. "India and Pakistan as Factors in Each Other's Foreign Policies." *International Studies* 8, nos. 1–2 (July–October):49–63.

Sager, Peter. 1966. *Moscow's Hand in India, An Analysis of Soviet Propaganda.* Berne: Swiss Eastern Institute.

Sastri, Khandrika Venkata Subtahmanya. 1967. *Federal-State Fiscal Relations in India: A Study of the Finance Commission and the Techniques of Fiscal Adjustment.* Bombay: Oxford University Press. (Indian Branch) Tables, p. 143.

Sastry, S. V. S. 1967. "The Case for Nonalignment." *Indian and Foreign Review* 4, no. 8 (February 1):18–19.

Seth, Nareshavern Dayal. 1966. "India's Policy towards China and Pakistan in the Light of Kautilya's Arthasastra." *Mobern Review* 120, no. 3, Whole no. 717 (September):200–203.

Shah, A. B., ed. 1966. *India's Defense and Foreign Policies,* vol. 9. Bombay: Manaktala. P. 169.

Singh, Balgit. 1955. "The United States and the India-Pakistan Conflict." *Parliamentary Studies* 9, no. 12 (December):15–19.

Singh, Gopal. 1967. "India's Relations with Pakistan." *Parliamentary Studies* 11, no. 5 (May):11–13.

Sinha, Shyam Nandan. 1967. "Union-State Relations in a New Key." *AICC Economic Review* 19, no. 8 (November 1):625–629.

Smoker, Paul. 1967. "The Arms Race as an Open and Closed System." *Peace Reseach Society Papers,* no. 7.

Srinivasan, N. 1966. "Union State Relations in Agricultural Development." *Indian Journal of Public Administration* 12, no. 3 (July–September):389–406.

Stein, Arthur. 1964. "India's Relations with the U.S.S.R. 1953–63." *Orbis* (Philadelphia) (Summer):357–373.

Subbaiah, M. J. 1967. "Ecafe and Regional Economic Cooperation." *Foreign Affairs Reports* 16 (July):75–81.

"Summary of the Report on Inter-State Relations by Syndicate Group no. X, 1963." 1964. *National Academy of Administration Journal* 9, no. 3 (July):99–134.

Than, S. 1966. "Indo-Africa Cooperation." *Africa Quarterly* 6, Supplement (July–September):54–60.

Tripathi, P. K. "Legislative Relations between the Union and the States and Educational Planning." 1965. *Indian Advocate* 5, nos. 3, 4 (July–December):4–12.

Vaidyanathan, R. 1966. "Some Recent Trends in Soviet Policies towards India and Pakistan." *International Studies* 7, no. 3 (January):429–447.

Zhukov, Yuri. 1967. "India and the Struggle for World Peace." *Indian and Foreign Review* 4, no. 24 (October 1):10–13.

7 MANAGEMENT OF REGIONAL PLANNING

Role of Management Science in Development

Over the last three decades the theoretical structure of regional planning has become more sophisticated, but its application to developing countries has met with little success. One reason for this situation is that although the planning methodology is satisfactory, implementation of the plans has been very weak. There is an urgent need to use different techniques of management science to implement the planning decisions.

For example, the subject of accounting—both financial and management accounting—can be used in deciding to allocate funds and investigating whether they have been used effectively. Just as accounting statements tell us whether a private business or organization is running profitably, the same can be true for the planning organization, except that the profit in this case is measured by the attainment of goals as postulated by the plans.

The main bottleneck of the plan is financial resources. The income level of the developing countries is low; and most of it is used up by consumption, leaving a small amount for investment. The subject of finance can help us decide how best to develop the private and public money markets so as to reap the maximum benefit of the available financial resources. The role of the international financial institutions in providing resources can also be expanded if domestic financial planning is made more efficient. Gathering information and processing it in suitable form is the key to a realistic plan. We need the development of regional and interregional information systems using the latest technology. Many of these countries have a long background in information gathering and its applications; however, this was not done in a way that will facilitate the formation and application of regional planning.

There have been important developments in the field of decision science that can help us adopt appropriate strategies in the face of uncertainties. One such area is the centralization and decentralization of decision making—that is, determination of the magnitude and the type of decision to be made at each mode so that the participation of the members in the organization is at a satisfactory level, with the stipulation that the demand of such a plan meets the constraints of the system. For example, an important feature of the recent Indian political scene is center-state and interstate relations. The future of democracy in India will be very much determined by the harmony in these relations and also by the participation of the people as a whole in decision making at different levels.

Center-state relations have attained increased prominence in recent years as parties with different ideologies have come to control the government at the center and a number of governments in key states. Although interstate feuds have a longer history, only after independence did they assume their present form. The nature of the problems is too well known to be emphasized here. One basic factor that accentuates this friction (and that, if properly utilized, can result in reduction of its intensity) is the allocation of authority to make decisions related to administration, planning, and so on at different levels in the hierarchical system of center, zone, state, local, and other administrative areas (Maass 1958). Thus a study of the proper spatial organization of the decision making is vital. In fact, it can be shown easily that the proper degree of spatial decentralization of decision making and the efficient allocation of industry and other economic activity of the afore-mentioned administrative units are mutually interdependent. Spatial patterns of economic activities may well be different for different spatial degrees of decentralization and the optimum spatial organization of decision making. Similarly, administration and planning also may vary with different spatial allocations of industry and economic activity. More concretely, the optimal locational distribution of, say, steel and the steel-fabricating industry's capacity is, other things being equal, not unrelated to spatial degrees of decentralization of decision making in governmental administration and vice versa. The objective of this study is to identify a pattern of decision making that will minimize frictions among decision-making units and allow an optimum amount of participation to the interested parties. For this purpose we will adopt a gravity-type model,[a] given as:

$$I_{ij} = G \frac{P_i P_j}{d_{ij}^b} ,$$ (7.1)

where I_{ij} = the actual attraction between the ith and jth area.
P_i and P_j = the population for the ith and jth subareas.
$\qquad d_{ij}$ = the distance.
$\qquad b$ = a constant.
The most general form of the gravity model is:

$$I_{ij} = G \frac{w_i(p)_i^a w_j(p)_j^c}{d_{ij}^b} ,$$ (7.2)

where w_i and w_j represent per capita weights in regions i and j, respectively; and a and c are measures of agglomeration or deglomeration economies. Another important tool is the method of potential, which is as follows:

$$V_j = G \sum_i^n \frac{P_{ij}}{d_{ij}^b} .$$ (7.3)

This states that the potential at a point from all other points is the sum of the individual potentials—namely, the population divided by the distance between two areas. The gravity and potential models have found wide application in such areas as marketing, migration, transportation studies, and organizational structure. (Warntz 1959; Harris 1954; Anderson 1956).

Application of the Gravity Model for the Indian Federation

The states in the Indian Union have been placed in the following groupings for the sake of convenience: (1) Andhra Pradesh, (2) Assam and Nagaland, (3) Bihar, (4) Gujarat, (5) Haryana, (6) Jammu and Kashmir, (7) Kerala, (8) Madhya Pradesh, (9) Maharastra, (10) Mysore, (11) Orissa, (12) Punjab, (13) Rajasthan, (14) Tamil Nadu, (15) Uttar Pradesh, and (16) West Bengal.

Although the number of states has increased over time, for simplicity we

---

[a]This analysis is heavily based on Isard (1969, Chapter 3).

are limiting our discussion to sixteen states as an example. On the basis of a number of criteria, these states can be divided into the following four zones:

Zones		Population (1961) (millions)
North:		
1. Jammu and Kashmir		3.5
2. Uttar Pradesh		73.7
3. Punjab		
4. Haryana		20.3
	Total	97.5
West:		
1. Gujarat		20.6
2. Maharastra		39.6
3. Rajasthan		20.2
4. Madhya Pradesh		32.4
	Total	112.8
South:		
1. Andhra Pradesh		35.9
2. Tamil Nadu		33.7
3. Mysore		23.6
4. Kerala		16.9
	Total	110.1
East:		
1. Bihar		46.5
2. Assam and Nagaland		11.9
3. Orissa		17.5
4. West Bengal		36.9
	Total	112.8

For each of the aforementioned states, we can identify, say, four subregions within each state. Districts can be combined to form such units, or some similar meaningful areas can be taken. Thus we can have the following hierarchical system: (1) center, (2) zone, (3) state, and (4) local. The system can be portrayed by a treelike hierarchy, as shown in Figure 7–1. Each node, starting from the peak, leads to four subordinate nodes. The tree consists of four orders. The number of nodes of the first, second, third, and fourth orders are 1, 4, 16, and 64, respectively. Their numbers run from 1 in the first order, from 2 to 5 in the second, from 6 to 21 in the third, and from 22 to 85 in the fourth. It is not necessary for this structure to be a symmetrical four-node hierarchy. For simplicity, however, let us assume that this is the case.

For each member of the hierarchy (say, at i) we can attach a mass M_i, $i = 1, 2, \ldots 85$. This mass can be considered a vector having, say, k components, as follows:

$$M_i = (M_{1i}, M_{2i}, \ldots M_{ei}, \ldots M_{ki}). \qquad (7.4)$$

The components of this vector can denote different social, economic, and political characteristics of the nodes; and, geometrically, it will be a point in a k-dimensional space. At this stage we will not be concerned with measurement of these components. As a crude approximation, a ranking system with a meaningful base can be utilized for this purpose. For example, the components can be of the following types: (1) population, (2) birthrate, (3) death rate, (4) density of population, (5) percentage of urban population, (6) population growth rates, (7) infant mortality rates, (8) percentage of land under cultivation, (9) total food grain production, (10) per capita food grain production, (11) KWh of energy consumption, (12) Km of railways per unit

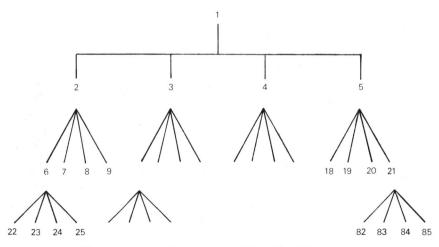

Figure 7–1. A Symmetrical Treelike Hierarchy

area, (13) percentage of literates, (14) percentage of people speaking the national language, (15) industrial production, (16) number of trained executives, and so on. Instead of dealing with all these variables in their totality, we can conduct a factor-analysis study to identify a number of factors F_{1i}, F_{2i}, ... F_{mi} and express the original variables M_{ji} with the following relation:

$$M_{ji} = a_{j1} F_{1i} + a_{j2} F_{2i} + \ldots + a_{jm} F_{mi}, \qquad (7.5)$$

where i refers to node.
and j refers to variable.
When the factor equation 7.5 has been estimated, the factor score for any node can be used in place of the values of the variables (Harman 1960).

In the following we shall assume that the measurements on k component mass vector have been obtained directly or that they have been replaced by factor scores resulting from a factor-analysis study. For any characteristic (component)—say, e—we define:

$$I_{ij} = \frac{G \cdot W_{ie}(M_{ie})^{\alpha} W_{je}(M_{je})^{\beta}}{d_{ije}^{b}} \qquad (7.6)$$

and

$$I_i^e = I_{i1}^e + \ldots + I_{ij}^e + I_n^e = \sum_{j=1}^{n} \frac{G W_{ie}(M_{ie})^{\alpha} W_{ie}(M_{ie})^{\beta}}{d_{ije}^{b}}$$

$$= G W_{ie}(M_{ie})^{\alpha} \sum_{j=1}^{n} \frac{W_{je}(M_{je})^{\beta}}{d_{ije}^{b}} \qquad (7.7)$$

Dividing both sides of definitional equation 7.7 by the weighted adjusted mass at i—namely, $W_{it}(M_i)^{a}$—we obtain

$$_iV^e = \frac{I_i^e}{W_{ie}(M_{ie})^{\alpha}} = G \sum_{j=1}^{n} \frac{W_{je}(M_{je})^{\beta}}{d_{ije}^{b}} . \qquad (7.8)$$

By definition, $_iV^e$ represents total interaction at i per unit of weighted mass at i. The term $_iV^e$ is designated as potential at i (Isard 1969). For each component of the mass vector M, a potential can thus be computed; and the total potential may be obtained by summing these potentials; that is:

$$_iV = \sum_{e=1}^{k} {}_iV^e \qquad (7.9)$$

Equation 7.9 gives the total potential (with respect to all characteristics) generated at i by all other members in the system. In the Indian context (when $i = 1$), it will denote the influence of all the eighty-four remaining units at local, state, and zonal levels on the center with respect to a set of social, economic, and political factors.

In the context of the federal structure of Indian democracy, this influence on potential can be viewed as being generated at different levels. The Indian constitution clearly defines the jurisdiction of authority in Central, State, and Concurrent Lists. The potential is thus generated, and efforts should be made to force its generation at the following levels:

1. Between the center and the zones, $_cV_z^e$

2. Between zones, $_zV_z^e$

3. Between the center and the states, $_cV_s^e$

4. Between states within a zone, $_zV_s^e$

5. Of the local units at the state, $_sV_L^e$

6. Between local units within a state, $_LV_L^e$

In symbols (see Figure 7–1),

$$_cV_z^e = G \sum_{j=2}^{5} \frac{W_{je}M_{je}^2}{d_{jce}^b} \tag{7.10}$$

$$_zV_z^e = G \sum_{z=2}^{5}\sum_{\substack{j=2 \\ z \neq j}}^{5} \frac{W_{je}M_{je}^2}{d_{zje}^b} \tag{7.11}$$

$$_cV_s^e = G \sum_{j=6}^{21} W_{je}M_{je}^2/d_{jce}^b \tag{7.12}$$

$$_zV_s^e = G \sum_{j=6}^{21} W_{je}M_{je}^2/d_{jze}^b \tag{7.13}$$

where $z = 2$ when $j < 9$.

$z = 3$ when $j < 13$.
$z = 4$ when $j < 17$.
$z = 5$ when $j < 21$.

$$_sV_L^e = G \sum_{j=22}^{85} W_{je} M_{je}^2 / d_{jze}^b \qquad (7.14)$$

where $z = 6$ when $j < 25$.
$z = 7$ when $j < 29$.
$z = 21$ when $j < 85$.

Finally:

$$_LV_L^e = \sum_{i=22}^{85} \sum_{j=22}^{85} W_{je} M_{je}^2 / d_{ije}^b \qquad (7.15)$$

The total potential generated in the system is:

$$V^e = {_cV_z^e} + {_zV_z^e} + {_cV_s^e} + {_sV_L^e} + {_LV_L^e} + {_zV_s^e}. \qquad (7.16)$$

Equation 7.16 states that for any component—say, language—the potential for the country as a whole can be obtained by summing the individual potentials generated at the foregoing levels.

To clarify our definitions, we can use the following example. We start with the relationship of the center to different zones with respect to the first component of the mass vector M, as depicted in Figure 7-2. The first component may denote the population.

In calculating $_1V^i$ for the situation—that is, potential at 1 (center) from all zones with respect to the first component (namely, population), we get:

$$a = 1 \qquad M_{11} = 9 \qquad W_{11} = 1$$
$$B = 1 \qquad M_{12} = 6 \qquad W_{12} = 1$$
$$b = 1 \qquad M_{13} = 8 \qquad W_{13} = 1$$
$$G = 1 \qquad M_{14} = 2 \qquad W_{14} = 1$$
$$M_{15} = 4 \qquad W_{15} = 1$$

We also define the number of distance units corresponding to any d_{ij} as the smallest number of intervening links between i and j; $i = 1; j = 2, 3, 4,$ and 5. Thus:

$$d_{31} = 1 \qquad d_{21} = 2 \qquad d_{41} = 2 \qquad d_{51} = 3.$$

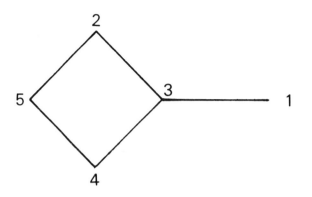

Figure 7-2.   A Graphical Representation of a Central State Relationship

Finally, we define $d_{11} = e$, a small arbitrary positive number that we set at 1/5.
Then, by definition:

$$_1V^1 = \frac{M_{11}}{d_{11}} + \frac{M_{12}}{d_{21}} + \frac{M_{13}}{d_{31}} + \frac{M_{14}}{d_{41}} + \frac{M_{15}}{d_{51}} =$$

$$(7.17)$$

$$\frac{9}{1/5} + \frac{6}{2} + \frac{8}{1} + \frac{2}{2} + \frac{4}{3} = 58\frac{1}{3} = \frac{175}{3},$$

and

$$\frac{M_{11}}{_1v^1d_{11}} = \frac{45}{175/3} = \frac{135}{175} = \frac{27}{35}.$$

So the potential generated by all the zones at the center with respect to population is 175/3, and the participation in or interference on a unit (representative) decision at i by the mass at i is 27/35, indicating the degree of centralization in decision making.

In the aforementioned example it was assumed that the link flows in both directions. If some component of the mass vector—say, language—permits flows in one direction, as indicated in Figure 7–3, we have a new set of relevant distances, namely,

$$d_{21} = 2, \qquad d_{31} = 1, \qquad d_{41} = 2, \qquad d_{51} = a.$$

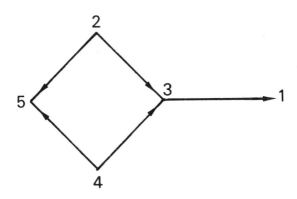

Figure 7-3. A Graphical Representation of a Central State Relationship Taking Direction into Consideration

We now recalculate:

$$_1 V^1 = \frac{M_{11}}{d_{11}} + \frac{M_{12}}{d_{21}} + \frac{M_{13}}{d_{31}} + \frac{M_{14}}{d_{41}} + \frac{M_{15}}{d_{51}}$$

$$(7.18)$$

$$= \frac{9}{1/5} + \frac{6}{2} + \frac{8}{1} + \frac{2}{2} + \frac{4}{2} = 57$$

Thus restrictions on the direction of flow in general tend to decrease participation and interference of masses at a distance.

After computing the potential at the center created by the zones, we can consider the potential created by the zones among themselves. The procedure is similar except that we calculate the potential at each zone (with respect to population) by the remaining three zones and take the sum (equation 7.11). The potential created by the states within a zone is calculated similarly and summed for all the zones (equation 7.13) The potential created by the states at the center can be computed by equation 7.9 and intrastate potentials by equations 7.14 and 7.15.

At this point some clarification is necessary to assure that there is no duplication. Consider, for example, one component of the mass vector—namely, the percentage of people speaking the national language, Hindi. Here the potential of the zones at the center or the potential generated among the zones is meaningful, whereas intrastate potential may not mean anything. So when this component is considered for intrastate component units, the weights assigned—that is, W_i—can be zero. Obviously, when we are considering such a component as interstate cooperation in resource utilization, then a local node bordering two states may contribute a certain amount of potential.

Participation Potential

We now wish to consider participation and influences with respect to the regular hierarchy, as shown in Figure 7–1. It is difficult to define the term *participation in decision making* in an Indian context. Notwithstanding these difficulties, we are interested in defining a concept of participation potential that might be directly related to and testable in terms of some operational measure of participation. For example, we may wish to employ a measure of the degree of

1. Participation of any individual in any given decision.
2. Participation of a population of the system in this given decision.
3. Participation of a population of a system in all decisions of that system.

For item 1 we might, for example, define *degree* of participation in terms of number of votes cast for a political party with a given ideology, number of letters written in newspapers, number of meetings attended, or some other act of communication. If the individual participated in, say, 4 percent of all communication acts taken by all individuals, then his or her degree of participation in that decision would be 4 percent. For item 2 we might, for example, measure average participation of individuals, where the participation of any one individual is defined and where total population numbers are explicit. For item 3 we might, for example, measure the average degree (or probability) of participation by any individual in any decision, which is simply the mean of the average population participation in each decision, keeping explicit the total number of decisions and population.

Whatever the level of abstraction, we will define the participation potential P for a system as the sum of the products of the potential generated by each node and the amount of decisions made therein. This can be explained with reference to the Indian hierarchical structure assumed in Figure 7–1. For simplicity let us assume that a given component of the mass vector, the mass = 1, with weights = 1 at all nodes. Further, we assume $d_{fg} = 1$ when $f > g$, and $d_{fg} = 0$ when $f < g$. The sense of the last assumption is that only upward flow of participation and exercise of influence are permitted. A person cannot affect decisions at any node of higher order than the one at which he is located. Consider all decisions made in their totality and without any loss of generality. The total number of decisions is assumed to be unity.

With these assumptions, the participation potential P is defined (Isard 1969) as the sum of the product of the potential generated at each node and the amount of decisions to be made at that node. Symbolically,

$$P = \sum_{i=1}^{n} r_i \cdot {}_iV, \qquad (7.19)$$

where r_i is the proportion of all decisions to be made at node i, and $_iV$ is the participation potential generated at the ith node defined in equation 7.9. Choosing different values for r_i at $i(i = 1, 2, \ldots n)$, we shall get different patterns of decentralization. For example, for $r_i = 1$ at $i = 1$, and $r_i = 0$ elsewhere, we have the case of absolute centralization. Similarly, when $r_j = 1$, where j is the lowest-order node, and $r_j = 0$ elsewhere, we have absolute decentralization. Between these extremes different patterns of decentralization will be obtained by assigning different values of r_i at $i = 1$, $2, \ldots n$.

Centralization and Decentralization: Decision Matrix

In this scheme of analysis, a number of remarks seem to be in order. In the measurement of centralization or decentralization, we are using the percentage of decisions made at different nodes; but it is the nature of the decision and not its number that is relevant. Again, when we have more than two nodes, it is difficult to decide which pattern is more decentralized since we shall be comparing two sets. Each set contains more than two numbers, and each type of decision is not made by all nodes of different orders. Of course, the masses and distances need not be 1 for all nodes. The scope of the previous analysis can be extended by relaxing these assumptions. For example, the decisions can be divided into the following groups:

1. International: defense, foreign policy, foreign trade, and so on.
2. National: language, industrial policy, transportation, national planning, taxation, and so on.
3. Regional and interregional: sharing of resources, interregional industrial ventures, zonal trade, mutual problems, and so on.

4. State: state planning, state taxation, law and order, education, health, community planning, and so on.
5. Local: Panchayats, local self-government, village development, and so on.

In the case of international decisions, it is conceivable that all the decisions will be made by the center. However, in some international decisions participation by a state may be necessary. For example, when the defense of the country is concerned, a border state's opinion with respect to some decisions may be of value. Even in this case, some decision-making power can be entrusted to the local people with respect to military training and the like.

Similarly, all national decisions need not be made by the central government alone. For example, in the case of language, participation by different zones may be crucial. Where regional and interregional decision making are concerned—as with a boundary dispute, sharing of river water, and so on—the central government need not be left out completely. Similarly, although it is desirable that the center keep out of all state decisions, it is always easy to identify some state decision where the center must have some power to protect the democracy and integrity of the Indian Union. The same type of argument applies in the case of local decisions. The following matrix will explain the argument:

Type of Decision	Authority			
	Center	Zone	State	Local
International	0.7	0.1	0.1	0.1
National	0.6	0.2	0.2	0
Regional	0.3	0.3	0.4	0
State	0.1	0	0.6	0.3
Local	0	0	0.2	0.8

Each cell of the abovementioned matrix shows the percentage of a particular type of decision made at a given level. For example, with respect to international decisions, 70 percent of them are made by the central authority. Admittedly, the use of percentages is quite crude. However, if the question of resource use (in millions of rupees) is concerned, it will mean that 70 percent of it will be controlled by the center. Again, if a joint committee administers the decision, then 70 percent of the members will be appointed by the center, and so on. Obviously, different members can be put in the cells of the matrix, indicating different degrees of decentralization.

Let us take the decision matrix in more general form, as follows:

Type of Decision   *Authority*

	Center	*Zone*	*State*	*Local*
International	r_{Ic}	0	r_{IS}	0
National	r_{cc}	r_{cz}	r_{cs}	r_{cL}
Regional and interregional	r_{zc}	r_{zz}	0	0
State	r_{sc}	0	r_{ss}	r_{sL}
Local	0	0	r_{Ls}	r_{LL}

Since we are dealing with a decision matrix, the problems of comparing two patterns with respect to decentralization becomes more complicated. Let us assume that the higher the value of $(r_{Ic} + r_{cc} + r_{zc} + r_{sc} + r_{ss})$, the greater the degree of centralization.

With this in mind, we can define *participation potential* as the sum of products of the potentials by the percentage of decisions of different types left to that order to perform. In symbols:

$$P = (r_{Ic} + r_{cc} + r_{zc} + r_{sc})\,({}_cV_z + {}_cV_s)$$
$$+ (r_{cz} + r_{zz})\,({}_zV_z + {}_zV_s) + (r_{Is} + r_{ss} + r_{Ls} + r_{cs})_s V_L$$
$$+ (r_{LL} + r_{SL} + r_{CL})_L V_L \qquad (7.20)$$

We shall explain the whole procedure with reference to the Indian situation as depicted in Figure 7–4. In this hypothetical example the masses and the distances are ranked from 1 to 4. The rank-mass of the nodes is shown at the bottom of each node, and the distances are indicated at the arm. For example, the mass of Uttar Pradesh is taken as 1, and the distance from it to the zone is also taken as equal to 1. The distances between the four zones are taken as follows:

$$d_{12} = 1 \qquad d_{23} = 5$$
$$d_{13} = 6 \qquad d_{24} = 3$$
$$d_{14} = 2 \qquad d_{34} = 4$$

The masses of the states and the corresponding distances to the center are given as follows:

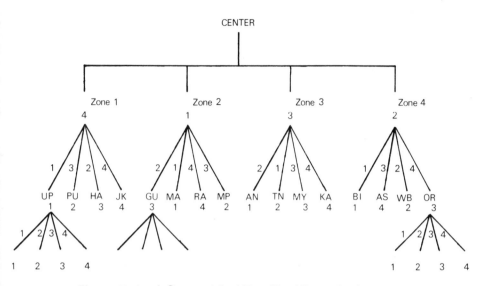

Figure 7–4.   A Symmetrical Treelike Hierarchy for India

State Number	States	Rank-Mass	Rank-Distance
1.	Andhra	4	4
2.	Assam and Nagaland	13	9
3.	Bihar	2	11
4.	Gujarat	9	1
5.	Haryana	15	7
6.	Jammu and Kashmir	16	10
7.	Kerala	12	16
8.	Madhya Pradesh	7	8
9.	Maharashtra	3	2
10.	Mysore	8	3
11.	Orissa	11	13
12.	Punjab	14	12
13.	Rajasthan	10	5
14.	Tamil Nadu	6	14
15.	Uttar Pradesh	1	6
16.	West Bengal	5	15

For this hypothetical example, the values of the potentials were calculated with and without weights. The weight system is as follows:

1. The weight of zone 4 is 2. The weight of all other zones is 1.
2. When we are considering the center-state potential, the weights of
    Jammu and Kashmir $= 2$, Maharashtra $= 2$, Tamil Nadu $= 3$, Kerala
    $= 2$, West Bengal $= 3$, Assam $= 2$, and all other states $= 1$.

The potentials are given as:

	Without Weights	With Weights
$_cV_z =$	5.916 7	9.916 7
$_zV_z =$	62.083 4	88.750 0
$_cV_s =$	27.102 1	106.67
$_zV_s =$	16.916 7	
$_sV_L =$	64.00	
$_LV_L =$	224.00	

Table 7–1 shows twenty-five patterns of decentralization. For example, in
pattern A all the international decisions are made at the central level; 100
percent of the national decisions are made at the central level; all zonal
decisions are made at the zonal level, as are the state and local decisions. For
these patterns of decentralization, the participation potential P has been
calculated (see Table 7–2). The behavior of P for different patterns of
decentralization is shown in Figure 7–5.

Calculations in the tables were done with respect to one component of the
mass vector, namely, population. The same type of calculations can be
repeated with other components and summed to get the total participation
potentials with respect to all the components. From Figure 7–5 it is seen that
as centralization increases, participation potential decreases.

For each decision matrix a certain value of the participation potential P
will result, and it will reflect a certain amount of productivity of the system. It
is true that measurement of the productivity will be difficult since it must be a
combination of growth of income, internal peace, social welfare, national
integration, and so on. Although choosing a pattern for which this productivity is maximum is a desirable objective, it may not be feasible since a certain
amount of social, political, and economic cost must be incurred. For
example, if the central government makes a decision that is completely local
because of lack of information and its distance from the local area, it is likely
to make a wrong decision. On the other hand, for a zonal decision, such as
sharing river water, the central government may have an unbiased solution,
whereas the contending parties may not. It is undeniable that a major portion
of the costs involved may be qualitative in nature and that exp. essing the cost
function in terms of visible policy parameters is immensely difficult. Assum-

Table 7-1 Decentralization Patterns

Patterns	International		National				Regional		State			Local	
	r_{IC}	r_{IS}	r_{cc}	r_{cz}	r_{cs}	r_{cL}	r_{zc}	r_{zz}	r_{sc}	r_{ss}	r_{sL}	r_{LS}	r_{LL}
A	1.0	0	1.0	0	0	0	0	1.0	0	1.0	0	1	0
B	0.9	0.1	0.9	0.1	0	0	0.1	0.9	0.1	0.9	0	0.9	0.1
C	0.9	0.1	0.8	0.1	0.1	0	0.1	0.9	0.1	0.8	0.1	0.8	0.2
D	0.9	0.1	0.7	0.1	0.1	0.1	0.1	0.9	0.1	0.8	0.1	0.8	0.2
E	0.9	0.1	0.6	0.1	0.2	0.1	0.1	0.9	0.1	0.7	0.2	0.8	0.2
F	0.9	0.1	0.6	0.1	0.2	0.1	0.1	0.9	0.1	0.7	0.2	0.8	0.2
G	0.9	0.1	0.6	0.2	0.1	0.1	0.1	0.9	0.1	0.7	0.2	0.8	0.2
H	0.9	0.1	0.5	0.3	0.1	0.1	0.1	0.9	0.2	0.6	0.2	0.8	0.2
I	0.9	0.1	0.5	0.3	0.1	0.1	0.1	0.9	0.2	0.6	0.2	0.8	0.2
J	0.9	0.1	0.5	0.3	0.1	0.1	0.2	0.8	0.2	0.6	0.2	0.8	0.2
K	0.9	0.1	0.4	0.3	0.2	0.1	0.3	0.7	0.2	0.5	0.3	0.7	0.3
L	0.9	0.1	0.3	0.3	0.3	0.1	0.4	0.6	0.2	0.4	0.4	0.7	0.3
M	0.9	0.1	0.2	0.4	0.3	0.1	0.5	0.5	0.2	0.3	0.5	0.7	0.3
N	0.9	0.1	0.1	0.5	0.3	0.1	0.6	0.4	0.2	0.3	0.5	0.7	0.3
O	0.9	0.1	0.1	0.4	0.4	0.2	0.6	0.4	0.2	0.2	0.6	0.7	0.3
P	0.9	0.1	0.1	0.3	0.5	0.1	0.6	0.4	0.2	0.1	0.7	0.6	0.4
Q	0.9	0.1	0.1	0.2	0.6	0.1	0.6	0.4	0.2	0.1	0.7	0.6	0.4
R	0.9	0.1	0.1	0.1	0.7	0.1	0.6	0.4	0.2	0.1	0.7	0.6	0.4
S	0.9	0.1	0.1	0.1	0.8	0	0.6	0.4	0.2	0.1	0.7	0.5	0.5
T	0.9	0.1	0.1	0.2	0.8	0	0	1.0	0.1	0.1	0.8	0.4	0.6
U	0.8	0.2	0	0.2	0.8	0	0	1.0	0	0	1.0	0.3	0.7
V	0.7	0.2	0	0	0	0.9	0	1.0	0	0	1.0	0.2	0.8
W	0.6	0.4	0	0.1	0	0.9	0	1.0	0	0.1	0.9	0.1	0.9
X	0.5	0.5	0	0.1	0	0.9	0	1.0	0	0.2	0.8	0.1	0.9
Z	0	1.0	0	0	0	1.0	0	1.0	0	0	1.0	0	1.0

Table 7–2   Participation Potential for Different Decentralization Patterns

Decentralization Pattern	Centralization Index $r_{Ic} + r_{cc} + r_{zc} + r_{sc} + r_{ss}$	Participation Potential (P)	
		nonweighted	weighted
A	3.0	273.0	466.9
B	2.9	281.1	472.3
C	2.7	324.1	509.6
D	2.6	343.2	520.4
E	2.5	354.2	525.7
F	2.4	370.2	541.7
G	2.4	355.9	524.7
H	2.3	352.6	513.1
I	2.3	349.5	518.1
J	2.4	344.9	519.4
K	2.4	367.3	541.8
L	2.3	389.7	564.2
M	2.2	397.8	569.6
N	2.1	405.9	575.1
O	2.1	442.6	614.4
P	2.0	466.5	641.0
Q	1.0	496.8	674.0
R	1.9	511.1	691.0
S	1.9	519.0	701.5
T	1.1	578.4	710.1
U	0.8	632.6	747.5
V	0.7	732.5	817.7
W	0.7	742.0	818.9
X	0.7	729.1	797.6
Z	0.0	815.0	841.7

ing that such an estimate of the cost has been made, a programming interpretation of the model can be given. The problem is to choose the level of the decision parameters $r_{Ic}, r_{cc}, r_{zc}, r_{sc}, r_{zz}, r_{zs}, r_{SL}$ for each time period (say, at five-year intervals) in such a manner that the total participation potential generated at the terminal year T (say, 2000) is maximum, subject to the fact that the cost of decentralization in each period does not exceed a given amount. Good decisions will decrease the distance and increase the force of integration. Symbolically, this can be stated as follows:

Choose the decision parameters r_{Ic}, r_{cc}, r_{zc}, and so on in such a manner that at time period T,

$$D = [(r_{Ic} + r_{cc} + r_{zc} + r_{sc})\,(_cV_z + {}_cV_s) + (r_{cz} + r_{zz})\,(_zV_z + {}_cV_s)$$

$$+ (r_{Is} + r_{ss} + r_{Ls} + r_{sc})_s V_L$$

$$+ (r_{LL} + r_{SL} + r_{CL}) + {}_LV_L]$$

maximum, subject to, for each t

$$\left. \begin{array}{l} \text{Total cost} < C_0 \\[4pt] 1 > r_{Is}, \, r_{Ic}, \, r_{cc}, \, r_{zc}, \, r_{sc}, \, r_{cc}, \, r_{zz} > 0 \\[4pt] r_{Ic} + r_{IS} = 1 \\[4pt] r_{sc} + r_{cz} + r_{cs} + r_{cL} = 1 \\[4pt] r_{zc} + r_{zz} = 1 \\[4pt] r_{sc} + r_{ss} + r_{sL} = 1 \\[4pt] r_{Ls} + r_{LL} = 1 \end{array} \right\} \qquad (7.21)$$

It is true that the model in this form is too theoretical to be of any practical value. Even the theoretical notions also should be improved in many respects. However, this model is only a suggestion. It is hoped that its critical evaluation and modification will lead to a more refined and operational procedure.

Regional and Interregional Growth and Allocation Theory

The subject matter of regional and interregional growth and allocation theory is the distribution of investment funds at different points in time so that the system (the developing country) can be uplifted from a point S_0 (underdevelopment) to a point S_1 (high-income point). Starting from the Harrod/Domar theory, it has been very well developed up to turnpike theorems. New formulations in both time and space have also been made (Fujita 1978). Rahman (1963) first studied the problem in a rigorous fashion. Then Intriligator (1969), Takayama (1967), and Sakashita (1967) reformulated it in terms of Pontryagin's (1962) maximum principle. Sakashita also went further, dividing the funds into public and private investment. The public investment was divided into productive government investment (for example, in a steel mill) and social overhead investment. Assuming there are two regions, the problem is to decide the tax rate γ and the percentage allocation to the first region (u) such that the total income generated at the future time

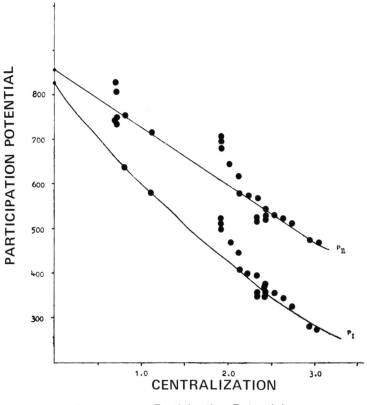

Figure 7–5. Participation Potential

period (T) is maximized. In his analysis he did not consider the production functions of the two regions. He simply used the output-capital ratio to transform the investment in private and public sectors into output figures. He also did not consider the question of interregional migration. His model was later generalized for n regions by Ohtsuki (1971). The solution in each was Rahman's "bang-bang" solution, where the decision is to invest in one region (and make no investment in the other region) for some period $t \leq t_0$, and then, after t_0, to switch the investment to the other region.

Another avenue of research is carried out by Fukuchi and Nobukuni (1970). Here the authors are interested in the relationship between differences in regional productivity and the interregional movement of production factors. As mentioned before, Sakashita considered the first factor marginally through the inequality of output-capital ratios and completely neglected the second factor. On the other hand, Fukuchi and Nobukuni were not involved in any maximum conditions. They only derived the stability condition of the balanced growth path. Here we shall combine the approach of Sakashita and that of Fukuchi and Nobukuni.

Modified Formulation of a Regional Allocation Model

Let $X_i (i = 1, 2)$ denote the output of the ith region. The production function of the ith region is given by

$$X_i = E_i^{1-r} K_i^r = E_i q_i^r \qquad i = 1, 2, \ldots \qquad (7.22)$$

where $q_i = K_i / E_i$.

In the Cobb-Douglas production (equation 7.22), E_i and K_i denote the employment and investment in the ith region, respectively.

Differentiating equation 7.22 with respect to E_i, we get

$$\frac{\delta X_i}{\delta E_i} = (1 - r) E_i^{-r} K_i^r = \left(\frac{K_i}{E_i} \right)^r (1 - r) = q_i^r (1 - r). \qquad (7.23)$$

Let the growth path of income of the two regions be given by

$$\frac{\delta X_i}{\delta t} = \sigma_1 \left(\frac{1}{2} + \eta \lambda \right) (1 - \gamma) (s_1 X_1 + s_2 X_2) +$$

$$\qquad (7.24)$$

$$\delta_1 \left(\frac{1}{2} + u + p \right) (s_1 X_1 + s_2 X_2) \gamma.$$

We are assuming that taxation is imposed only on savings and not on consumption, which in a poor country is at a subsistence level. Thus,

$$\frac{\delta X_2}{\delta t} = \sigma_2 \left(\frac{1}{2} - \eta \lambda \right) (1 - \gamma) (s_1 X_1 + s_2 X_2)$$

$$\qquad (7.25)$$

$$+ \delta_2 \left(\frac{1}{2} - u - p \right) (s_1 X_1 + s_2 X_2) \gamma.$$

In equations 7.24 and 7.25, we have the following notational system:

s_i = average propensity to save in the ith region. ($i = 1, 2$).

γ = tax rate.

σ = output capital ratio in the public sector in the ith region (i = 1, 2).

σ_2 = output-capital ratio in the private sector in the ith region.

p = differential population growth in region 1 compared with the national population growth. Without any loss of generality, p can be assumed to be greater than zero.

$(\frac{1}{2} + u + p)$ = proportion of the total public investment fund spent in region 1.

$(\frac{1}{2} - u - p)$ = proportion of the total public investment fund spent in region 2.

$(\frac{1}{2} + \eta\lambda)$ = proportion of the total private investment fund spend in region 1.

$(\frac{1}{2} - \eta\lambda)$ = proportion of the total private investment fund spent in region 2.

From the foregoing it is clear that we must have

$$0 \le u < \tfrac{1}{2} - p,$$
$$0 \le \eta\lambda < \tfrac{1}{2}.$$

We define

$$\lambda = \frac{\dfrac{\partial X_1}{\partial K_1} - \dfrac{\partial \bar{X}}{\partial K}}{\dfrac{\partial \bar{X}}{\partial K}}$$

as marginal productivity of capital in the first region compared with that of the nation as a whole (η = an adjustment factor, $\bar{X}$ = national output). Remembering that

$$\frac{\delta X_i}{\delta t} = \frac{\delta X_i}{\delta E_i} \cdot \frac{\delta E_i}{\delta t} = q_i^r (1 - r) \frac{\delta E_i}{\delta t},$$

equations 7.24 and 7.25 can be written as

$$\frac{\delta E_1}{\delta t} = \frac{[\sigma_1(\frac{1}{2} + \eta\lambda)(1 - \theta_1 - \theta_2) + \delta_1\theta_1][s_1 E_1 q_i^r + s_2 E_2 q_2^r]}{(1 - r)q_1^r}, \quad (7.26)$$

$$\frac{\delta E_2}{\delta t} = \frac{[\sigma_2(\frac{1}{2} - \eta\lambda)(1 - \theta_1 - \theta_2) + \delta_2\theta_2][s_1 E_1 q_i^r + s_2 E_2 q_2^r]}{(1 - r)q_2^r}, \quad (7.27)$$

where $\theta_1 = (\frac{1}{2} + u + p)\gamma$
and $\theta_2 = (\frac{1}{2} - u - p)\gamma$.

Since u, γ, and p are dependent on time, θ_1 and θ_2 (which are the transformed policy variables) also depend on time, t. Let us denote them by $\theta_1(t)$ and $\theta_2(t)$. The problem then is to choose the policy variables $\theta_1(t)$ and $\theta_2(t)$ such that the total employment generated for the nation at the time period T is maximum. Therefore, we maximize

$$[F_1(T) + E_2(T)] = \int_0^T \left[\frac{\delta E_1}{\delta t} + \frac{\delta E_2}{\delta t} + (E_1{}^0 + E_2{}^0) \right]. \qquad (7.28)$$

It is to be noted here that the objective is to maximize total employment at a future date, subject to technological and financial restriction. This objective may be inconsistent with that of maximizing income, but for some countries (particularly overpopulated developing countries) the first objective may be desirable. Note also that our policy variables θ_1 and θ_2 are *not* the same as $\mu\gamma$ and $(1 - \mu)\gamma$, respectively, of Sakashita's model. The maximization is performed with respect to $\theta_1(t)$ and $\theta_2(t)$, subject to equations 7.26 and 7.27 and

$$\left. \begin{array}{l} 0 \leq \lambda \leq \theta \\[2mm] 0 \leq \lambda \leq \frac{1}{2}\eta \\[6mm] 0 \leq u \leq \frac{1}{2}p \end{array} \right\} \qquad \left. \begin{array}{l} 0 \leq \theta_1 \\[2mm] 0 \leq \theta_2 \\[2mm] \theta_1 + \theta_2 \leq \theta \\[2mm] 0 \leq t \leq T \end{array} \right\} \qquad (7.29)$$

where θ is the upper limit of γ. This is a problem in dynamic programming that can be approached from Pontryagin's maximum principle. The Hamiltonian of the maximum problem is

$$H = -\psi_0 \left[\frac{\delta E_i}{\delta t} + \frac{\delta E_2}{\delta t} \right] + \psi_1 \frac{\delta E_1}{\delta t} + \psi_2 \frac{\delta E_2}{\delta t}. \qquad (7.30)$$

From its definition,

$$\left. \begin{array}{l} \dfrac{\delta \psi_0}{\delta t} = 0 \\[6mm] \dfrac{\delta \psi_1}{\delta t} = \dfrac{\delta H}{\delta E_1} \\[6mm] \dfrac{\delta \psi_2}{\delta t} = \dfrac{-\delta H}{\delta E_2} \end{array} \right\} \qquad (7.31)$$

At $t = T$, we have $\psi_0(T) = -1$, $\psi_1(T) = \psi_2(T) = 0$. Putting $\Phi = 1 + \psi_1$, and $\Phi_2 = 1 + \psi_2$ from equation 7.30, we get

$$H = [\{\sigma_1(\tfrac{1}{2} + \eta\lambda)\,\phi_1|_{q_1{}^r(1-r)} + \sigma_2(\tfrac{1}{2} - \eta\lambda)\,\phi_2|_{q_2{}^r(1-r)}\}$$

$$+ \theta_1\{(\delta_1 - \sigma_1(\tfrac{1}{2} + \eta\lambda))\,\phi_1/q_1{}^r(1 - r) - \sigma_2(\tfrac{1}{2} - \eta\lambda)\phi_2/q_2{}^r(1-r)\}$$

$$+ \theta_2\{-\sigma_1(\tfrac{1}{2} + \eta\lambda)\,\phi_1|_{q_1{}^r(1-r)} + (\delta_2 - \sigma_2(\tfrac{1}{2} - \lambda\eta))\phi_2/q_2^r(1 - r)\}].$$

$$[s_1 E_1 q_1{}^r + s_2 E_2 q_2{}^r] \tag{7.32}$$

$$\frac{\delta\phi_1}{\partial t} = \frac{-\partial H}{\partial E_1} = -s_1 q_1{}^r \left[\frac{\sigma_1(\tfrac{1}{2} + \eta\lambda)\,(1 - \theta_1 - \theta_2) + \delta_1\theta_1}{q_1{}^r(1 - r)} \phi_1 \right.$$

$$\left. + \frac{\sigma_2(\tfrac{1}{2} - \eta\lambda)\,(1 - \theta_1 - \theta_2) + \delta_2\theta_2}{q_2{}^r(1 - r)} \Phi_2 \right].$$
$$\tag{7.33}$$

Similarly,

$$\frac{\delta\phi_2}{\delta t} = -s_2 q_2{}^r \left[\frac{\sigma_1(\tfrac{1}{2} + \eta\lambda)\,(1 - \theta_1 - \theta_2) + \delta_1\theta_1}{q_1{}^r(1 - r)} \phi_1 + \right.$$

$$\left. \frac{s_2(\tfrac{1}{2} - \eta\lambda)\,(1 - \theta_1 - \theta_2) + \delta_2\theta_2}{q_2^r(1 - r)} \phi_2 \right].$$
$$\tag{7.34}$$

Let the multiplicative factor of θ_i in equation 7.33 be denoted by $P_i (i = 1, 2)$. Then the maximum principle tells us

1. $\theta_i = 0$ if $P_i < 0$ $(i = 1, 2)$
2. $\theta_i = 0$ and $\theta_j < \theta$ if $P_i < P_j$

Let us write explicitly the expression for P_i $(i = 1, 2)$

$$P_1 = \left[\left\{ \delta_1 - \sigma_1 \left(\frac{1}{2} + \eta\lambda \right) \right\} \frac{\phi_1}{q_1^r(1 - r)} \right.$$

$$\left. - \left\{ \sigma_2 \left(\frac{1}{2} - \eta\lambda \right) \frac{\phi_2}{q_2^r(1 - r)} \right\} \right]. \tag{7.35}$$

$$P_2 = [\{- \sigma_1(\tfrac{1}{2} + \eta\lambda) \phi_1 |_{q_1^r(1-r)}\} + \{(\delta_2 - \sigma_2(\tfrac{1}{2} - \lambda\eta) \phi_2 |_{q_2^r(1-r)}\}]. \quad (7.36)$$

$$\therefore P_1 - P_2 = \frac{\phi_1}{q_1^r(1 - r)}{}_{31} - \frac{\phi_2}{q_2^r(1 - r)} \Delta_2 \quad (7.37)$$

$$P_1 - P_2 > 0$$

if (from equation 7.37)

$$\phi_1 > \frac{q_1^r}{q_2^r} \frac{\delta_2}{\delta_1} \phi_2. \quad (7.38)$$

Now, from equations 7.33 and 7.34 we see that by solving the simple differential equation

$$\phi_2 = \frac{s_2 q_2^r}{s_1 q_1^r} \phi_1 + c, \quad (7.39)$$

where c is a constant of integration.

At $t = T$, $\phi_1 = \phi_2 = 1$. So from equation 7.39 we get

$$c = \frac{s_1 q_1^r - s_2 q_2^r}{s_1 q_1^r}.$$

Then the complete solution of equation 7.39 is

$$\phi_2 = \frac{s_2 q_2^r}{s_1 q_1^r} \phi_1 + \frac{s_1 q_1^r - s_2 q_2^r}{s_1 q_1^r}. \quad (7.40)$$

Substituting equation 7.40 in equation 7.38, we see $P_1 - P_2 > 0$ if

$$\phi_1 > \frac{q_1^r}{q_2^r} \frac{\delta_2}{\delta_1} \frac{s_2 q_2^r}{s_1 q_1^r} \phi_1 + \left(\frac{q_1}{q_2}\right)^r \frac{\delta_2}{\delta_1} \left(\frac{s_1 q_1^r - s_2 q_2^r}{s_1 q_1^r}\right), \quad (7.41)$$

or

$$\phi_1 > \frac{g_2^{\frac{1}{2}}}{g_1^{\frac{1}{2}}} \phi_1 + \frac{\delta_2(s_1 q_1^r - s_2 q_2^r)}{g_1^{\frac{1}{2}} q_2^r}, \quad (7.42)$$

where $g_1^1 = g_i \delta_i (i = 1, 2)$, or

$$\phi_1 > \frac{\delta_2(s_1 q_1^r - s_2 q_2^r)}{g_1^1 - g_2^1}. \tag{7.43}$$

At $t = T$, $\phi_1(T) = 1$. So $P_1 \} P_2$ if R.H.S. of equation 7.43 < 1 which after simplification gives

$$g_1^1 / g_2^1 \leq \frac{q_2^r - 1}{\delta_2 / \delta_1 q_1^r - 1} \tag{7.44}$$

If $t \neq T$, then approximately,

$$\phi_1 = (T - t) [s_1 q_1^r \sigma_1 \lambda + s_2 q_2^r \sigma_2 (1 - \lambda)] = h(T - t), \text{ say.}$$

Then the condition corresponding to equation 7.44 is

$$g_1^1 \leq g_2^1 \left[\frac{q_2^r - 1 - h(T - t)}{\delta_2 / \delta_1 q_1^r - 1 - h(T - t)} \right]. \tag{7.45}$$

If equation 7.45 is satisfied, it means that

1. For the time interval $0 \leq t \leq t^*$, where t^* is the solution of equation 7.45 with equal signs, impose a tax rate θ on both regions and concentrate public investment in the first region.
2. For the time interval $t^* \leq t \leq T$ there should be no tax and no public investment. From equation 7.44 it will be seen that the inequality condition depends on the following parameters, and whether the conditions will be satisfied will depend on the values of the parameters.
   $g_i^1 = s_i \delta_i$ = growth rate due to public investment $(i = 1, 2)$.
   q_i = capital-labor ratio in the ith region $(i = 1, 2)$.
   σ_i = output-capital ratio in the private sector $(i = 1, 2)$.
   λ = the productivity of capital in the first region compared with the country as a whole

The foregoing analysis is an extension of the combined approach of Sakashita and Fukuchi-Nobukuni. However, the model can be generalized by considering other factors that are faced in real situations, such as political pressures, defense needs, and national integrity. Even many economic factors such as interregional trade, industry linkages, and allocation by sectors can be taken into consideration. This model has been extended by Fujita (1973) as follows:

Maximize

$$\sum_{L=r,s} \sum_{i=1,2} p_i^{-L}(N)X_i^L(N)$$

Subject to:

$$0 \le X_1^L(t+1) \le X_1^L(t) + \theta_1^L(t)(y_1^r + y_1^s)t$$

$$0 \le X_2^L(t+1) \le \theta_2^L(t)(y_2^r + y_2^S)_t$$

for some

$$\theta_i^r(t) + \theta_i^s(t) = 1, \; \theta_i^r(t), \qquad \theta_i^s(t) \ge 0$$
$$i = 1,2$$

and

$$(y_1^L, y_2^L) \in f_1(X_1^L, X_2^L)_t$$

$$t = 0, 1, \dots N - 1$$

where X_1^L = amount of capital used in region L.
X_2^L = amount of material good used in region L.
y_1^L = amount of investment good produced in region L.
y_2^L = amount of material good produced in region L.

In this extension there is only one kind of investment good, which can be moved between locations without transport inputs, and only two locations, regions r and s; θ is the ratio of investment good allocated to region r, and p^L ($L = r, s$) is the efficiency prices of capital in region L. This model can be extended to m regions and n goods (Fujita 1973; Isard and Liossatos 1979).

The foregoing formulation was based purely on economic grounds; but in practice the solution, even if optimum, cannot be implemented because regions compete for funds using political pressure. Although such pressures and other noneconomic factors will make the realistic solution nonoptimal, nevertheless we must choose the best among the nonoptimal solutions. In this purpose we can use the veto-incremax solution (Isard 1969).

References

Anderson, Theodore. 1956. "Potential Models and Spatial Distribution of Population," *Papers and Proceedings of the Regional Science Association* 2:175–178.

Fujita, Masahisa. 1973. "Optimum Growth in Two-Region Two-Good Space Systems: The Final State Problem." *Journal of Regional Science* 13, no. 3:385–408.

————. 1978. *Spatial Development Planning: A Dynamic Convex Programming Approach.* Amsterdam: North-Holland.

Fukuchi, Takao, and Nobukuni, Makoto. 1970. "An Econometric Analysis of National Growth and Regional Income Inequality." *International Economic Review* 11 (February):84–100.

Harmon, Harry H. 1960. *Modern Factor Analysis.* Chicago: University of Chicago Press.

Harris, Chauncy. 1954. "The Market as a Factor in the Localization of Industry in the United States." *Annals of the Association of American Geographers* 44:517.

Intriligator, Michael. 1969. "Regional Allocation of Investment Comment." *Quarterly Journal of Economics* 78, no. 4:659–662.

Isard, Walter. 1969. *General Theory: Social, Political, Economic, Regional.* Cambridge, Mass.: MIT Press.

Isard, Walter, and Liossatos, Panagis. 1979. *Spatial Dynamics and Optimal Space-Time Development.* Amsterdam: North-Holland.

Maass, Arthur A. 1958. *Area and Power: A Theory of Local Government.* Glencoe, Ill.: Free Press.

Ohtsuki, Yashitaka. 1971. "Regional Allocation of Public Investment in a n-Region Economy." *Journal of Regional Science* 11, no. 2:225–234.

Pontryagin, Lev S., et al. 1962. *The Mathematical Theory of Optimal Process,* trans. K. N. Trirogoff. London: Wiley Interscience.

Rahman, Anisur. 1963. "Regional Allocation of Investment." *Quarterly Journal of Economics* 77, no. 1:26–39.

Sakashita, Noburu. 1967. "Regional Allocation of Investment." *Papers of the Regional Science Association* 19:161–182.

Takayama, Akira. 1967. "Regional Allocation of Public Investment." *Quarterly Journal of Economics* 81, no. 2:330–337.

Warntz, William. 1959. *Towards a Geography of Price.* Philadelphia: University of Pennsylvania Press.

8 RETROSPECT AND PROSPECT

The Future of Regional Science

In some countries in the East, a horoscope is usually made when a child is born. If it is a boy, the horoscope specifies how healthy and wealthy he will be or in the case of a girl, how beautiful she will be, what type of husband she will have, and whether she will prevail over the husband in the family.

For regional science, we have no such horoscope. What we do have is the timing of its birth and its growth pattern over the last two decades. Regional science was born at an auspicious moment, when, in all the social sciences (including management education) new ideas and techniques were cropping up and many fields of specialization were being established. This was largely the result of the development of the computer. This era is now coming to a close, and for a while there will be some degree of stabilization. Although thirty years is not enough time to allow us to judge the performance of a new discipline, we have some evidence to judge whether regional science will stay or not, and how much flexibility (if any) in its definition and scope should be allowed to give it a better probability of survival. Therefore, on the basis of a priori probabilities at the time of birth and information on growth for the two decades, I will venture to make some sort of speculation using Bayesian probability statements.

The question today is not whether or not there is a case for a new area called regional science among the different social science disciplines. This argument has been settled. It is generally accepted that there is a subject like regional science, but the task of the regional scientists will be to invent new ideas and techniques to justify its continued existence. Otherwise, for a social scientist of the twenty-first century, it will be a historical fact that a discipline called regional science developed in the 1950s and had a gradual demise by the end of the twentieth century. The same concern has been expressed vividly by Walter Isard (1956):

> I will not be able to point to an established and reputable body of doctrine. All there is to display are some budding theories, a stock of solid empirical studies and large quantities of data, a number of techniques and tools of other social sciences which are refashioned for regional use, and considerable promise. Yet I insist we must boldly paint that promise, strive for more appropriate conceptual frameworks, venture new hypotheses and models of interrelations, explore new arrangements and processing of data and otherwise thrust forward with vigor. Unless we do so, by adhering to a traditional, outmoded slicing of the regional body which yields the standard, social science fields of investigation, we may preclude the identification of the very basic interaction matrix of this live dynamic organism, which we seek. Of course, I cannot invoke any objective studies to support these views, only posterity can attest to their validity.

Some scholars have suggested that the name *regional science* is not appropriate. Another name, such as areal/spatial science or urban science, may be the proper one. It is true that these terms have connotations that are easily understood, but they do not express the true nature of the philosophy behind this dicipline. Regional science gives equal attention to both urban and rural (geographical as well as environmental) areas. Again, the words *spatial/areal* somehow give the impression that we are interested only in those features of activities that are pursued on the face of the earth. Regional science goes beyond that.

Regional Science and Other Disciplines

In its present form, regional science is basically a social science or, more properly, an integration of parts of a number of social sciences. However, this does not mean that it has no connection with the physical and biological sciences. It must be identified with physiography because regional scientists are concerned with areal groupings of human activities and natural phenomena such as climate and topography. In the coming decades, regional science will draw heavily on the science of ecology.

Regional science was organized as a discipline in the 1950s. If we look at the literature of geography, economics, and so on in different countries, however, we shall see that many writers were trying to make similar hypotheses, emphasizing the same type of interdependence that we now often do in our area. Their modes of analysis may have been different. All of them were not mathematical; and, of course, they did not have the computer. When I talk about regional science, I include these contributions. The definition of the discipline, then, is not restricted to the activities of regional science associations and articles published in journals and papers of the associations. Any analysis involving some spatial dimension and where the process of decision making consists in developing objective scientific hypotheses and testing them with logical and consistent reasoning, with or without empirical observations, automatically belongs to this science. Consequently, a large portion of urban and regional studies belongs to this field.

I know that to some, particularly those outside the profession of regional science, this will appear to be a drastic change in the definition postulated by its founders; they may find it an encroachment on other disciplines. However, this definition seems quite consistent with Isard's definition of regional science as a discipline stretching from "abstract-mathematical model constructions to empiric field type enquiry." With respect to encroachment, I would like to point out that there is no boundary in social science disciplines; the same accusations can be made about many other *sciences* and specializations. My definition will imply a narrowing of the gap between regional science and objectively conducted regional studies.

Future Directions for Regional Science

In the literature on regional science and city and regional planning, numerous studies are available on the subjects mentioned in previous chapters; but it must be admitted that not all of them are really *spatial*. These studies start by denouncing the notion of a one-point economy. In the final analysis, however, these correspond to a multiple-point economy (with the central places as the bases). For practical purposes, this is not unsatisfactory; but we have really failed to capture the essential multidimensional linkages of the points on the space. The development of spatial statistics and social physics was a start in the right direction, but few significant new contributions have been made recently.

In the field of regional population studies, little work (compared with the total volume of work in demography) has been done concerning the redefinition of different indexes, population growth models, life table construction, migration, and so on for urban and regional units. In the field of demography, excellent studies in different countries on migration are available; but regional scientists so far have failed to develop an overall theory of migration. We have placed a proportionally high importance on distance, rather than on psychological behavior, thus hardly mentioning the relationship between information systems and migration. A promising direction has been pioneered by Rogers (1968) and Rees and Wilson (1977).

In the case of input-output analysis, regional tables have been constructed; but their features are essentially those of national tables, and input-output coefficients are rarely given separately for inputs from within and from outside the region. It is understandable that this is a very difficult task since data do not exist; theoretically, however, it can be introduced in the overall input-output analysis. The same type of argument can be advanced for other techniques as well. Even on a theoretical level, little work has been done in the field of dynamic interregional input-output analysis; nor has regional science been linked with regional growth theory, a subject much better handled by national growth economists than by regional scientists.

Another potential area of development is the regional econometric models. There is ample scope to conduct significant new theoretical research in this field. The type of regional econometric models available are not really regional because they do not portray the spatial interconnection that is the most crucial factor in regional science. They are really national models, except that a small geographical area has been substituted for the word *nation* In the field of regional social accounts, we have followed national accounts too closely and have not used the theories and principles of capital accounting.

Another important variable is the question of time. Regional activities and regional structure change over time. There is an interaction not only between activities and space but also between space-time and activities. Techniques like the gravity model have very little use in predicting the structure of the future unless we bring forth this dynamic aspect. There have been favorable developments in regional and urban complex/system analysis, but in many situations these are based on technical relationships rather than principles of social sciences. Simulation techniques have followed too closely those used in business and offer very little connection with real-life situations in society. There have also been good contributions of abstract theoretical constructs with respect to space; but, compared with the potential opportunity to enrich this area, these studies have been few. Although over the years new problems in political science and sociology have cropped up, no significant contribution in geopolitics has been made—that is, the development of regional conflict, regional political organization, and power structure. Isard's (1969) contribution to the development of interregional general systems is a significant exception. Again, in the field of management of public and nonprofit organizations, government administration, and education and health administration, new problems related to spatial organization have developed; unfortunately, no original ideas have been forthcoming from regional scientists to cope with them.

In short, we are lagging behind in our attempt to attack new problems. Our efforts to modify the well-developed theories of economics and other social sciences by injecting the notion of space are far from satisfactory.

Another topic that is not often emphasized is regional data collection. It is true that the available data on a regional level are meager. Even with what data we have, however, we can reorganize them, check them, and present them in a form that will be useful for further analysis. Again, for many situations we can devise means by which to avoid the requirement of extensive regional data. For example, if data for regional econometric models do not exist, then we can construct sectoral models for the major industries in the region (for which time-series and cross-section data are usually available) and link the model with some overall aggregates such as gross regional product, employment, salaries, and so on.

The foregoing criticism of the progress in regional science does not imply that little has been done in this field. On the contrary, its growth over the past three decades has been phenomenal. However, much of it has involved the repetition of the same techniques over and over again. That is not to say that this has not happened to other social sciences. The difference is that as a young discipline, regional science cannot afford it. We not only have to keep up with other social sciences, but we must also innovate in our field.

There are untapped areas in operations research, mathematics, economics, and other social sciences in which regional scientists not only can look for new and more powerful ideas and techniques but also can modify them to suit their purposes. For example, the whole area of topology in mathematics should be of great interest to the regional scientist, who is concerned with the multidimensional nature of the distribution of points in space, and the interrelationships of these points over time. It is in this area that we should concentrate our attention heavily if we want to develop the abstract theoretical base or core of regional science.

Coming back to economics, we find there has been a tremendous increase of new ideas in the field of econometrics—say, in growth models and welfare economics. In regional science literature we have few regional growth models parallel to the national growth model. Little work has been done in the fields of regional welfare economics and choice theory—that is, the formulation of regional goals and their relation to national goals, and so on. Again it may be possible to develop a methodology for constructing regional econometric models, modifying the established procedure with the help of location and space economics.

Financial variables such as interest rates, inflation, money supply, demand deposits, mortgage money availability, and so on have important spatial dimensions that are intricately related to the economic structure of a region. Considerable work can be pursued in this area. Other promising areas include resource management (agricultural, mineral, and ecological), particularly energy management.

We shall mention a number of directions in which regional science has been moving in recent years and also some new avenues of research. The location theory that forms the basis of regional science can be further developed in new directions. First of all, as a result of the development of multinational corporations, the geographic dimension has changed. Although the attraction of the market is still predominant, the cost and transportation of resources are reemerging as crucial factors. The movement toward reindustrialization in, for example, the northeastern United States demands some new modes of locational analysis.

Population redistribution through migration is now the source of regional population growth in the developed countries, and the change in the age structure of the population will lead to a different type of demand for services. Thus it is necessary for us to reformulate our migration theory. There are also a number of facilities, such as nuclear power generating plants, sewerage treatment plants, and chemical treatment plants, near which no one wants to locate, but whose benefit everyone wishes to enjoy. What criteria are we going to use for locating such facilities? Environmental factors such as international diffusion of air pollution also point to the need for reformulating location theory.

The greatest challenge with respect to location theory is to make it consistent with conflict theory. The optimum location point in economic space may not be acceptable in the policy of space. For example, from the point of view of Weberian location theory, a steel plant may not be justified for South India; but this decision may not be the best one from the point of view of internal conflicts in India.

There can be different types of conflict in both the developed and the developing countries, but all types of conflict usually have a spatial dimension. Tribal conflicts in some countries in Asia and Africa arise primarily because of the existence of different racial stocks in those countries. For a country such as the United States, the locations of the racial conflicts are the central cities. Political conflict also grows from a specific point in space and usually spreads through the total system. Economic class conflict within nations also generally arises because of uneven economic development over space. To locate an optimum point in space, we need to consider the economic space in conjunction with the policy space and to develop a fused conflict-location theory. For the development of such a conflict theory we need to have a macromodel based on the microbehavior of organizational theory, using such concepts as group dynamics.

Before we think about a scheme of conflict resolution, we need to have an accounting system that we can build with the help of the emerging theories of accounting. Marketing the ideas of conflict resolution is another new concern. The use of system designs and information systems for the development of conflict theory is also emphasized. The use of Bayesian probability theory for the development of a step-by-step incremax process to solve the problem, as mentioned in Chapter 6, is also a worthwhile venture. Except for Isard's (1979) research on the time and space dimension of development, no new ideas seem to be forthcoming. There is a golden opportunity to apply the theory of mathematical biology and statistical ecology in the field of regional science. The role of catastrophe theory in the framework of conflict theory needs to be developed. After Wilson (1970) showed how entropy theory could be used in urban and regional planning, there was a spurt of research papers but in recent years this has subsided.

Although regional science had considerable impetus from management science in the development of new theory, there are some areas, such as finance and accounting, that have made very little contribution to regional science.

Regional Science and the Developing Countries

The area that has the highest potential of development is regional science for developing countries. Many of these countries, however, are trying to reverse the trend of underdevelopment by relying on national economic planning. This consists of formulating economic and social goals for the people at a future date, expressing them in quantifiable money values, and suggesting the most efficient strategy to attain these goals with available internal and external resources. There have been many experiments, and numerous studies on the theory and practices of national planning are available in economic literature. However, over the years it has been increasingly realized that national planning is not leading to a balanced development of the country. One reason is that in most economic planning strategies, we abstract the notion of space. We are thinking in terms of one-point economy and trying to devise policies to make economic growth optimal over time. In reality, however, we do not live in a one-point economy. All parts of a country do not have the same characteristics with respect to resource orientation, manpower, economics, and social and political history. Some areas are urban, others rural. Some got an earlier start in economic growth. The situation is further complicated by the existence of different languages, ethnic groups, and conflicting regional interest. Thus particular attention is needed in specific areas and regions. This does not necessarily mean that the country should be divided into smaller areas, each with a separate planning authority. What is needed, along with a national framework, is a series of interconnected regional plans consistent with national plans.

The need for regional planning can be realized when we look to the individual countries. The regional dimension of Indian planning problems is too well known to be reemphasized here. India is a vast country with an uneven distribution of natural resources. Climatic conditions and soil types are varied, requiring different approaches to economic development. Although the people are strongly bound with a common heritage, language and cultural barriers sometimes pose an insurmountable problem. The planning commission of the government of India explicitly recognizes this need and aims to have a balanced regional development within the available resources.

The civil war in Pakistan and the creation of Bangladesh serve as very good examples in this respect. Here was a country with two wings (East Pakistan and West Pakistan) separated by 1,000 miles of hostile Indian territory. The people in these two areas were different in many ways, with religion as the only common bond. The political instability in Pakistan was a direct result of this regional difference. Consider also the case of the Republic of Phillipines. Here the unbalanced development is highlighted by the fact that about 75 percent of the manufacturing industries are concentrated in the metropolitan Manila area and adjoining provinces. Thus it is not surprising that 85 percent of the national taxes are collected in this area.

Regional disparity in the level of development is also very pronounced for a highly industrialized country like Japan. The Japanese population is much more congested than would be expected on the basis of the national average density. The population is concentrated in narrow coastal plains and small valley bottoms. Examples of this phenomenon can be multiplied for countries in Asia, Africa, and Latin America. In terms of application to real problems, regional science is most suited to these developing countries struggling to raise the standard of living within the framework of a regional structure of society. Although the techniques of regional science have been developed in highly industrialized Western countries, they are widely used in these countries without regard for the validity of the assumptions involved, the peculiar situations existing there, and the value systems of the society. If we take some specific examples, the foregoing points can be understood more clearly. It is generally assured in regional studies that the population is the dependent variable and employment the independent variable. If the employment of the region at a future date can be determined, then, using multiplier or regression techniques, the population will be determined. This mode of analysis is untenable for those countries in which the population is an exogenous factor and the employment is generated as a result of decisions of government agencies in most situations.

As for the question of migration, it is not always a question of distance or attraction of opportunities that bring people to a certain place. The so-called push factors (overpopulation and underemployment for the villages, for example) are responsible for the migration to the cities. Other factors, such as the caste systems and marriage customs, have an overriding influence on migration. This is not to say that traditional factors (attractions of urbanization, and so on) do not play any role, or that people in these countries are not mobile.

In the case of input-output analysis, there has to be a clear distinction between large- and small-scale industries. We must treat the system as some sort of aggregation of a number of individual complexes, each of which should be studied separately and then put back into an input-output scheme. When we consider applying regional science techniques in developing countries, we have a completely different perspective. Cultural aspects, social systems, government structure, goal formulation, and the definition of optimum decisions are some of the factors that are becoming more and more important. In short, the emphasis should be more on social, cultural, and political factors and less on economic considerations. Regional science appears to be a tool of regional planning, just as economic models are mere tools of economic planning. The ultimate object of regional planning—more so than is the case with national planning—is man and his community, but this perspective is likely to be lost because of an unusually heavy reliance on the tools of economic planning. In the crowd of eocnomic tools, not only is man missing, but there may even be conflicts about goals, as Lalwani (1965) states:

If science means a basic consistency, we welcome it, but if science means breaking away from reality then there is a great danger. Science takes shape where process is repetitive and variables very few. But where variables are innumerable and fresh variables crop up too often and where repetition is a chance, each problem having novelty not only over time but also over space, a too much standarized thing ruins the risk of giving wrong guidance or even inadequate guidance.

The United States, the USSR, and the industrialized countries of Europe have gone through this process; but a different kind of regionalization based on urbanization has resulted. If we look at the settlement patterns; their economic, political, and social systems; and their interconnections, we find that they resemble a series of nets over space connected by transport and other communication systems. Within each one of the nets a highly complicated interdependence system has developed on the basis of the development of the regional history of activities and the value system of the region. This system is under constant stress through external competition and impacts. The situation is further complicated by ecological factors, such as air pollution, water pollution, sewage disposal, noise pollution, mental health, crime, etc. These problems are too well known to be emphasized here. In fact, we are facing an urban crisis in these countries. Thus, the potential of research in the developed countries lies in the field of environmental planning. A start has been made by the regional scientists in this area, but the number of people working in the field is small and the pace of work is slow. In urban areas of the developing country, we get the same picture. In addition, in the agricultural regions of these countries, there is intense population pressure on the land and environment, leading to ecological imbalance. Fortunately, however, the per capita demand of man on environment in these countries is much lower than in the Western world. In sum, the problem is worldwide and it will assume serious proportions unless we begin to look for solutions.

I am fully aware that the development of abstract theoretical concepts may not and will not solve the practical problems in the short run. But common sense experience, backed by powerful analytical tools are thus necessary, and theoretical constructs can take us further than pure common sense experience. Further developments in management science and more inter-actions between management science and regional science are needed to design practical policies to alleviate the poverty and destitution to which a great part of humanity is subject.

References

Isard, Walter. 1956. *Location and Space Economics*. Cambridge, Mass.: MIT Press.

Isard, Walter. 1969. *General Theory: Social, Political, Economic, and Regional.* Cambridge, Mass.: MIT Press.

Lalwani, Kasturchand. 1965. *Economics of Industrial Labor: Theory and Practice.* Calcutta: Artha Vanijya Gabesana Mandir.

Rees, P. H., and Wilson, Alan Geoffrey. 1977. *Spatial Demographic Analysis.* London: Arnold.

Rogers, Andrei. 1968. *Matrix Analysis of Interregional Population Growth.* Berkeley: University of California Press.

Wilson, Alan Geoffrey. 1970. *Entropy in Urban and Regional Modelling.* London: Pion.

Author Index

Subject Index